Pro ADO.NET Data Services

Working with RESTful Data

John Shaw and Simon Evans

Apress®

Pro ADO.NET Data Services: Working with RESTful Data

Copyright © 2009 by John Shaw and Simon Evans

ISBN-13 (pbk): 978-1-4302-1614-8

ISBN-13 (electronic): 978-1-4302-1615-5

Printed and bound in the United States of America 9 8 7 6 5 4 3 2 1

Lead Editor: Tony Campbell
Technical Reviewer: Damien Foggon
Editorial Board: Clay Andres, Steve Anglin, Mark Beckner, Ewan Buckingham, Tony Campbell, Gary
    Cornell, Jonathan Gennick, Michelle Lowman, Matthew Moodie, Duncan Parkes, Jeffrey Pepper, Frank
    Pohlmann, Ben Renow-Clarke, Dominic Shakeshaft, Matt Wade, Tom Welsh
Project Manager: Sofia Marchant
Copy Editors: Ami Knox, Heather Lang
Associate Production Director: Kari Brooks-Copony
Production Editor: Laura Cheu
Compositor: Kinetic Publishing Services, LLC
Proofreader: Nancy Bell
Indexer: Broccoli Information Management
Artist: Kinetic Publishing Services, LLC
Cover Designer: Kurt Krames
Manufacturing Director: Tom Debolski

Distributed to the book trade worldwide by Springer-Verlag New York, Inc., 233 Spring Street, 6th Floor, New York, NY 10013. Phone 1-800-SPRINGER, fax 201-348-4505, e-mail orders-ny@springer-sbm.com, or visit http://www.springeronline.com.

For information on translations, please contact Apress directly at 2855 Telegraph Avenue, Suite 600, Berkeley, CA 94705. Phone 510-549-5930, fax 510-549-5939, e-mail info@apress.com, or visit http://www. apress.com.

Apress and friends of ED books may be purchased in bulk for academic, corporate, or promotional use. eBook versions and licenses are also available for most titles. For more information, reference our Special Bulk Sales–eBook Licensing web page at http://www.apress.com/info/bulksales.

The source code for this book is available to readers at http://www.apress.com.

To Lori
Thanks for being understanding while I worked on this during
our honeymoon . . . it proves to me how much you love me.
—John Shaw

To Angharad
Your soul makes me complete and your true friendship
makes me love you more each passing day.
—Simon Evans

Contents at a Glance

PART 1 ▦ ▦ ▦ ADO.NET Data Service Fundamentals

PART 2 ▦ ▦ ▦ ADO.NET Data Services in the Real World

PART 3 ▦ ▦ ▦ ADO.NET Data Services from the Outside

PART 4 ▦ ▦ ▦ The Future of ADO.NET Data Services

Contents

PART 1 ■■■ ADO.NET Data Service Fundamentals

PART 2 ■ ■ ■ ADO.NET Data Services in the Real World

PART 3 ■ ■ ■ ADO.NET Data Services from the Outside

PART 4 ▪▪▪ The Future of ADO.NET Data Services

Foreword

It's amazing to see the things you can build with a mashup today. You run into a mashup tool, grab a couple of data sources, feed them into one of these fancy display options, and you end up with a working application that would have been really hard to build just a few years ago. Statistical data, visual maps, real-time activity of social networks, all right there, consolidated and displayed nicely after just 5 minutes of work.

When you think about the example of mashups, the technology to move data around and display it in nice visual representations has been around for a long time. The key element that enables all of these scenarios is availability of data. Ubiquity and simplicity add to the broad availability to complete the picture of a game-changing scenario where mashups are not only possible, but also trivial to build and effective in their application.

While this may sound easy and natural, sharing data effectively at the scale of the Web comes with its challenges. First of all, the Web is a big place, with lots of people and computers in it, so scalability is a big challenge. It's also a very diverse place, where keeping things simple and using low coupling is important. Finally, it's made of a bunch of smaller pieces, making composability and layering essential to make things work.

A number of folks have spent a lot of time reflecting about all this and documenting what makes the Web work well and what gets in the way of that. Things such as the REST architectural style observe and articulate the traits of applications that can satisfy the scale, layering, and long-term availability requirements of good web applications and services.

The goal of Project Astoria, which has become the ADO.NET Data Services framework, was to bridge the world of data locked in databases and other traditionally proprietary data sources with the world of the Web. We wanted to make it easy to create systems that expose data in a way that naturally followed the principles that make the Web work. We picked a resource model such that items of interesting granularity would become *resources* and the associations between those resources would be *links*. Every resource in the system is addressable with a URL, like any other web resource. Agents act on resources by using well-known verbs that client and server systems, as well as intermediaries, can understand and consider.

We tried hard not to invent anything. That way we could reuse everything out there, from proxies to authentication to representations. This could open the door to more data being available on the Web for applications to build on top of. Sometimes these will be simple applications in closed systems, sometimes large systems made of clients and servers exchanging data with minimum coupling, and sometimes they will involve shared data for anybody out there to use.

A small set of core principles is what makes the Web tick. We tried hard to capture them in the data services framework. But in order to successfully build applications that are good web citizens and benefit from its architecture, you must know these principles explicitly and know how the various APIs and options in the data services framework help you implement them.

In this book you'll find a discussion of these principles followed by a practical description of what the ADO.NET Data Services framework can do, how it does it, and what it means for your application. Hopefully the combination of principles, framework, and the guidance in this book will help you in your next data application or service undertaking, and you'll have the Web and its goodness working for you.

Pablo Castro
Software Architect
Microsoft Corporation

About the Authors

SIMON EVANS has worked for ten years as a software developer and technical architect. He has architected enterprise-scale applications and services for clients that are household names. Simon is a managing consultant for Conchango in the U.K., part of EMC Consulting Services. He is an expert in .NET development, and more specifically in WCF and ASP.NET, having participated in several Microsoft early adoption programs. Simon believes deeply that a broad understanding of key technology concepts is an essential foundation to being a gifted designer and builder of solutions. Simon is a regular contributor to the blogosphere through his blog at http://blogs. conchango.com/simonevans, where he writes about all .NET technologies including ADO.NET Data Services.

JOHN SHAW has worked in business processing and integration for over ten years and has architected some of the largest Microsoft integration projects in the U.S., U.K., and Australia. His technical expertise includes implementing Microsoft BizTalk and messaging standards for a variety of clients in finance, supply chain, and other sectors. Most recently, he founded SphereGen, a niche company that provides a blended model of low-cost onshore and offshore solutions for its clients. Prior to that, John worked as the U.S. BizTalk Practice Lead for Conchango Plc., where he obtained BizTalk Virtual Technical Specialist (VTS) status within Microsoft.

John is a regular contributor to the blogosphere through his blog at http://blogs. spheregen.com/johnshaw, where he writes about all .NET technologies including ADO.NET Data Services.

About the Technical Reviewer

DAMIEN FOGGON is a freelance developer and technical author based in Newcastle, England. When not wondering why the Newcastle Falcons can never win at home or away, he spends his spare time writing, playing rugby, scuba diving, or pretending that he can cook.

If he could be consistent (or interesting), his blog might not be three months out of date. You never know, you may be lucky. See for yourself at `http://www.littlepond.co.uk`.

Acknowledgments

I would like to thank my partner, Angharad, for her continuous help and support throughout the highs and lows of writing this book. I would also like to thank my parents for buying me my first computer at the age of eight and helping me learn to program it. Without this investment, I would not be in my chosen career.

Several people have helped in reading and providing opinion on the content of this book. Beyond everyone at Apress who have turned a rambling text into a coherent body of work, I would also like to thank my colleagues at Conchango who have provided valuable opinion. In particular I would like to thank Owain Wragg for providing an extra pair of eyes over much of the content of this book.

Simon Evans

I would like to thank my wife, Lori, for her love and support and her inspiration. Thanks also to my family and friends who have stuck by me over the years, particularly my parents, who helped me emerge from a little-known town called Warrington. Similar to Simon's parents, mine bought me a ZX spectrum when I was five years old, providing a solid programming foundation.

Additionally, I would like to thank Mark Beckner, Damien Foggon, Ami Knox, and the rest of the team at Apress, as well as Mike Taulty and Jon Flanders, who provided valuable early insights into ADO.NET Data Services. Lastly I would like to thank the Astoria team, particularly Pablo Castro and Mike Flasko, who have put together a great piece of software.

John Shaw

PART 1

ADO.NET Data Service Fundamentals

What does the word "elegant" mean to you? According to one dictionary, it is defined as "gracefully concise and simple; admirably succinct." Elegant is great way to describe ADO.NET Data Services and the underlying concepts of REST.

Paradoxically, ADO.NET Data Services is big on concepts and fuses together many technologies in the Microsoft stack. Therefore, let us not confuse elegance with simplicity; developing a data service is a hugely productive yet deceptively complex undertaking that requires no less consideration than developing any other kind of service.

The elegance of ADO.NET Data Services is demonstrated by the fact that the core technology stack is covered in a single part of the book over three chapters. These chapters take you on a journey through the big concepts that have shaped ADO.NET Data Services as a technology, and describe the fundamental knowledge you need to get working with developing and testing your own data services.

CHAPTER 1

■ ■ ■

The Foundations of ADO.NET Data Services

Software development is hard; one year in development is equivalent to a dog year's worth of change. The problem of rapid change is exacerbated by those in the industry who incessantly call the latest innovation the silver bullet that will solve the world's ills. While this is never the case, innovations in technology, if used appropriately, do deliver better solutions that improve the bottom line of the businesses we serve.

Underpinning technology innovations are concepts, which evolve at a much slower rate than the specifics of a new technology. Concepts help us solve many of the requirements that are common to most of the solutions that we as software developers have to deliver in the enterprise.

ADO.NET Data Services is a new technology designed to meet one of the most common requirements in software development: access to data over a network. Developers use three key concepts to meet this requirement, each of which we'll discuss in this chapter:

- The concept of **set-based logic** to access data from a data source

- The concept of **object orientation** to apply business logic to data

- The concept of **service orientation** to communicate data using messages across a network

This chapter will describe the key Microsoft technologies that apply to using these concepts and explore how ADO.NET Data Services builds on top of these foundations to make working with data over a network more productive than ever before.

The Concept of Set-Based Logic

Set-based logic is about solving a problem in terms of sets of data, where a set of data is defined by statements that limit, group, and order the data in the set. For example, you may wish to retrieve a set of customers where the customers' first names equal "Joe" and order the set of customers by their last names. When developers think of set-based logic, they normally think of Structured Query Language (SQL), which is the most common way of implementing set-based logic. A limitation of SQL as a technology is that it is only used to retrieve data from a data source (usually a relational database) such as SQL Server. To give developers a way to carry out set-based operations in code, Microsoft introduced Language Integrated Query (LINQ) in .NET 3.5, which applies the concept of set-based logic to work with all forms of data, whether the information comes from SQL Server or XML, or is in memory.

Under the covers, LINQ uses technologies such as SQL to work with data from the data source, but it abstracts the need for developers to learn several technologies when they have to perform set-based logic. Flavors of LINQ include LINQ to Objects, LINQ to SQL, and LINQ to XML.

The Concept of Object Orientation

Whereas set-based logic is used to access data, object orientation is used to provide a representation of that data to some real-world entities (objects). The reason that object orientation is so important to writing maintainable solutions is that the representation of data as it is stored in a database does not describe the behavior of that information. For example, you could have customers modeled in a Customer table in SQL Server, each with a customer type, such as buyer and vendor. Clearly, some ways in which you need to interact with buyers and vendors will be the same, as they are both customers; but in other ways, the business rules you use with buyers may well differ from those customers who are vendors. For example, you may want to provide vendors with access to sales on your web site, but this information must be withheld from buyers because it is sensitive information. Yet both buyers and vendors would need to log in to the web site, so business rules dealing with authentication and authorization would need to apply to all customers.

Object orientation allows both buyer and vendor entities to inherit from a base customer entity, meaning that they can both behave as customers, but also extend this common behavior with buyer- or vendor-specific properties and methods. Figure 1-1 shows this principle, with the Buyer and Vendor classes inheriting from the Customer abstract class. The Buyer and Vendor classes extend the base class, each adding a property and method associated with how buyers and vendors handle products. Without object orientation, it would not be possible to treat both the Buyer and Vendor objects as customers.

Figure 1-1. *Simple example of the object-oriented principle of inheritance*

In moving between data as it is structured in a relational database and entities, there is clearly a need to map the data between its representation in a table and its representation in an entity. This difference in structure is sometimes referred to as an **impedance mismatch**. Traditionally, this problem would have been solved by writing mapping code in the data access layer, but recent innovations have led to the use of object relational mappers to perform the mapping between databases and objects. By using object relational mapping, the developer does not need to write tedious code to achieve this aim. Several object relational mappers are available to .NET developers, such as NHibernate, but this book will focus on Microsoft's own ADO.NET Entity Framework, because of its close relationship with ADO.NET Data Services and LINQ, using LINQ to Entities.

The Concept of Service Orientation

With set-based logic helping us access data and object orientation helping us implement business logic on that data, the final problem that needs to be solved in order to meet the original requirement is moving this data across a network. The concept of service orientation deals with this requirement by communicating data in discrete messages between a sender and a receiver application. The sender is commonly called the **client** or **proxy** and the receiver is the **service**.

The sent messages must conform to a contract dictated by the service. The contract defines exactly what structure of data is accepted by the service and how the data can be used. The format (such as XML) and encoding (such as text) of the message may differ, and the low-level protocol (transport) used for communication may differ also; however, by considering communication of data as encoded messages being sent and received over a transport using a set contract, service orientation loosely couples the sender and receiver, and acknowledges that the technology implementation of the transport and encoding may change over time. Indeed, we may also want to use different transports and encodings for different clients. For example, we may want to expose a service to external customers over the Internet using the Hypertext Transfer Protocol (HTTP) transport with a text encoding, but internally we may want to communicate using TCP/IP and a binary encoding, because internally we have control of the development of our own clients and the security of our network.

In .NET, the concept of service orientation is delivered using Windows Communication Foundation (WCF), and ADO.NET Data Services is built on top of this foundation. WCF is described in detail later on in this chapter in the section "The ABCs of Windows Communication Foundation."

RESTful Thinking

If you have designed components or services in the past, you are most likely to have developed an interface or service contract, where you define what operations a component is allowed to perform. For example, you might design a contract that contains three operations: GetProductById, PersistProduct, and DeleteProduct. Each of these operations deals with a product entity and defines what you can do with a product. In other words, each operation is a **verb**, and it deals with the product entity, which is a **noun**.

Why do we write service contracts containing operations describing what a client can do with the service? It is because there is commonly no other mechanism for understanding how a service can be consumed. But the majority of **web** services use HTTP as their transport. This protocol specifies HTTP verbs that must be sent in the request message. Therefore, if we are only exposing our service over HTTP, it is possible to use the protocol itself to understand the intent. This is the architecture proposed by Roy Fielding when he first described a style of service-oriented architecture (SOA) known as representational state transfer (REST).

REST services do not require you to design your own service contracts, because you can rely on HTTP verbs to describe intent. This radically simplifies your service's design. HTTP defines the verbs GET, PUT, POST, and DELETE. By using these built-in verbs, REST services provide access to resources (our nouns) via a Uniform Resource Indicator (URI) and an HTTP verb. For example, you could get a product by its ID by specifying `http://myservice.com/Products(1)` using an HTTP GET verb.

By focusing on resources rather than intent, REST services expose a behavior that is unique to this style of SOA; every resource exposed by a service is accessible to the client if the client decides to address it. This open architecture for services is much more akin to how the world uses the Internet as a whole: a pool of resources where consumers decide what they want to access.

The ABCs of Windows Communication Foundation

Anyone who has built software on any scale is likely to have had to work with APIs that deal with communicating information between two or more computers. All forms of communication involve creating messages that are transported over the wire from one computer to another. If you look at this concept from a far enough distance, all applications have similar communication requirements, and yet up until recently developers have had to learn different APIs for different forms of communication. For example, a developer using .NET 1.1 would use ASMX web services (`System.Web.Services`) for communication over HTTP using SOAP messages, the `System.Messaging` namespace for communications over TCP/IP or RPC using MSMQ messages, and remoting (`System.Remoting`) for communications over TCP/IP using binary messages to remoting applications.

While this proliferation of APIs makes the developer's life much harder, meaning they have to learn and relearn a list of APIs that keeps growing as the communication protocols evolve, it has a more damaging impact on the investment made by the owner of your software; as your business changes, the requirements you have of your software inevitably change, which can include changing how your solutions need to communicate with other solutions. This inevitably means switching communication APIs and throwing away much of your existing investment. Furthermore, if you want to extend your application to support more than one form of communication, you will have to duplicate effort in your architecture by supporting more than one API.

In .NET 3.0, Microsoft introduced WCF to provide a universal API for communications to and from the Windows platform. This rich framework is able to serve as such an API because it abstracts all the common behaviors that communication protocols share into its architecture, and provides extensibility points to accommodate future changes and additions to communication protocols.

You may well be wondering why such an undertaking has not been conducted before. While the concept of communications via messages is simple to grasp, the intricate differences between each communication protocol make the job of abstraction a monumental task. WCF was over two years in the making before the first version was released. When this work was started back in 2003, many in the industry thought that all web services would adopt SOAP over HTTP as the standard communications protocol for web services.

WHAT IS SOAP?

SOAP, which stands for Simple Object Access Protocol, is a W3C messaging specification based on XML. The specification defines three major parts to a message structure: the envelope, the header, and the body. The SOAP header and the body are both contained within the envelope, which is the root element of a SOAP message. The header contains important metadata that relates to how the message should be used by a service. For example, one common header is the Action header used to address a SOAP message. The body contains the core information that is consumed by a service.

However, in recent years, REST has become more ubiquitous than SOAP as a standard for public services available across the Internet. Fortunately, the WCF team's investment in abstracting the concepts of communication paid dividends, as they were easily able to accommodate the communication requirements of REST in .NET 3.5.

WCF abstracts the communication of messages into three key pillars: address, binding, and contract (ABC). An **address** identifies **who** the intended recipient for the message is. In the Internet world, this is most commonly a URI, but in other communication protocols, the address may take on other forms. A **binding** describes **how** the message will be communicated, including which transport and encoding to use, as well as any other policies such as security that apply to how the message is communicated. For example, a SOAP-formatted message may be sent over an HTTP transport using text encoding. A **contract** describes **what** format the message(s) will take, what a service can do, and what format any faults in the service will take.

Addresses

For anyone who uses the Internet, the concept of an address is most easily associated with entering a Uniform Resource Locator (URL) into a browser to retrieve a web page. The URL points to the location of a resource on the Internet. The URL is a subset of a URI, which defines both the location and the Uniform Resource Name (URN) for the resource. This URI is the address of the web page, which is coupled to the transport you are using (HTTP). REST services such as those you develop using ADO.NET Data Services are entirely reliant on the addressing capabilities of HTTP; once you strip away the semantics of a message sent using HTTP, the content of the message does not include the address of the intended recipient.

While addressing for REST services is a simple matter of understanding that the URI is the address, it is worth understanding the importance of addressing within the broader sphere of messaging architectures and message topologies. REST-based services are broadly used by consumers that adopt a request-reply message exchange pattern; this means the client (such as a browser) sends a request message to a URI address and waits for a response from that URI. However, other important message exchange patterns exist, such as one-way (datagram) messaging, where the client sends a message without waiting for a reply. One-way messaging is an important pattern because it allows high-scale messaging for circumstances where the client need not wait for a response from the service.

A message topology often used with one-way messaging is a **service intermediary**. Consider a service intermediary to be a similar concept to a postman, who delivers your mail without knowing or caring about the content. For example, a service intermediary may be used to take a text-encoded message sent via HTTP over the Internet and forward the message on using binary encoding over TCP/IP. Service intermediaries are only concerned with whom the recipient of the message is, and thus they must understand the address of the message. Because REST services rely on the URI for addressing, it is assumed that this URI is the ultimate recipient of the message, because the message does not contain any other address. Therefore, intermediaries cannot be easily employed using solely REST-based architectures.

■**Note** Another important message topology that relies heavily on the concept of addressing is the **service broker topology**, where the broker acts as a hub to messages published to it and then broadcasts messages to subscribers of the published message. An important example of a service broker is BizTalk Server.

Bindings

In WCF a binding describes how messages are sent and received. The binding is used to create a **channel stack**, where each channel in the stack is a facet of the overall method of communication. A channel stack must always include an encoding and a transport (such as text sent over HTTP), but it can also include other information, such as security or WS-* policies as described by the binding.

WHAT IS WS-*?

WS-* is a set of standardized web service policies for SOAP-based messages. The policies have a number of contributors including Microsoft, IBM, and Sun Microsystems, which ensure their adoption across platforms.

WS-* policies handle common messaging requirements that are not standardized by the SOAP protocol itself. Such policies include WS-Addressing, which standardizes the method used to address a message, WS-Security, which applies message-level security, and WS-ReliableMessaging, which can be used to guarantee message ordering between sender and receiver.

In WCF you can create a binding from scratch, but several commonly used bindings come out the box, including WebHttpBinding (since .NET 3.5), which is used by ADO.NET Data Services to describe how RESTful messages are sent and received. Bindings can be configured either in code or, more commonly, within a configuration file. Listing 1-1 shows example bindings for both a WebHttpBinding (used for REST services) and WsHttpBinding (used by SOAP services that use WS-* policies).

Listing 1-1. *Example WCF Configurations for a REST and WS-* Service*

```
<configuration>
  <system.serviceModel>
    <bindings>
      <wsHttpBinding>
        <binding name="SampleWsHttpBinding">
          <reliableSession enabled="true" />
```

```xml
          <security mode="None">
            <message clientCredentialType="None" negotiateServiceCredential="false"
                establishSecurityContext="false" />
          </security>
        </binding>
      </wsHttpBinding>
    </bindings>
    <services>
      <service behaviorConfiguration="Apress.Services.SampleWebServiceBehavior"
        name="Apress.Services.SampleWebService">
        <endpoint behaviorConfiguration="Apress.Services.SampleWebEndpointBehavior"
          binding="webHttpBinding" name="WebEndpoint"
bindingNamespace="http://schemas.apress.com/"
          contract="Apress.Services.ISampleWebService" />
      </service>
      <service behaviorConfiguration="Apress.Services.SampleWsServiceBehavior"
        name="Apress.Services.SampleWsService">
        <endpoint binding="wsHttpBinding" bindingConfiguration="SampleWsHttpBinding"
          name="WsEndpoint" contract="Apress.Services.ISampleWsService" />
        <host>
          <baseAddresses>
            <add baseAddress="http://localhost/SampleWsService" />
          </baseAddresses>
        </host>
      </service>
    </services>
    <serviceHostingEnvironment aspNetCompatibilityEnabled="true"/>
    <behaviors>
      <endpointBehaviors>
        <behavior name="Apress.Services.SampleWebEndpointBehavior">
          <enableWebScript/>
        </behavior>
      </endpointBehaviors>
      <serviceBehaviors>
        <behavior name="Apress.Services.SampleWebServiceBehavior">
          <serviceMetadata httpGetEnabled="true"/>
          <serviceDebug includeExceptionDetailInFaults="true"/>
        </behavior>
        <behavior name="Apress.Services.SampleWsServiceBehavior">
          <serviceMetadata httpGetEnabled="true"/>
          <serviceSecurityAudit auditLogLocation="Application"/>
        </behavior>
      </serviceBehaviors>
    </behaviors>
  </system.serviceModel>
</configuration>
```

WebHttpBinding defines a channel stack with HTTP/HTTPS as its transport and text as its encoding. It differs from other HTTP-based bindings such as BasicHttpBinding in that it does not assume the semantics of a SOAP message. Therefore, it does not wrap the contents of the message inside an envelope, and it does not set the address of the message using a URI defined in an action header. Instead, it relies on the URI used by the HTTP protocol itself to address the message.

An encoding is a core part of all channel stacks created by WCF for any binding. It is important to understand that an encoding is not the same concept as serialization. **Serialization** is the process of taking an in-memory object and writing the contents of the object into a message. During object serialization, the serializer will format the message in a particular way, such as in XML or JSON format. Once the message has been serialized, an encoding is then required to specify how the message will be streamed over the wire. For example, an object may be serialized to XML and then encoded into a binary message sent over the wire. In the context of ADO.NET Data Services, all data is transmitted using a text encoding and is serialized either into JSON or Atom format. This is controlled by specifying an Accept HTTP header on the request message.

Contracts

Contracts describe the messages that are exchanged between a client and a service. WCF enables you to design contracts that define the types of data passed using data contracts and how this data can be used through service contracts, which contain one or more operations describing what methods a service supports. An easy way to consider service contracts is that they are the verbs that describe what a service does, and data contracts are the nouns that describe the objects passed between services.

In SOAP services, data contracts and service contracts are represented by XML Schema Definitions (XSDs) that you define. The service exposes a Web Service Definition Language (WSDL) that a client can examine to understand how to consume these contracts.

REST services differ from SOAP services in that they use the HTTP verbs and the URI to describe the service operations (what a service can do). Therefore, REST services have no need for a WSDL to describe service operations. REST services use the verbs of HTTP to describe the action of the message in terms of Create, Read, Update, and Delete (CRUD) semantics. So, for example, if you are reading data from a REST service, the message will use the HTTP GET verb along with the URI called to identify what information to read from the service. Alternatively, if you are updating data from a REST service, you will use the HTTP POST verb and post the data to the service in the request message.

When messages are received by a service's channel stack, the message needs to be passed on to the correct service operation as defined in the service's contract. WCF conducts this wiring job in a class called the ChannelDispatcher. In WCF services that use WebHttpBinding, the ChannelDispatcher handles wiring a URI and HTTP verb to a service operation in a service contract by examining the WebGet (for HTTP GET) and WebInvoke (for other HTTP verbs) attributes of the operations in a service contract. WCF also provides a class named UriTemplate, which can be used to understand URI patterns, defining the format of arguments passed into the service operation via the URI. This is in contrast to SOAP messages that use BasicHttpBinding, where the ChannelDispatcher examines the message's Action header to determine which service operation to execute.

Endpoint = Address + Binding + Contract

By using the constructs of address, binding, and contract, WCF delivers a conceptual model for building systems that need to communicate using messages. These three collectively describe an endpoint for a service. A service may expose many endpoints, either because the service exposes many contracts or because the service exposes the same contract using different bindings. For example, a service may want to expose a contract using one endpoint configured to use a WsHttpBinding for clients consuming the service from the Internet, and a different endpoint exposing the same contract using NetTcpBinding for internal clients, where security requirements are different and internal clients are able to take advantage of binary encoding across the LAN.

■**Note** WCF comes with a configuration editor in the SDK to help you safely edit the bindings you use to expose your service endpoints.

Hosting Endpoints

For a service to expose one or more endpoints to clients, the service needs a host in which to control instances of each endpoint at runtime. WCF defines a ServiceHost class that reads the description of the endpoint's binding, constructs a channel stack, and opens and closes communications for the service at a given address. In WCF, a host can be any AppDomain, from a console application to a web site running in IIS. IIS is a common choice to host HTTP-based bindings, because it manages process recycling and failure. In Windows Server 2008, Windows Activation Services (WAS) provides similar hosting semantics for non-HTTP-based endpoints. Alternatively, you can host a service outside of IIS or WAS, but you are responsible for keeping that process running and restarting the process after failure.

■**Note** During testing, it is quite common to use a console application as a host for ease of debugging, but in production, services are commonly hosted in IIS or WAS.

In addition to requiring a service host, WCF also defines a factory class called ServiceHostFactory, which is used by WCF in managed environments such as IIS to instantiate the ServiceHost class from a declarative statement placed in a service host file (an SVC file). You can subclass both the ServiceHost and ServiceHostFactory classes to add code specific to your hosting requirements. Data services have a predefined service host called DataServiceHost and a factory called DataServiceHostFactory that together contain all the extra ADO.NET Data Services–specific wiring for hosts of data services. ADO.NET Data Services assumes that you will host your service in IIS (or Visual Studio Web Development Server), which is a fair assumption given that ADO.NET Data Services is tightly coupled to the HTTP transport. Therefore a data service is called by addressing a SVC host file.

Don't Forget the Client

When considering service design, it is equally as important to consider the design of the service from the perspective of a calling client; if your service's contracts are difficult to consume, you will dissuade developers from using your service. Regardless of how you design a service, a client needs to understand how to send and receive messages to and from a service in the correct format over the correct transport to the correct address.

Most WCF clients address this requirement by creating a set of proxy classes, which can be handwritten or generated using svcutil.exe (a tool that comes with the SDK). These proxy classes serialize and deserialize to the correct message format and deal with creating the correct channel stack in order to communicate with the service.

Putting It All Together

A summary of all the preceding discussion on WFC leaves us with a generic WCF architecture that looks the one in Figure 1-2.

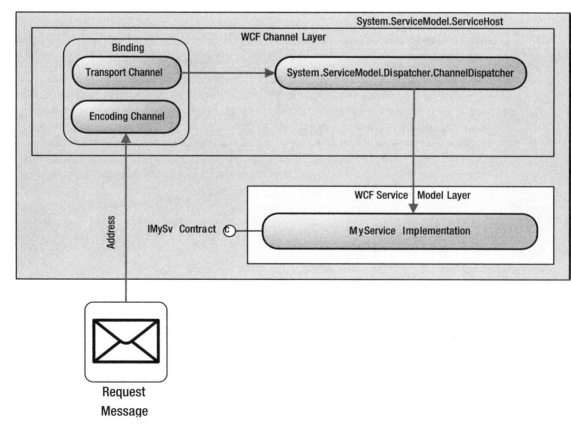

Figure 1-2. *Overview of a generic WCF architecture*

Understanding how WCF defines address, binding, and contract helps you to understand how ADO.NET Data Services has built on top of this foundation, and how this can fit into your broader enterprise SOA.

Standing on the Shoulders of Giants

So what exactly is ADO.NET Data Services? It is best described as the marriage of the technologies that together meet the requirement of accessing data over a network. ADO.NET Data Services uses WCF's ability to create REST-style services, coupled with LINQ's ability to perform set-based logic on a data source such as the Entity Framework, which maps data between a relational database and entities.

So ADO.NET Data Services is standing on the shoulders of giants in the .NET universe. What it adds to this already rich technology stack is simplicity. While WCF, LINQ, and the Entity Framework could be used without ADO.NET Data Services to meet our requirement, ADO.NET Data Services adds an extra layer to the architecture that simplifies the marriage of these technologies. ADO.NET Data Services makes several assumptions about exactly how the requirement of remote data access will be delivered using REST-based services that

- **Only** work using HTTP/HTTPS

- **Only** work using Atom or JSON format messages using a text encoding

- **Only** work using a REST-based URI structure that is dictated for you

- **Only** work using operations that return the LINQ interface IQueryable

On the face of it, this may seem very limiting, but in reality most of these limitations are intrinsic to REST services themselves. REST services assume that you are designing services for the Web (and are thus reliant on HTTP as the underlying protocol). While this clearly doesn't apply to all services, it does to the vast majority, and for all other services you can still leverage WCF and build an architecture sympathetic to both needs.

Data services are composed of REST services, and these services use the URI for addressing and calling a service operation, together with a corresponding HTTP verb (such as GET). They use WebHttpBinding, which defines text-encoded messages transported over HTTP or HTTPS without any form of message envelope. These services have a predefined format for how to pass arguments via a service URI (similar in concept to a prewritten UriTemplate).

The Universal Service Contract

It is well known in software development that the cost of changing code increases dramatically once a version of the software has gone into production. Although change is something that we must all embrace, we should also be aware of any reasonable measures we can take while designing a solution that will limit this cost.

The most costly aspect to developing and evolving services is undoubtedly the cost of changing contracts in production. One of the reasons for such a cost to changing contracts is that you may need to support clients that consume an older version of the contract, while you roll out your new version of the service.

With SOAP services you define what you **can** do with a service; in ADO.NET Data Services you define what you **cannot** do with a service by locking down resources you do not want a client to access and making all accessible resources queryable and addressable. The impact of this REST-based architecture on contract design is that you do not need to specify lots of service operations that define what your service does, and locking down service resources does not involve any contract changes. Thus this architecture reduces the chances of changing your service contracts, because your contracts will only be affected by changes to the resources themselves.

ADO.NET Data Services defines a service contract out of the box named IRequestHandler. This contract defines only one service operation called ProcessRequestForMessage and is implemented by a class called DataService<T>, where T is a LINQ data source that implements IQueryable<T>. The service operation ProcessRequestForMessage enables you to access any information from the underlying data source via a URI and HTTP verb. Therefore, the URI becomes programmable using set-based logic, much like SQL. You define in DataService<T> what is not accessible by setting up access rules in the InitializeService method.

Atom and JSON

ADO.NET Data Services serializes messages into either Atom or JSON format, depending on the Accept HTTP header in the request message. Atom is a subset of XML, which is defined by a prewritten XML schema. JSON is not XML based, but it is defined by a standard contained in RFC 4627. Both of these message formats have one thing in common, which is that every data item in a **message** contains both the data and the type of data being sent or received. This is in contrast to SOAP services, where the types are defined by a separate XML schema rather than being part of the message itself.

The impact of using either Atom or JSON for serialization is that so long as your client understands the serialization format, it will be able to understand the types of data in the message without needing to refer to a separate contract. Additionally, ADO.NET Data Services makes all related data easily addressable, by exposing URIs for any related resources not returned in the response. Listing 1-2 shows an ADO.NET Data Services raw-text response serialized into Atom format, while Listing 1-3 shows the equivalent data in JSON format.

Listing 1-2. *Example ADO.NET Data Service Response Using Atom format*

```
<?xml version="1.0" encoding="utf-8" standalone="yes"?>
<feed
xml:base="http://localhost.:1478/Apress.Data.Services.CustomerService.Host/
CustomerDataService.svc/" xmlns:d="http://schemas.microsoft.com/ado/2007/08/
dataservices" xmlns:m="http://schemas.microsoft.com/ado/2007/08/
dataservices/metadata" xmlns="http://www.w3.org/2005/Atom">
  <title type="text">Customers</title>
  <id>http://localhost.:1478/Apress.Data.Services.CustomerService.Host/
CustomerDataService.svc/Customers</id>
  <updated>2008-09-07T20:00:41Z</updated>
  <link rel="self" title="Customers" href="Customers" />
  <entry>
    <id>http://localhost.:1478/Apress.Data.Services.CustomerService.Host/
CustomerDataService.svc/Customers(3)</id>
    <title type="text"></title>
    <updated>2008-09-07T20:00:41Z</updated>
    <author>
      <name />
    </author>
    <link rel="edit" title="Customer" href="Customers(3)" />
```

```
    <link rel="http://schemas.microsoft.com/ado/2007/08/dataservices/related/Gender"
type="application/atom+xml;type=entry" title="Gender" href="Customers(3)/Gender" />
    <link rel="http://schemas.microsoft.com/ado/2007/08/dataservices/related/
Salutation" type="application/atom+xml;type=entry" title="Salutation"
href="Customers(3)/Salutation" />
    <link rel="http://schemas.microsoft.com/ado/2007/08/dataservices/
related/Address" type="application/atom+xml;type=feed" title="Address"
href="Customers(3)/Address" />
    <link
rel="http://schemas.microsoft.com/ado/2007/08/dataservices/related/TelephoneNumber"
type="application/atom+xml;type=feed" title="TelephoneNumber"
href="Customers(3)/TelephoneNumber" />
    <category term="CustomerModel.Customer"
scheme="http://schemas.microsoft.com/ado/2007/08/dataservices/scheme" />
    <content type="application/xml">
      <m:properties>
        <d:CustomerId m:type="Edm.Int32">3</d:CustomerId>
        <d:FirstName>Jane</d:FirstName>
        <d:LastName>Smith</d:LastName>
        <d:DateOfBirth m:type="Edm.DateTime">1982-03-01T00:00:00</d:DateOfBirth>
      </m:properties>
    </content>
  </entry>
  <entry>
    <id>http://localhost.:1478/Apress.Data.Services.CustomerService.Host/
CustomerDataService.svc/Customers(5)</id>
    <title type="text"></title>
    <updated>2008-09-07T20:00:41Z</updated>
    <author>
      <name />
    </author>
    <link rel="edit" title="Customer" href="Customers(5)" />
    <link rel="http://schemas.microsoft.com/ado/2007/08/dataservices/related/Gender"
type="application/atom+xml;type=entry" title="Gender" href="Customers(5)/Gender" />
    <link rel="http://schemas.microsoft.com/ado/2007/08/dataservices/related/
Salutation" type="application/atom+xml;type=entry" title="Salutation"
href="Customers(5)/Salutation" />
    <link rel="http://schemas.microsoft.com/ado/2007/08/dataservices/related/
Address" type="application/atom+xml;type=feed" title="Address"
href="Customers(5)/Address" />
    <link rel="http://schemas.microsoft.com/ado/2007/08/dataservices/related/
TelephoneNumber" type="application/atom+xml;type=feed" title="TelephoneNumber"
href="Customers(5)/TelephoneNumber" />
    <category term="CustomerModel.Customer"
scheme="http://schemas.microsoft.com/ado/2007/08/dataservices/scheme" />
    <content type="application/xml">
      <m:properties>
```

```
        <d:CustomerId m:type="Edm.Int32">5</d:CustomerId>
        <d:FirstName>John</d:FirstName>
        <d:LastName>Smith</d:LastName>
        <d:DateOfBirth m:type="Edm.DateTime">1963-09-09T00:00:00</d:DateOfBirth>
      </m:properties>
    </content>
  </entry>
</feed>
```

Listing 1-3. *Example ADO.NET Data Service Response Using JSON Format*

```
{ "d" : [
{
"__metadata": {
"uri": "http://localhost.:1478/Apress.Data.Services.CustomerService.Host/
CustomerDataService.svc/Customers(3)", "type": "CustomerModel.Customer"
}, "CustomerId": 3, "FirstName": "Jane", "LastName": "Smith", "DateOfBirth":
"\/Date(383788800000)\/", "Gender": {
"__deferred": {
"uri": "http://localhost.:1478/Apress.Data.Services.CustomerService.Host/
CustomerDataService.svc/Customers(3)/Gender"
}
}, "Salutation": {
"__deferred": {
"uri": "http://localhost.:1478/Apress.Data.Services.CustomerService.Host/
CustomerDataService.svc/Customers(3)/Salutation"
}
}, "Address": {
"__deferred": {
"uri": "http://localhost.:1478/Apress.Data.Services.CustomerService.Host/
CustomerDataService.svc/Customers(3)/Address"
}
}, "TelephoneNumber": {
"__deferred": {
"uri": "http://localhost.:1478/Apress.Data.Services.CustomerService.Host/
CustomerDataService.svc/Customers(3)/TelephoneNumber"
}
}
}, {
"__metadata": {
"uri": "http://localhost.:1478/Apress.Data.Services.CustomerService.Host/
CustomerDataService.svc/Customers(5)", "type": "CustomerModel.Customer"
}, "CustomerId": 5, "FirstName": "John", "LastName": "Smith",
```

```
"DateOfBirth": "\/Date(-199238400000)\/", "Gender": {
"__deferred": {
"uri": "http://localhost.:1478/Apress.Data.Services.CustomerService.Host/
CustomerDataService.svc/Customers(5)/Gender"
}
}, "Salutation": {
"__deferred": {
"uri": "http://localhost.:1478/Apress.Data.Services.CustomerService.Host/
CustomerDataService.svc/Customers(5)/Salutation"
}
}, "Address": {
"__deferred": {
"uri": "http://localhost.:1478/Apress.Data.Services.CustomerService.Host/
CustomerDataService.svc/Customers(5)/Address"
}
}, "TelephoneNumber": {
"__deferred": {
"uri": "http://localhost.:1478/Apress.Data.Services.CustomerService.Host/
CustomerDataService.svc/Customers(5)/TelephoneNumber"
}
}
}
] }
```

A data service is able to understand the types of data from the underlying data source and emit these types within messages serialized into Atom or JSON format. This means that there is no need to develop your own data contracts as you would have done with SOAP services because the serialization format and the data source define these contracts for you.

■**Note** You should be aware however, that making changes to your underlying data source (such as the Entity Framework) will still effectively force you to version your service for customers who are still consuming the older data model.

The reason ADO.NET Data Services supports both Atom and JSON formats is that they are both useful in different circumstances. Atom-formatted messages are useful in cases where the client can work most effectively with XML (such as a Silverlight 2.0 client). The JSON format serializes messages into an object array format native to JavaScript clients (such as an HTML web page running in a browser). Browsers are therefore able to work with JSON-formatted data more efficiently than XML-formatted data because the former can be manipulated natively in JavaScript.

Data Service Hosting

ADO.NET Data Services assumes that your service will be hosted in IIS (or Visual Studio Web Development Server) and provide a DataServiceHost<T>, which supplies that additional wiring for building an ADO.NET Data Services host.

Data Service Clients

ADO.NET Data Services clients need to concern themselves with amending the HTTP Accept header in their HTTP request to ensure that a response is returned using the required data format (Atom or JSON). Additionally, with REST services such as those built using ADO.NET Data Services, it is not essential to create a set of proxy classes, because the address and transport are defined by HTTP. As most clients understand how to communicate over HTTP using a URI, it is possible to just create a simple HTTP request and parse the response. For example, you could use the WebClient class in the .NET Framework to create a simple HTTP request using HTTP GET.

Whether or not you use a set of proxy classes will depend on the type of client you are developing; a client developed for Ajax use (using JSON-formatted messages) will send a request using the browser's XMLHTTP capabilities. In this case, communications will be instigated by JavaScript running in a browser. Frameworks such as ASP.NET AJAX simplify the consumption of data services in JavaScript by providing prebuilt JavaScript libraries that deal with issues such as those relating to browser compatibility.

If you are consuming a data service from .NET code, you can use a tool provided with the ADO.NET Data Services SDK named DataSvcUtil.exe, which generates a .NET proxy for your service. The additional benefit this proxy has over just creating an HTTP request is that it understands how to serialize and deserialize Atom, and also provides LINQ to Data Services, which enables you to query your data service as though it were any other LINQ-based data source.

Putting It All Together

A summary of all the discussion of how ADO.NET Data Services fits in WCF leaves us with an ADO.NET Data Services–WCF architecture that looks like Figure 1-3.

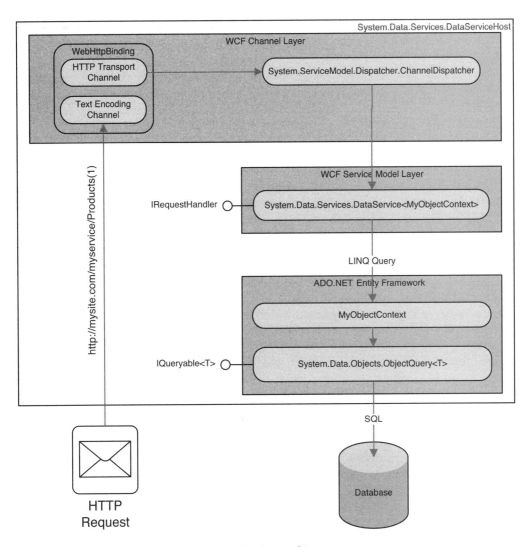

Figure 1-3. *Overview of the ADO.NET Data Services architecture*

From the preceding figure you can see how ADO.NET Data Services fits into broader technology stack of WCF and LINQ.

Reports of My Death Have Been Greatly Exaggerated

Looking at the architecture of REST services and how ADO.NET Data Services implements this approach to designing services, you would be forgiven for thinking that there is no future for SOAP, or at least architectures that operate along the lines of discrete service operations. The greatest asset of a REST-based architecture is its pure elegance; like all the best ideas, it is devastatingly and beautifully simple. Yet you must consider what it cannot do, which is both its strength and its weakness.

When Microsoft and other big vendors backed SOAP and WS-* standards, all parties were looking for standards that could work in any number of complex scenarios. It is the classic "But what if?" mindset that many architects adopt when they try to build future-proofed systems. The reality of building an extensible model that can deal with all scenarios is that you build complexity into your architecture. This one-size-fits-all bloat is something you definitely feel when you implement services using SOAP, and fans of REST architectures will cry "You ain't gonna need it" from the rooftops.

But be clear here. By choosing to design a service using REST, you are making some big decisions about what you will not need in the future. Table 1-1 looks at key differences between REST services and SOAP/WS-* service capabilities.

Table 1-1. *Capabilities of REST and WS-* Services*

Capability	REST Services	WS-* Services
Addressing	Limited to simple topologies addressed via URI and HTTP verb	Available via WS-Addressing
Transport	HTTP and HTTPS	Any (for example, RPC and TCP/IP)
Encoding	Text only	Any (for example, binary)
Message Exchange Pattern	Request-reply only	Any (for example, duplex)
Topology	Peer to peer	Any (for example, service broker)
Ordering	No support	Available via WS-ReliableMessaging
Transactions	No support	Available via WS-AtomicTransactions
Security	Only transport security via HTTPS	HTTPS, WS-Security, WS-SecureConversation, and WS-Trust

When you look at this table, it is not surprising to see why REST services have become so commonplace for public-facing services on the Internet. In these scenarios, you only ever want to expose your service via HTTP, and you do not want to secure access to your services. You are not interested in atomic transactional support, or the order in which messages are sent and received. You are only interested in supporting simple request-response scenarios. However, services designed for internal consumption within an enterprise or business-to-business can look very different, and some of the additional capabilities of WS-* may be necessary in specific scenarios.

The reality is WS-* is not dead, nor is REST only suitable for public Internet-facing services. As an architect, you have to look at the scenarios you face, determine the probability of change, and choose the appropriate tool for the job. The reality of future enterprise SOAs is that they will mix and match all these technologies, and in the Microsoft space they will share WCF as the common foundation for all services, regardless of which implementation best suits your current needs.

LINQ to Something

So far this chapter has largely focused on describing ADO.NET Data Services from the outside: what ADO.NET Data Services looks like to design and consumes from a messaging perspective. Internal to any service is an implementation, which in ADO.NET Data Services is achieved through a class named DataService<T>.

The service contract IRequestHandler that DataService<T> implements only one operation called ProcessRequestForMessage, and the implementation for this method is already written within the DataService<T> class as part of ADO.NET Data Services. This operation wires up an HTTP verb and the inbound URI to executing a method in an interface called IQueryable<T>, which is defined in the System.Linq subsystem of the .NET Framework.

The importance of executing queries against IQueryable<T> is that it enables developers to choose which underlying LINQ-based provider they wish to expose as a service through ADO.NET Data Services. Since .NET 3.5 SP1, the framework provides two implementations of IQueryable<T>: LINQ to SQL and LINQ to Entities. LINQ to SQL enables you to query a SQL Server database, and LINQ to Entities uses the ADO.NET Entity Framework to enable you to query the conceptual model to manipulate data in an underlying data source. Alternatively, you can also write your own LINQ provider or use some of the many LINQ provider implementations freely available on the Internet, such as LINQ to LDAP for querying an LDAP data source.

Before describing IQueryable<T> further, it is important to understand some key technology concepts specific to LINQ.

■**Note** The general term "LINQ," as mentioned previously, groups together several underlying implementations such as LINQ to Objects, LINQ to SQL, LINQ to Entities, LINQ to Datasets, and LINQ to XML. When you read the term LINQ, it is important to understand which implementation of LINQ is being referred to, as different flavors of LINQ have subtly different characteristics.

Defining LINQ

The beginning of this chapter described the key concept of set-based logic, where a set of data is manipulated using queries (such as those written in SQL). LINQ is a new feature of .NET 3.5 that brings the concepts of set-based logic into the .NET world.

At the heart of LINQ is a framework defined under the System.Linq namespace, which when coupled with the new language constructs of C# 3.0 provides the ability to write LINQ queries, either over objects held locally or over remote data sources.

The key features of C# 3.0 that are important to writing LINQ queries are extension methods and lambda expressions. **Extension methods** enable you to extend the methods of an existing type. For example, you could create an extension method to the String class called ToStringArray(), which when called turns a string variable into a string array. **Lambda expressions** enable you to write an expression within a method signature that is evaluated at runtime. Lambda expressions are a shorthand way of writing a delegate.

LINQ provides classes that contain extension methods commonly referred to as **query operators**. Examples of LINQ query operators are Select, Where, and GroupBy. Many of these methods will feel familiar to SQL developers as much of the set-based logic in LINQ follows the same semantics as SQL. Query operators accept lambda expressions as a way of evaluating the input to the query operator to return an output.

LINQ to Local Data

LINQ defines a class named `Enumerable`, which contains the query operators used to write LINQ queries over local objects in memory. These query operators are extension methods to the `IEnumerable<T>` interface, which is an existing .NET interface inherited by all generic collections, such as `List<T>`. Using extension methods in this way means that any type that inherits `IEnumerable<T>` can be queried using LINQ. Objects that implement `IEnumerable<T>` are collections of objects or XML documents loaded into memory. These two flavors of LINQ are commonly referred to as LINQ to Objects and LINQ to XML, respectively.

Query operators defined in the `Enumerable` class typically accept an input collection and return an output collection. The contents of the output collection would depend on the conditions of the Lambda expression. A simple LINQ query is shown in Listing 1-4.

Listing 1-4. *Example LINQ Query Using Extension Methods and Lambda Expressions*

```
using System;
using System.Linq;

namespace Apress.Data.Web.Samples.NameGenerator
{
    class Program
    {
        static void Main(string[] args)
        {
            string[] names = new string[] { "Simon", "John", "Angharad", "Tim" };

            string[] longnames = GetLongNames(names);

            foreach (string name in longnames)
            {
                Console.WriteLine(name);
            }
        }

        static string[] GetLongNames(string[] names)
        {
            var longnames = names.Where(n => n.Length > 4);

            return longnames.ToArray();
        }
    }
}
```

Executing this code would return two names: Simon and Angharad. The `Where()` method is a query operator defined in `Enumerable`. The lambda expression it executes returns an output collection of string objects longer than four characters. The n variable is of type `string` because the array `names` is a string array. The `Where()` query operator is able to be executed directly from the `names` string array, because the string array inherits `IEnumerable<T>`.

Notice that the object `longnames` is declared as type var. The var keyword in C# 3.0 is an implicit type. This means that it is strongly typed, taking the return type of the `Where()` method, which is the output collection of type `IEnumerable<string>`. Finally, the query operator `ToArray()` is called to cast the output sequence to the type `string[]`. This is an important step in the preceding code, because it is only here that the query is actually executed; this process is known as **deferred execution**, which can mislead developers who think that the result of the query is set on the line of code that returns the original output sequence.

LINQ to Remote Data

LINQ defines a class named `Queryable`, which contains the query operators used to write LINQ queries to remote data. These query operators are extension methods to the `IQueryable<T>` interface, which is an interface inherited by collections that **represent** the remote data source. The query operators under the `Queryable` class largely mirror those in the `Enumerable` class, meaning that to developers, the syntax for writing LINQ queries is the same whether you are querying local objects or remote data.

The `IQueryable<T>` objects that represent the underlying data source are objects provided by a LINQ implementation. The two LINQ implementations that come out the box with the .NET Framework are LINQ to SQL and LINQ to Entities. LINQ to SQL translates LINQ queries into Transact SQL (T-SQL) for SQL Server. LINQ to Entities translate a LINQ query into Entity SQL (E-SQL) for the ADO.NET Entity Framework. E-SQL is a special form of SQL used by the ADO.NET Entity Framework to query the conceptual model defined by the ORM.

■**Note** It is possible to write your own LINQ provider by inheriting `IQueryable<T>`. Alternatively, as mentioned previously, many LINQ providers are freely available on the Internet, such as LINQ to LDAP, used to translate LINQ queries into LDAP queries.

A LINQ implementation provides `IQueryable<T>` classes containing implementation details to interpret a query for a specific data source. For example, LINQ to SQL provides classes such as `Table<T>` to represent tables of data in SQL Server, providing specific methods to execute against a table of SQL Server data.

Using LINQ to query remote data sources is very similar to querying in-memory objects, but for one extra task; you must develop special entity classes that represent the entities stored in your underlying database. These entities map C# types to the underlying data structure. In LINQ to SQL, this is achieved by attaching attributes to the types in your entity, specifying the columns and key constraints in the underlying tables. This metadata is used by LINQ to SQL to understand how to translate the LINQ query into T-SQL.

The extra work of generating entity types for your data source is alleviated by the provision of tools to automatically generate these classes based on the structure of the data source itself. From within Visual Studio you can generate LINQ to SQL classes from a SQL Server database and use the visual designer to manipulate the created classes. Similarly, the ADO.NET Entity Framework provides a designer for creating a conceptual model of your entities, which inherit from `IQueryable<T>`.

The `IQueryable<T>` classes generated either by using LINQ to SQL or LINQ to Entities are wrapped in a context class (named `DataContext` for LINQ to SQL or `ObjectContext` for LINQ to

Entities). It is this class that is wired into the ADO.NET Data Services `DataService<T>` service implementation, where T is your strongly typed context object. The WCF service implementation of ADO.NET Data Services translates the inbound URI and HTTP verb to a LINQ query against your chosen `IQueryable` data source within the `ProcessRequestForMessage` method. This LINQ query is then interpreted by the underlying LINQ implementation to execute the query native to the data source.

LINQ TO SQL VS. LINQ TO ENTITIES

You may be wondering at this point why there are two implementations of LINQ that work for databases in the .NET Framework? Either will work with ADO.NET Data Services, but which one should you choose?

The key difference between LINQ to SQL and LINQ to Entities is that LINQ to Entities provides a conceptual model for your database, whereas LINQ to SQL works much more closely with the relational data model of your database. The extra layer of abstraction LINQ to Entities provides from the structure of the database itself enables you to design an object-oriented representation (conceptual model) of your relational database. Queries written in LINQ to Entities are executed against this conceptual model using E-SQL. The entity framework handles mapping between the conceptual model of your entities and the relational model in your database using an ORM, thus addressing an impedance mismatch that can occur between how you ideally want to model the data in the database and how you want represent an object model in your code.

LINQ to SQL has limited mapping capabilities and unlike LINQ to Entities only works with SQL Server. However, if you do not have a big impedance mismatch between your database design and your object model and you are using SQL Server, LINQ to SQL is a simpler and therefore quicker option to use for development.

Summary

This chapter covers a lot of ground in the .NET field because ADO.NET Data Services touches so many concepts and technologies. Clearly, there is much to take in and think about here: the ramifications of REST on the world of service orientation, and the contribution of both WCF and LINQ to the architecture of ADO.NET Data Services and the wider enterprise.

ADO.NET Data Services is a great example of the whole being more valuable than the sum of its parts; the concepts of REST and the implementation of ADO.NET Data Services are devastatingly elegant. When you write your first REST service and come to terms with what it really means to your world, you may well ask yourself, "What do I do now?" It does indeed feel so very simple, but it is always possible to create a bad design regardless of the technologies you are using.

Developing services using ADO.NET Data Services enables you to focus on important aspects of service design that in the past may have been ignored due to the amount of heavy lifting needed elsewhere. Focus on the relational database design to ensure the best structure for your data store. Focus on the object model design to ensure the most natural programming model. Focus on the design of your service for easy client consumption by targeting the best data formats and URI structures. Finally, learn when and when not to apply a REST service architecture.

■ ■ ■

CHAPTER 2

Addressing RESTful ADO.NET Data Services

If you're a developer, you probably want to learn everything about ADO.NET Data Services as quickly as possible so you can implement it in your company. However, as with most software development that is undertaken, you should observe certain principles. Architecturally, ADO. NET Data Services is a strange beast because it's a technology that really makes you think about your resources as assets and how to exploit them. In fact, the way that you expose these is actually quite easy. To understand ADO.NET Data Services, you need to forget how you'd traditionally expose services as RPC calls. Luckily, guidelines exist for covering the design of your service.

The initial part of this chapter sets the scene by examining the differences between REST and traditional web service programming, as well as the RESTful design tenets that should be applied when developing your services.

The chapter goes on to explain on how to configure your environment with the "latest and greatest" technology from Microsoft. An introductory exercise then shows you how to create your first data service. Through an examination of this data service, you'll learn about the features of the query string that is the heart of ADO.NET Data Services and how it provides RESTful addressability features through URLs. A thorough understanding of this query string and its expression language is required before you can attempt to write your own data service interface.

The topics that will be discussed in this chapter are as follows:

- **Brief history of where we are**: In this discussion, you'll learn how services have evolved to what they are today and where the RESTful service fits into modern services.

- **Getting started**: Set up your environment so you can follow along with the rest of this book.

- **Creating your first data service**: This exercise provides a step-by-step guide to create the Northwind service that will be used throughout this chapter and the book.

- **Addressing data**: See how data is described by ADO.NET Data Services in the form of resource sets, resources, and links in order to promote a uniform addressable interface for the data.

- **Data representation**: The format of data exposed by the service can be changed without changing any server-side code.

- **Formulating data service queries**: Learn how to formulate URL queries using all the standard query operations: $filter, $expand, $orderby, $top, and $skip.

Brief History of the Web Service

If we look at how services on the Web have evolved over the last 15 years, they have actually been built in layers, with each layer solving different issues and being more advanced than the last. It all started when corporations realized that the Web is essentially a network that they could use to freely exchange data internally between their offices and trading partners. Many of these corporations chose the HTTP protocol as the mechanism to transfer data over the Web. This was partly because of the protocol's abilities to penetrate corporate firewalls as well as being SGML based, so it was essentially platform/language agnostic. However, using HTTP as a remote programming model caused its own problems because the protocol is essentially very simple and doesn't contain all the attributes required to call objects remotely. The big software corporations, recognizing this limitation, began working on the Simple Object Access Protocol (SOAP), which would extend HTTP capabilities to allow objects to be called remotely over HTTP. This was the first layer added atop HTTP. In subsequent years, other challenges arose around transaction handling, addressability, large payloads, and so on that required yet another set of standards to be introduced (WS*). This again added another layer as shown in Figure 2-1.

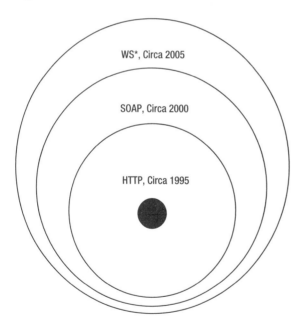

Figure 2-1. *HTTP protocol layers over the years*

As an analogy to describe the current state of web services, nowadays the service architectures for many corporations reassemble that of Rome, which is built upon so many generations of different architectures that road engineers sometimes have to wait years to dig up certain parts of the city while archeologists study the implication of doing so. In fact, to even create a simple modern web service such as WCF requires an understanding of various protocols and architectural styles. This has caused some software developers to ignore new standards and stick with what they know. If you take a look at the Web Services 3.0 .NET programming model shown in Figure 2-2, this point is underscored: even excluding the ADO.NET Data Services assemblies, the diagram is extremely complex.

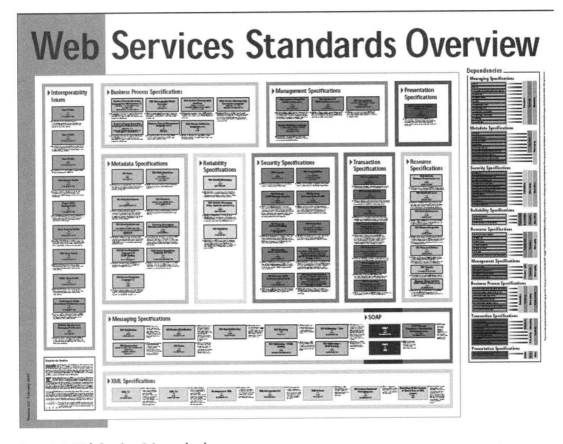

Figure 2-2. *Web Services 3.0 standards*

Finally, the biggest problem with traditional web services is they don't interact well with the Web, for two primary reasons: HTTP verb usage and the scoping information of the request.

HTTP Verb Usage

There is no way to determine the actual operation of a traditional web service call without looking into the body of the message. This is because web service SOAP requests use the HTTP POST verb to transport requests to endpoints. In these requests, the actual method name is stored in a special HTTP header called SOAPMethodName, as shown in Listing 2-1. The SOAP parser takes the SOAPMethodName and the parameters of the call and executes this against the service. In this example, a GET type request is being performed against the data source, as indicated by the get included in the method name, but the request could easily be something else like `RetrieveBalance`, `GetFooBalance`, `ObtainBalance`, and so forth. The only way for the outside world to know the type of operation that is being performed against the underlying data source is to have a standard convention for naming SOAP methods. The issue here is that developers have full control of this name, and many don't follow the same conventions. Another potential problem is that developers can program what they like in the execution of the operation, and the SOAP parser will freely allow this. For example, a `DELETE` operation could be executed even though the method name has something to do with data retrieval. These points cause confusion for the consumer of the service.

Listing 2-1. *SOAP Request Header*

```
POST /objectURI HTTP/1.1
Host: www.foo.com
SOAPMethodName: urn:develop-com:IBank#getBalance
Content-Type: text/xml
Content-Length: 300
```

Scoping Information

The second reason traditional web services don't interact well with the Web is that the scope of the request being made to the traditional web service isn't clear. This is because SOAP methods are constructed using verbs that act upon the resources. Table 2-1 shows some examples of typical web service methods.

Table 2-1. *Typicial Web Service Methods*

Method	Action
getUser()	Gets a single user
addUser()	Adds a single user
deleteUser()	Deletes a user
saveUser()	Saves a user
listUsers()	Lists users
getFlightDetails()	Gets flight details
bookFlight()	Books a flight

As you go down the list, it's increasing difficult to determine the scope of the request being performed. For instance, in the first three examples, you can safety assume that the requesting application is acting on data for a single user. However, what if the user object has the following shape:

```
User Object
Personal Details
Addresses
Home
Billing
```

This is where the scoping information is difficult to determine because the application may only be allowed to update the address details part of the user object. If the method name is called SaveUser(), you can guess that this is for saving user details, but which details aren't clearly defined in the method. The omission can be overcome by having a separate method for each operation against each part of the user object. However, this isn't practical or efficient.

These issues make it difficult for firewall and security administrators to determine which requests should be allowed into the network: essentially everything is a POST with an unclear scope. What normally happens is that network administrators just allow all HTTP traffic in, which negates the original reason for allowing HTTP traffic to flow through corporate firewalls in the first place.

What Makes a Service RESTful?

As outlined in the first chapter, we try to avoid a debate of whether REST services are better than traditional web services; instead, we prefer to believe that web services can live side by side with RESTful services. Revisiting the history of web services, we can see that these services have been built in layers for a reason: they primarily solve problems in the application services space. RESTful services, on the other hand, are quite different because they expose data-centric services to clients. In some cases traditional web services should be used, and in other cases, RESTful services should be used. The main benefit of ADO.NET Data Services is that it is built upon the WCF framework, which allows extensibility so that you can plug in features of a traditional web service that might be required. To learn how to develop RESTful services, the first step is to understand what makes a service RESTful. The term "representational state transfer (REST)" was first coined in a dissertation by Roy Thomas Fielding.[1] In his work, Fielding reviewed today's modern web architecture to drive a different architecture style that would enable developers to work with the Web instead of against it.

The best practical description for Fielding's work comes from Sam Ruby and Leonard Richardson.[2] These authors acknowledge that REST is only a design approach that should be applied as a general guideline to HTTP-based service development. To describe the architecture approach, they formalize the term **Resource-Oriented Architecture**. Resource-Oriented Architecture describes the tenets or rules behind creating RESTful services. These tenets are outlined in Table 2-2 and discussed in a little more detail next.

---

1. Roy Thomas Fielding, "Architectural Styles and the Design of Network-Based Software Architectures" (PhD dissertation, University of California, Irvine, 2000), Chapter 5.

2. Sam Ruby and Leonard Richardson, *RESTful Web Services* (Sebastopol, CA: O'Reilly, 2007)

Table 2-2. *Tenets of REST*

Tenet	Overview
HTTP method	Method information is kept in the HTTP header, not in the body of the request.
Resource based	Resources are expressed as "services" that clients consume.
Addressability	The scoping information is kept in the URL.
Relationships	How the data relates to each other is expressed in ADO.NET Data Services by resource links according to the CSDL.
Statelessness	No stateful messages are exchanged between resources.

HTTP Method

In ADO.NET Data Services, the method information that describes the operation being performed follows the HTTP standard and is kept in the HTTP header. These operations, such as HTTP GET, DELETE, PUT, and POST, relate directly to the CRUD operation that is being performed against the resource.

Resources

Anything can be a resource: user, address, product, product categories, and so on. These resources are expressed in ADO.NET Data Services as entities according to the Conceptual Schema Definition Language (CSDL) specified in the Entity Data Model (EDM).

Addressability

The addressability of resources is specified in the URL with the ability to navigate and filter different resources using data services operations such as $filter, $top, $skip, and $orderby.

Relationships

This refers to how data relates to each other, which is specified by a collection of URLs that are returned against each entity. These URLs act as links that describe how to navigate to related entities. For example, a customer might contain a relationship link element such as <link href="Customers('ALFKI')/Orders">, which a consumer of the service can put into a URL to navigate to the orders of a customer.

Statelessness

Each HTTP request in data services is stateless, which promotes scalability of a solution. There is some overhead to this because of the repeatable data that must be sent in each request. This problem is combated by caching requests on the client using a data context to avoid repeated requests and smaller payloads to the server.

Getting Started: Setting Up the Environment

The first step in creating your first data service is to ensure that you have all the prerequisites that are required for your machine. Throughout this book, you will undertake two types of development exercises: local and enterprise. Local development doesn't consist of any of the enterprise server products such as BizTalk, so the Windows operating system can be either Vista or XP. We recommend that you install a server-level operating system such as Windows 2003 for enterprise development, which is outlined in later chapters. Therefore, it makes sense to install Windows 2003 now for local development instead of later.

The local development environment should consist of the following software and hardware components:

- **Hardware**:
    - 2 GHz processor
    - At least 1GB of RAM
    - 30GB Hard drive space
- **Software**:
    - Microsoft Windows XP SP2/Microsoft Windows Vista SP1/Microsoft Windows 2003 R2 (Enterprise)
    - Internet Information Services 6.0/7.0
    - Visual Studio 2008
    - Visual Studio SP1
    - SQL Server Express Edition with Advanced Services SP2
    - Microsoft .NET Framework 3.5 SP1
    - Internet Explorer 6.0 or later
    - Silverlight 2 SDK (required for Chapter 7)
    - Expression Blend (optional)

Visual Studio 2008 Components

ADO.NET Data Services is part of the ADO.NET 3.5 Service Pack 1 that resides in Visual Studio 2008 Service Pack 1. This service pack is more like a major release of Visual Studio due to the number of software updates and new concepts that are introduced in it. The service pack is outlined in detail in the following MSDN web page: `http://msdn.microsoft.com/en-us/vstudio/products/cc533447.aspx`. When the service pack is installed, it registers a number of ADO.NET 3.5 assemblies and new Visual Studio templates (shown as new project icons and project item icons). The ADO.NET Data Services Visual Studio project item can be added to new or existing ASP.NET 3.5 Web Site projects.

Development Approach

ADO.NET Data Services has a built-in synergy with WCF services because a WCF service contains binding configuration that is stored in the `web.config` file and the actual service runs within a host, which in ADO.NET Data Services' case is Internet Information Server (IIS). As discussed in Chapter 1, ADO.NET Data Services server operations consist of two parts. The first part is the static ADO.NET Data Services layer that implements URL translation, wire formats for data representations, and extensibility points using interceptors and service operations. The second part is the actual data source that is being surfaced to the data service. To promote a transparent layer that can be used to expose different types of sources, all communication between the data source and the data service is made by the provider implementing two interfaces: `IQueryable<T>` or `IUpdatable<T>`.

When developing a data service, you first must decide how you will expose your data source to the outside world. This choice is dependent upon the type of data source and the operations that you want to perform on the source. There are currently four ways to expose your data source to the data service:

1. Entity Framework

2. LINQ to SQL

3. Surfacing custom data sources using CLR classes

4. Creating a custom `IQueryable<T>` provider to surface a custom data source

Entity Framework

The first option is to use the Entity Framework. The Entity Framework is a first-class implementation of the EDM. When used, URLs are converted to Entity Framework Object Services calls, which then interact with the underlying data source. This approach is specific to the Entity Framework for when the underlying data model is a relational data source. ADO.NET Data Services enables this interaction by providing custom attributes that map the EDM to CLR objects. When a URL query is executed, it is then converted to a LINQ query, which returns a projected list of objects based upon the request. This topic will be discussed further in the "Language Integrated Query Support" section in Chapter 3. The Entity Framework is usually the easiest choice to surface a CRUD (Create, Read, Update, Delete) data service because it has built-in support for both the `IQueryable<T>` and `IUpdatable<T>` interfaces. In addition it has an extensive set of tools that can be used to change how entities are mapped to the underlying data source. An example of how to surface a data source using the Entity Framework provider is demonstrated in this chapter.

LINQ to SQL

The LINQ to SQL option can be used when the underlying data source is SQL Server and you don't want to have the extra configuration of the Entity Framework (i.e., you just want to expose your database model). The other reason could be that your company has a policy to not use Entity Framework because it is quite new compared to LINQ to SQL. When exposing a SQL Server data source the tool support for LINQ to SQL is similar to that of the Entity

Framework, and the data source can be quickly exposed. The key difference is that LINQ to SQL doesn't have a conceptual layer that can be used to change how the entities are mapped to the SQL Server tables. The main issue with using this provider is that the LINQ to SQL designer will only generate an IQueryable<T> interface. To enable update, insert, and delete operations, you must manually implement the IUpdatable<T> interface. In Chapter 4, we demonstrate how to expose a SQL Server data source using the LINQ to SQL provider along with a code sample of the IUpdatable<T> interface.

Surfacing Custom Data Sources Using CLR Classes

When the data source is something other than a relational database (e.g., an XML document, Excel spreadsheet, or another custom data sources), we need to manually query these data sources and return a collection of objects that support the IQueyable<T> interface. To do this we must manually craft CLR classes that form the entities that are exposed. We provide a walkthrough of how to expose such a data source in the final section of this chapter, "Surfacing Custom Data Sources Using CLR Classes." This method of surfacing a data source is limited because there is no way to capture what exactly is being queried on the data source, so what tends to happen is that you need to load a complete list of entities in memory by a static method. Therefore, this option should only be used for mocking up data sources or for small lightweight data services.

Implementing IQueryable<T> Custom Provider to Surface a Custom Data Source

Unfortunately, the final method of surfacing a data source is also the most complex. As indicated in the last method, there is no way of knowing what data is being queried because we cannot access the query expression tree that is sent to the data source. Therefore, we have to load the full collection of entities into our custom data store first. The way around this is to build an IQueryable<T> provider that can be used to intercept the query and transpose this into a query statement that the underlying data source understands. This is how the Entity Framework and LINQ to SQL providers work. Under the covers they both implement IQueryable<T> providers that take the query expression tree provided by data services and map this to either a SQL Server query or a stored procedure call. The logic behind how the query statement is constructed from the query expression tree involves implementing several interface layers and is by no means a small task (it could take months of development). This is the last option you should consider, and it could be used in the following situations:

- The underlying data source implements a non–SQL query language.

- There is no Entity Framework provider for the data source.

- The static-in-memory data source option needs to be implemented for a large data set.

A practical example that springs to mind is to implement an IQueryable<T> provider that maps a data service RESTful query to a Lightweight Directory Access Protocol (LDAP) query. LDAP is used to query Active Directory for users and computers in a domain. These entities (users and computers) are resources like customers and orders in a database, so having a standard RESTful interface that can be used from a browser becomes a useful tool for a system administrator.

An overview of the ADO.NET Data Services architecture is illustrated in Figure 2-3.

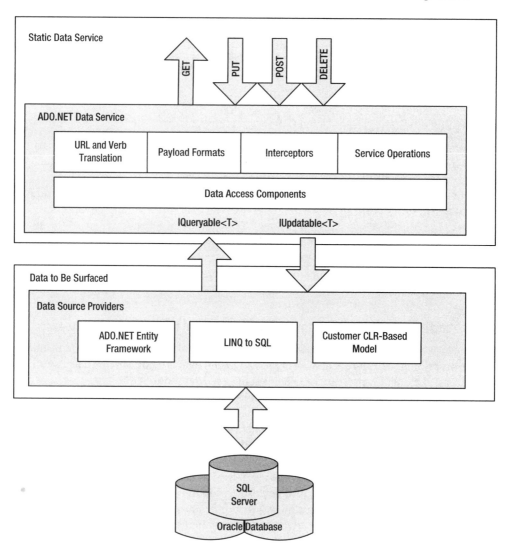

Figure 2-3. *ADO.NET Data Services Overview*

Following are exercises that provide step-by-step instructions on how to create your first data service using the Northwind database, which is exposed using the ADO.NET Entity Framework provider. These steps will work with any version of Visual Studio 2008 including Visual Studio Standard, Professional, and Team Edition. The Northwind database that the data service uses can reside on SQL Server 2005 Developer, Standard, or Enterprise Editions or the SQL Server Express Edition with Advanced Services SP2.

The Northwind data service that we create in these exercises will be consumed by various clients throughout the book. To promote reuse we have purposely not included any user interface (UI) components in the data services project. When creating your own data services, it is best practice to follow this approach and separate the UI and data services into their own projects. This enables the data service to be easily consumed by multiple UI interfaces such as .NET clients, Silverlight, and ASP.NET AJAX clients.

EXERCISE 2-1: CREATING THE ASP.NET DATA SERVICE PROJECT

This exercise outlines how to create a C# ASP.NET Web Site project that you will use to host your Northwind data service. When creating the service, you need to surface an underlying data source that the service operates on. To keep this exercise simple, you will use the Northwind database, which is included in most Microsoft examples. This database has a simple relational structure that consists of tables such as Products, Customers, Orders, Order Details, and Suppliers as shown in Figure 2-4. Please refer to this model to understand the shape of the responses from the service. You will use the Entity Framework, which will provide an autogenerated LINQ to Entities layer. The completed Northwind data service can be downloaded from the Apress web site (http://www.apress.com/book/sourcecode); you'll find it in the NorthwindService folder.

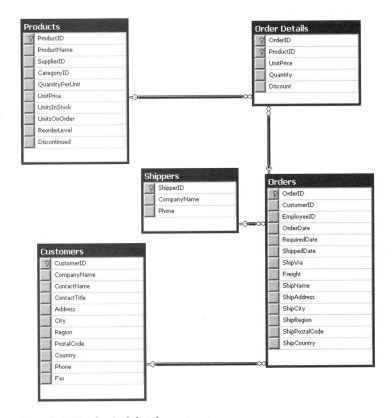

Figure 2-4. *Northwind database structure*

1. Download the Northwind and pubs sample databases from http://www.microsoft.com/downloadS/details.aspx?familyid=06616212-0356-46A0-8DA2-EEBC53A68034&displaylang=en, and install the sample databases by double-clicking the SQL2000SampleDb.msi file. Accept all default options in the installer and click Finish.

2. Attach the Northwind database to the SQL Server Express Edition instance by first opening SQL Server 2005 Management Studio Express: select File ➤ All Programs ➤ Microsoft SQL Server 2005 ➤ SQL Server Management Studio Express, and click the Connect button to establish a connection to the `.\sqlexpress` SQL Server Instance. In the left pane of the window you will see an explorer tree; right-click the Databases node and select Attach. The Attach Databases dialog will appear; click Add, browse to `c:\SQL Server 2000 Sample Databases\Northwind`, and click OK.

3. In Visual Studio 2008, create a new C# ASP.NET Web Site project by selecting File ➤ New ➤ Project. Select the ASP.NET Web Site Visual Studio project template and enter **NorthwindService** as the project name.

4. Remove the `default.aspx` page from Solution Explorer: right-click `default.aspx` and select Exclude from project.

5. Add a database connection to Visual Studio by selecting Tools ➤ Connect to Database. In the Add Connection dialog, enter your local SQL Server details and select the Northwind database from the Database name drop-down list. Click OK.

6. Add the Entity Data Model project item to the project from Solution Explorer by right-clicking the ASP.NET project name and selecting Add New Item. In the Visual Studio template dialog, select the Data project category. Highlight the ADO.NET Entity Data Model project item template and name the item `NorthwindModel.edx`.

7. The Entity Data Model Wizard dialog will appear. From this dialog select the Generate from Database option as shown in Figure 2-5, and click Next.

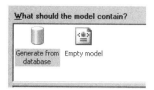

Figure 2-5. *Generate from Database option*

8. The next dialog in the wizard specifies the connection to the database and the name of the Data Services Entities connection string that will be placed in the `web.config` file. In this dialog, choose the Northwind database connection from the Data Connection drop-down and enter **NorthwindEntities** in the text box. Click Next.

9. The final dialog specifies what parts of the database need to be generated. Select all tables as shown in Figure 2-6. Enter **NorthwindModel** as the name of the model namespace that needs to be generated. Click Finish.

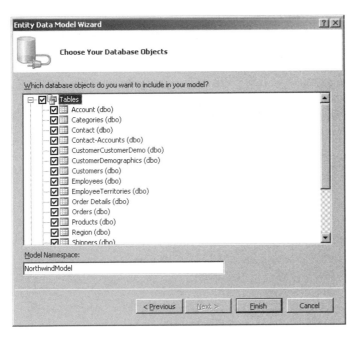

Figure 2-6. *Northwind database tables to generate*

■Note If you review the Entity Data Model that has been generated, you will notice that there isn't an entity for the `ContentAccount` and `CustomerCustomerDemo` tables. This is because many-to-many tables are automatically ignored by the Entity Framework in the conceptual model. This is similar to how you would create business objects because many-to-many database links are not normally created as separate objects, rather they are encapsulated within the object itself.

Now that you have added database access to the project, the next thing you have to do is create the actual data service and enable security access to it. The service is locked down by default and doesn't expose any entity set or metadata. For security purposes, you need to explicitly enable the access to the service in the `InitializeService()` method. When you specify the security permissions, you have the option to change read/write security settings for individual entity sets that are exposed. However, in the case of this example, you will grant full access to all entity sets by using "*" in the security settings.

EXERCISE 2-2: ENABLING ACCESS TO YOUR DATA SERVICE

The steps in this exercise outline how to create a data service and enable security access.

1. Add the ADO.NET Data Service item to the project from Solution Explorer by right-clicking the ASP.NET project name and selecting Add New Item. In the Visual Studio template dialog, select the Web category from the left-hand pane. Highlight the ADO.NET Data Service project item and name it `Northwind.svc`, as shown in Figure 2-7.

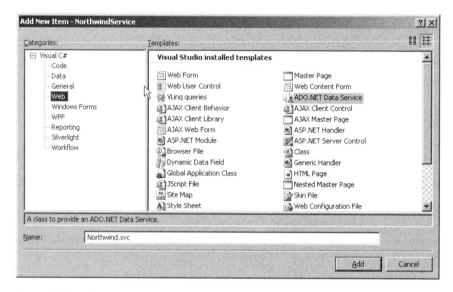

Figure 2-7. *ADO.NET Data Services component*

2. Open the `Northwind.cs` file and locate the `TODO` code section at the start of the class. This is the `ObjectContext` generic type that the service will operate upon. Replace the `TODO` with `NorthwindEntities`.

3. Now locate the `InitializeService` function and add the lines `config.SetEntitySetAccess-Rule("*", EntitySetRights.AllRead)` and `config.SetServiceOperationAccessRule("*", ServiceOperationRights.All)`; this is shown in Listing 2-2.

Listing 2-2. *Permissions Access Script*

```
using System;
using System.Collections.Generic;
using System.Data.Services;
using System.Linq;
using System.ServiceModel.Web;
using System.Web;

namespace NorthwindService
{
    public class Northwind : DataService< NorthwindEntities >
```

```
    {
        // This method is called only once to initialize service-wide policies.
        public static void InitializeService(IDataServiceConfiguration config)
        {
            config.SetEntitySetAccessRule("*", EntitySetRights.AllRead);
            config.SetServiceOperationAccessRule("*",
ServiceOperationRights.All);
        }
    }
}
```

4. To enable the project to navigate to the service, set the service to be the default project item from Solution Explorer by right-clicking Northwind.svc and selecting Set as Start Page from the context menu.

5. You need to turn off the automatic feed capability in IE 7 because the default data representation of the data service is Atom, which IE 7 will try to display using its feed reader, which will prevent you from reviewing the text of the service. To disable the feed reader in IE 7, from the Tools menu select Internet Options. Click the Content Tab. Click Settings and uncheck the Turn on feed reading view option as shown in Figure 2-8.

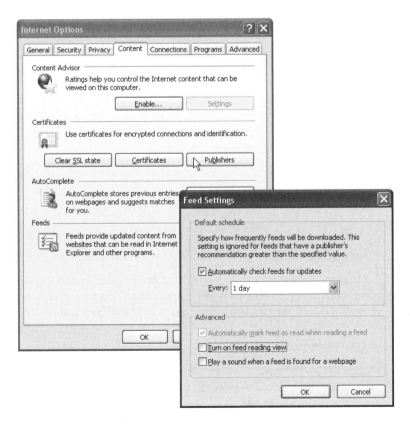

Figure 2-8. *Turning off the IE 7 feed reading view option*

Exercise 2-2 ends with a fully working data service. To test this service in Visual Studio 2008, simply press Ctrl+F5. The first impression that you probably have is "That was easy!" This is because the ADO.NET Data Services team has hidden the ABCs (address, binding, and contract) of WCF away from you.

Trying the New Data Service

Understandably you are probably itching to try out the new data service. A data service can be used by various .NET clients as discussed in later chapters. You'll see how to consume the service using a simple Windows Console (Chapter 3), an AJAX client (Chapter 5), a Popfly block (Chapter 6), Silverlight (Chapter 7), and BizTalk (Chapter 8). However, the easiest way to understand the data service is to simply query it using a browser. A data service URL has three main components:

- **Data Service URL**: This is typically the first part of the URL that points to the data service (e.g., `http://host/NorthwindService/Northwind.svc`). All data service URLs end by default with the `.svc` extension.

- **The entity set name**: The entity set name is an optional parameter to the URL. If the entity set name is included in the URL, all entities of that entity set are returned (e.g., `/Customers` would return all customers). To return a single entity, the entity keys can be included in parentheses after the entity set name. Additional query expressions are also allowed to further filter the data that is returned.

- **Navigation property**: The navigation property can be placed after the entity set to indicate traversal of a relationship, which is defined by a / (slash). The navigation to another entity then allows query strings to be executed against the traversed entity set. When traversing further relationships using the /, the data shape that is returned will change based upon the navigation property specified.

To interact with the data service you've created in the preceding exercises, just make sure that you have started the project by pressing Ctrl+F5, which will open up a browser, and navigate to the home page of the service, which will be `http://localhost:[random port]/Northwind.svc`.

Query 1: Entity Sets Exposed by the Service

The home page of the data service lists all the entity sets that are exposed by it as shown in Listing 2-3. The document is returned using the default serialization format, which is Atom. When the browser is used to query the data service, this is the only format supported.

Listing 2-3. *Entity Sets Exposed by the Data Service*

```
<service xml:base="http://localhost/NorthwindDataService➡
/Northwind.svc/" xmlns:atom="http://www.w3.org/2005/Atom" xmln➡
s:app="http://www.w3.org/2007/app" xmln➡
s="http://www.w3.org/2007/app">
  <workspace>
    <atom:title>Default</atom:title>
```

```xml
    <collection href="Account">
      <atom:title>Account</atom:title>
    </collection>
    <collection href="Categories">
      <atom:title>Categories</atom:title>
    </collection>
    <collection href="Contact">
      <atom:title>Contact</atom:title>
    </collection>
    <collection href="CustomerDemographics">
      <atom:title>CustomerDemographics</atom:title>
    </collection>
    <collection href="Customers">
      <atom:title>Customers</atom:title>
    </collection>
    <collection href="Employees">
      <atom:title>Employees</atom:title>
    </collection>
    <collection href="Order_Details">
      <atom:title>Order_Details</atom:title>
    </collection>
    <collection href="Orders">
      <atom:title>Orders</atom:title>
    </collection>
    <collection href="Products">
      <atom:title>Products</atom:title>
    </collection>
    <collection href="Region">
      <atom:title>Region</atom:title>
    </collection>
    <collection href="Shippers">
      <atom:title>Shippers</atom:title>
    </collection>
    <collection href="Suppliers">
      <atom:title>Suppliers</atom:title>
    </collection>
    <collection href="Territories">
      <atom:title>Territories</atom:title>
    </collection>
    <collection href="Transaction">
      <atom:title>Transaction</atom:title>
    </collection>
  </workspace>
</service>
```

Query 2: Querying Multiple Entities

The next query to try is to navigate to one of the entity sets that has been exposed. This is achieved by simply adding /Suppliers onto the end of the URL, resulting in http://localhost/ NorthwindDataService/Northwind.svc/Suppliers. This will return all the supplier entities that are stored in the Northwind database as shown in Listing 2-4.

Listing 2-4. *List of Entities Within an Entity Set*

```
<?xml version="1.0" encoding="utf-8" standalone="yes"?>
<feed xml:base="http://localhost/NorthwindDataService➥
/Northwind.svc/" xmlns:d="http:➥
//schemas.microsoft.com/ado/2007/08/dataservices" xmln➥
s:m="http://schemas.microsoft.➥
com/ado/2007/08/dataservices/metadata" xmlns="http://www.w3.org/2005/Atom">
  <title type="text">Suppliers</title>
  <id>http://localhost/NorthwindDataService/Northwind.svc/Suppliers</id>
  <updated>2008-09-17T22:12:14Z</updated>
  <link rel="self" title="Suppliers" href="Suppliers" />
  <entry>
    <id>http://localhost/NorthwindDataService/Northwind.svc/Suppliers(1)</id>
    <title type="text"></title>
    <updated>2008-09-17T22:12:14Z</updated>
    <author>
      <name />
    </author>
    <link rel="edit" title="Suppliers" href="Suppliers(1)" />
    <link rel="http://schemas.microsoft.com/ado/2007/08/dataservices➥
/related/Products" type="application/atom+xml;type=feed"➥
title="Products" href="Suppliers(1)/Products" />
    <category term="NorthwindModel.Suppliers"➥
scheme="http://schemas.microsoft.com/a➥
do/2007/08/dataservices/scheme" />
    <content type="application/xml">
      <m:properties>
        <d:Address>49 Gilbert St.1</d:Address>
        <d:City>LA</d:City>
        <d:CompanyName>Exotic Liquids</d:CompanyName>
        <d:ContactName>Charlotte Cooper</d:ContactName>
        <d:ContactTitle>Purchasing Manager</d:ContactTitle>
        <d:Country>UK</d:Country>
        <d:Fax m:null="true" />
        <d:HomePage m:null="true" />
        <d:Phone>(171) 555-2222</d:Phone>
        <d:PostalCode>EC1 4SD</d:PostalCode>
        <d:Region m:null="true" />
        <d:SupplierID m:type="Edm.Int32">1</d:SupplierID>
      </m:properties>
```

```
        </content>
      </entry>
      <entry>
        <id>http://localhost/NorthwindDataService/Northwind.svc/Suppliers(2)</id>
        <title type="text"></title>
        <updated>2008-09-17T22:12:14Z</updated>
        <author>
          <name />
        </author>
        <link rel="edit" title="Suppliers" href="Suppliers(2)" />
        <link rel="http://schemas.microsoft.com/ado/2007/08/dataservices➥
/related/Products" type="application/atom+xml;type=feed"➥
title="Products" href="Suppliers(2)/Products" />
        <category term="NorthwindModel.Suppliers" scheme=➥
"http://schemas.microsoft.com/ado/2007/08/dataservices/scheme" />
        <content type="application/xml">
          <m:properties>
            <d:Address>P.O. Box 78934</d:Address>
            <d:City>New Orleans</d:City>
            <d:CompanyName>New Orleans Cajun Delights</d:CompanyName>
            <d:ContactName>Shelley Burke</d:ContactName>
            <d:ContactTitle>Order Administrator</d:ContactTitle>
            <d:Country>USA</d:Country>
            <d:Fax m:null="true" />
            <d:HomePage>#CAJUN.HTM#</d:HomePage>
            <d:Phone>(100) 555-4822</d:Phone>
            <d:PostalCode>70117</d:PostalCode>
            <d:Region>LA</d:Region>
            <d:SupplierID m:type="Edm.Int32">2</d:SupplierID>
          </m:properties>
        </content>
      </entry>
      <entry>
        ...
      </entry>
    </feed>
```

Query 3: Querying a Single Entity Response

To construct a query that will navigate to one of the entities within the entity set shown in the last example, you need to add the entity key to the end of the URL query. If you aren't sure what the entity key is, you can get it from the <id> node. Using the last example, two suppliers are returned that contain a URL in the <id> node of http://.../Suppliers(1) and http://.../Suppliers(2). This basically means that the suppliers' IDs are 1 and 2. If you were to enter http://localhost/NorthwindDataService/Northwind.svc/Suppliers(1) as the URL, this would return just supplier 1. Also, notice that the <feed> node has now been removed from the output, due to the fact that this is a single item, not a feed of items. This is shown in Listing 2-5.

Listing 2-5. *Returning a Single Entity*

```
<?xml version="1.0" encoding="utf-8" standalone="yes"?>
<entry xml:base=http://localhost/NorthwindDataService/Northwind.svc➥
/ xmlns:d="http://schemas.microsoft.com/ado/2007/08/dataservices" xmln➥
s:m="http://schemas.microsoft.➥
com/ado/2007/08/dataservices/metadata" xmlns="http://www.w3.org/2005/Atom">
  <id>http://localhost/NorthwindDataService/Northwind.svc/Suppliers(1)</id>
  <title type="text"></title>
  <updated>2008-09-17T22:15:25Z</updated>
  <author>
    <name />
  </author>
  <link rel="edit" title="Suppliers" href="Suppliers(1)" />
  <link rel="http://schemas.microsoft.com/ado/2007/08/dataservices➥
/related/Products"type="application/atom+xml;type=feed" title="Products"➥
href="Suppliers(1)/Products" />
  <category term="NorthwindModel.Suppliers"➥
scheme="http://schemas.microsoft.com/ado➥
/2007/08/dataservices/scheme" />
  <content type="application/xml">
    <m:properties>
      <d:Address>49 Gilbert St.1</d:Address>
      <d:City>LA</d:City>
      <d:CompanyName>Exotic Liquids</d:CompanyName>
      <d:ContactName>Charlotte Cooper</d:ContactName>
      <d:ContactTitle>Purchasing Manager</d:ContactTitle>
      <d:Country>UK</d:Country>
      <d:Fax m:null="true" />
      <d:HomePage m:null="true" />
      <d:Phone>(171) 555-2222</d:Phone>
      <d:PostalCode>EC1 4SD</d:PostalCode>
      <d:Region m:null="true" />
      <d:SupplierID m:type="Edm.Int32">1</d:SupplierID>
    </m:properties>
  </content>
</entry>
```

Query 4: Navigating a Relationship

Data services are normally built upon a relational database that contains links between tables. In data services, these links are represented as navigation properties that can be added to a URL to navigate to a child of an entity. In the last example, notice there is a `<link rel=".."` `title="Products" href="Suppliers(1)/Products" />` node in the output. This node is the link to products that the supplier owns in a one-to-many relationship. To navigate to the products for this supplier, simply append this `href` attribute to the URL `http://localhost/` `NorthwindDataService/Northwind.svc/Suppliers(1)/Products`. This is shown in Listing 2-6.

Listing 2-6. *Returning Related Entities*

```
<?xml version="1.0" encoding="utf-8" standalone="yes"?>
<feed xml:base="http://localhost/NorthwindDataService/Northwind.svc/" xmln➥
s:d="http://schemas.microsoft.com/ado/2007/08/dataservices" xmln➥
s:m="http://schemas.microsoft.com/ado/2007/08/dataservices/metadata" xmln➥
s="http://www.w3.org/2005/Atom">
  <title type="text">Products</title>
  <id>http://localhost/NorthwindDataService/Northwind.svc/Suppliers(1)/Products</id>
  <updated>2008-09-17T22:49:48Z</updated>
  <link rel="self" title="Products" href="Products" />
  <entry>
    <id>http://localhost/NorthwindDataService/Northwind.svc/Products(1)</id>
    <title type="text"></title>
    <updated>2008-09-17T22:49:48Z</updated>
    <author>
      <name />
    </author>
    <link rel="edit" title="Products" href="Products(1)" />
    <link rel="http://schemas.microsoft.com/ado/2007/08/dataservices➥
/related/Categories" type="application/atom+xml;type=entry" title="Categories"➥
href="Products(1)/Categories" />
    <link rel="http://schemas.microsoft.com/ado/2007/08/dataservices/related➥
/Order_Details" type="application/atom+xml;type=feed" ➥
title="Order_Details" href="Products(1)/Order_Details" />
    <link rel="http://schemas.microsoft.com/ado/2007/08/dataservices/related➥
/Suppliers" type="application/atom+xml;type=entry" title="Suppliers"➥
href="Products(1)/Suppliers" />
    <category term="NorthwindModel.Products"➥
scheme="http://schemas.microsoft.com/ad➥
o/2007/08/dataservices/scheme" />
    <content type="application/xml">
      <m:properties>
        <d:Discontinued m:type="Edm.Boolean">false</d:Discontinued>
        <d:ProductID m:type="Edm.Int32">1</d:ProductID>
        <d:ProductName>Chai</d:ProductName>
        <d:QuantityPerUnit>10 boxes x 20 bags</d:QuantityPerUnit>
        <d:ReorderLevel m:type="Edm.Int16">10</d:ReorderLevel>
        <d:UnitPrice m:type="Edm.Decimal">18.0000</d:UnitPrice>
        <d:UnitsInStock m:type="Edm.Int16">39</d:UnitsInStock>
        <d:UnitsOnOrder m:type="Edm.Int16">0</d:UnitsOnOrder>
      </m:properties>
    </content>
  </entry>
  <entry>
    <id>http://localhost/NorthwindDataService/Northwind.svc/Products(2)</id>
    <title type="text"></title>
    <updated>2008-09-17T22:49:48Z</updated>
```

```
    <author>
      <name />
    </author>
    <link rel="edit" title="Products" href="Products(2)" />
    <link rel="http://schemas.microsoft.com/ado/2007/08/dataservices/related➥
/Categories" type="application/atom+xml;type=entry" title="Categories"➥
href="Products(2)/Categories" />
    <link rel="http://schemas.microsoft.com/ado/2007/08/dataservices/related➥
/Order_Details" type="application/atom+xml;type=feed" ➥
title="Order_Details" href="Products(2)/Order_Details" />
    <link rel="http://schemas.microsoft.com/ado/2007/08/dataservices/related➥
/Suppliers" type="application/atom+xml;type=entry" title="Suppliers"➥
href="Products(2)/Suppliers" />
    <category term="NorthwindModel.Products"➥
scheme="http://schemas.microsoft.com/ad➥
o/2007/08/dataservices/scheme" />
    <content type="application/xml">
      <m:properties>
        <d:Discontinued m:type="Edm.Boolean">false</d:Discontinued>
        <d:ProductID m:type="Edm.Int32">2</d:ProductID>
        <d:ProductName>Chang</d:ProductName>
        <d:QuantityPerUnit>24 - 12 oz bottles</d:QuantityPerUnit>
        <d:ReorderLevel m:type="Edm.Int16">25</d:ReorderLevel>
        <d:UnitPrice m:type="Edm.Decimal">19.0000</d:UnitPrice>
        <d:UnitsInStock m:type="Edm.Int16">17</d:UnitsInStock>
        <d:UnitsOnOrder m:type="Edm.Int16">40</d:UnitsOnOrder>
      </m:properties>
    </content>
  </entry>
  <entry>
    ...
  </entry>
</feed>
```

Addressing Data

Addressing data in an application has typically been time consuming, due to the amount of
code that would need to be written to expose each of the entities in the business tier and also
the logic required to interact with one or more data objects within each entity. To enable this
interaction, the data tier would then need to expose a CRUD interface that must be hooked
into a number of SQL-based operations against the data source. The work wouldn't necessary
end there, because you would also need extra code to shape how these business entities are
linked to other entities (e.g., customers and orders). Generally, it was difficult to navigate entities without adding a lot of code or by using concepts such as ADO.NET data sets to provide
this capability. Additionally, there were challenges concerning how large these entities should
be when exposed, so concepts such as shallow and deep loading of entities were introduced.

Over time, the amount of code has been reduced by implementing software concepts such as generics and tools such as CodeSmith that can be used to autogenerate ready-made tiers. The main issue with how business tiers were written is that they weren't uniform because everyone has a slightly different way of representing their particular business object to the outside world.

ADO.NET Data Services counters this problem by implementing an addressing scheme that uses URLs to locate data. URLs are specifically constructed so they promote a set of uniform and predicable patterns. The result is that you can address every piece of information in your system, and given the URL, you can also instantly understand exactly what part of the data is going to be returned as part of this request. This standard interface is achieved by modeling ADO.NET Data Services upon the EDM specification. The EDM specification is used by applications built upon the Entity Framework and provides definitions of how data is organized in entities and associations and how entities are logically grouped together. This model is defined by using an XML-based language called the Conceptual Schema Definition Language. Actually, due to ADO.NET Data Services being built on the Entity Framework, the ADO.NET Data Services team decided to reuse CSDL to describe their interfaces; an overview of the structure is shown in Figure 2-9. This forms the basis of the EDM elements that are exposed by data services.

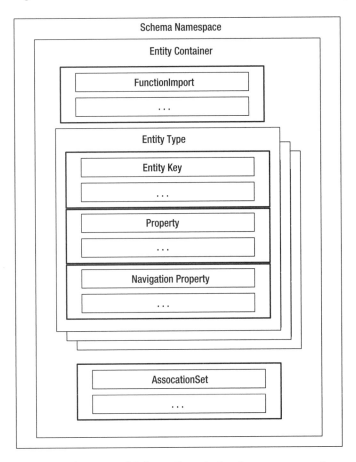

Figure 2-9. *Conceptual Schema Description Language overview*

To understand the EDM specification is to understand ADO.NET Data Services, so we'll explain briefly the key aspects of this specification and how this is implemented in ADO.NET Data Services. The EDM/ADO.NET Data Services components are outlined in Table 2-3.

Table 2-3. *ADO.NET Data Services/EDM Components*

ADO.NET Data Services Terminology	EDM Terminology	Overview
Resource type	Entity type	Domain-specific data type.
Resource key	Entity key	Key properties of the resource.
Resource property	Entity property	Unique name and type of a property defined on an entity type. In EDM, this is a simple type.
Resource complex type	Complex type	Grouping of simple type properties.
Resource container	Entity container	Scope of the entity sets and association sets that are defined.
Resource set	Entity set	A logical group of entity types.
Resource navigation property	Navigation property	The ends of a relationship between two entities.
Resource association set	Association set	A logical group of relationship definitions between entity types.
Resource namespace	Schema namespace	Namespace that contains entity types and complex types.

■**Note** As you can see in Table 2-3, ADO.NET Data Services terminology and EDM terminology are slightly different, but the concepts they encompass are fundamentally the same. EDM terminology will be used throughout the book, as these terms are more familiar to developers.

Entities (Resources)

Entity Data Model entities are defined as entity types for objects such as Customers, Orders, Suppliers, and so on. The entity type contains three main elements: name, properties, and key. Properties can be type agonistic or primitive types that are defined as either simple type or complex type. EDM simple types are defined from well-known abstract concepts such as integers, numbers, and strings. Simple type properties have their own definition of types that map onto CLR primitive types; a subset of these types is shown in Table 2-4. The EDM has no internal properties for these types and instead uses the semantics of the hosting type system. This allows clients that are not using the ADO.NET Data Services client library to interoperate with a data service.

Table 2-4. *EDM Properties to CLR Types*

EDM Type	CLR Type
Edm.Boolean	Bool
Edm.DateTime	DateTime
Edm.Double	Double
Edm.Int32	Int32
Edm.String	String

A complex type is a grouping of properties that are either simple type properties or property types that point to other defined complex types. It is used to implement a property that has internal properties of its own. The internal structure of the complex type is similar to that of an entity type except it doesn't have a key property. A special type of property is the navigation property, which is a simple type property that defines the relationships of an entity type. Listing 2-7 shows an entity type, Customer, that uses three types of properties. The Name property is a simple type, Address is a complex type, and Orders is a navigation property.

Listing 2-7. *Entity Type Definition*

```
<EntityType Name="Customer">
        <Key>
                        <PropertyRef Name="CustomerID"/>
        </Key>
        <Property Name="Name" Type="Edm.String"/>
            <Property Name="Address" Type="Self.Address"/>
            <NavigationProperty Name="Orders"
                        Relationship="NorthwindModel.FK_Orders_Customers"
                        FromRole="Customers" ToRole="Orders" />
</EntityType>

<ComplexType Name="Address">
            <Property Name="StreetAddress" Type="Edm.String"/>
            <Property Name="City" Type="Edm.String"/>
            <Property Name="Country" Type="Edm.String"/>
</ComplexType>
```

The entity types that are part of the same service are grouped together into entity sets. Entity sets that are part of the data service are displayed when you directly navigate to the data service's URL in the browser (e.g., /Northwind.svc) as follows:

```
<service>
        <workspace>
                <collection href="Customers">
                        <atom:title>Customers</atom:title>
                </collection>
<collection href="Suppliers">
                                <atom:title>Customers</atom:title>
                </collection>
        ...
        </workspace>
</service>
```

If you were to append `/Northwind.svc/Customers` to the URL in the browser, you would receive a <feed> of <entry>. A <feed> is essentially a collection of entity types. Each <entry> of the <feed> is a unique instance of an entity (entity type) for that collection.

Entity Keys (Resource Keys)

The entity key has an important role to play in ADO.NET Data Services as it is used to identify individual entity instances. In fact, in order for data services to operate with an entity, a key has to be defined. Entity keys are very similar to database keys as they can be made up of individual properties or composite keys containing one or more properties. There are a couple of restrictions on how entity keys can be defined:

- Must be nonnullable, immutable, simple type properties such as `string`, `integer`, and so forth.

- Must uniquely identify an individual instance of a resource within a resource set.

If the data service is surfaced from the Entity Framework, by default the keys that are defined on the database model are taken as the data service keys. When a data service is created using CLR types, the entity key must be decorated on the entity type class definition; this can be achieved by either explicitly defining the entity key(s) or having it surfaced implicitly by naming a property so it is recognized as an identity column. There are three ways to identify the entity keys on a class in order of precedence:

1. Specify a [`DataServiceKey`] attribute on the class and specify exactly which property/properties form the key, for example:

   ```
   [DataServiceKey("CompanyName")]
   Public class Suppliers..
   ```

2. If the type has a property named <typename>ID (case-sensitive), this property becomes the key for the type.

3. If the type has a property named ID (case-sensitive), this property becomes the key for the type.

To return a single entity instance, the entity key is added in parentheses to the URL; for example, `/Northwind.svc/Customers ('ALFKI')` would return the first customer record from the Northwind database, the infamous Alfreds Futterkiste. An example of the entity key defined on the `Customers` table is shown here:

```
<EntityType Name="Customers">
<Key>
  <PropertyRef Name="CustomerID" />
</Key>
...
```

Now that you are able to return a specific entity, you can access the properties of that entity by appending the name of the property to the end of the URL. For example, `/Northwind.svc/Customers ('ALFKI')/CompanyName` would return the company name for the `ALFKI` customer.

Entity Associations (Resource Navigations)

Relationships are logical connections between entities and are defined by associations, which outline the end points of the relationship and its multiplicity. An association has the following features:

- **Multiplicity**: Association end elements can be 0..n and the cardinality of either end may vary.

- **Nonexclusive**: An entity type can appear in multiple associations.

- **Direction**: Associations are bidirectional and can be navigated from either end.

An example of a relationship could be a customer who has one-to-many orders (1 to n). An entity type contains navigation properties that point to the association that defines this relationship, as shown here:

```
<EntityType Name="Customers">
        ...
        <NavigationProperty Name="Orders"
                Relationship="NorthwindModel.FK_Orders_Customers"
                FromRole="Customers" ToRole="Orders" />
        ...
</EntityType>

<Association Name="FK_Orders_Customers">
                <End Role="Customers" Type="NorthwindModel.Customers"➥
                Multiplicity="0..1" />
                <End Role="Orders" Type="NorthwindModel.Orders"➥
                Multiplicity="*"/>
</Association>
```

The multiplicity attribute is an important part of the relationship as it defines the cardinality. In the example, the `Customers` multiplicity is `0..1`, which means zero or one, and `Orders` is `*`, which means many. As outlined previously, a relationship can be navigated from either end, which means this could be many-to-one or one-to-many. The complete multiplication options available are as follows:

`0..1`: Zero or one entity

`1`: Exactly one entity only

`*`: Zero or more entities

In the "Trying the New Data Service" section, recall that when individual entities are returned in the Atom format, relationships are shown as <link> elements that point to the other entities that entity is associated to. The concept of the entity key defined earlier makes traversal these relationships simple. As an example, if you wanted to retrieve a <feed> of the orders for the ALFKI customer, you could use /Northwind.svc/Customers ('ALFKI')/Orders. If you were interested in a certain disputed order, you could just append the order number in parentheses at the end of the URL, for example, /Northwind.svc/Customers ('ALFKI')/Orders (10643). The traversal of relationships can be as deep as the Entity Data Model that has been defined.

ADO.NET Data Services provides the ability to interact with relationships directly by enabling the return of URL links from an entity. These URL links can then be used in HTTP DELETE and PUT operations to add, update, and remove relationships from the entity. To return the URL for a relationship of an entity, the keyword $links is used in the URL to return the relationship. For example, if you wanted to return the Order_Details that are associated with /Northwind.svc/Orders (10643), you could specify /Northwind.svc/Orders (10248)/$links/Order_Details, which would return three links for each of the Order_Details that are associated. The payload will only include the information for the association; other entity properties are not included as shown in Listing 2-8.

Listing 2-8. *Order Details Entity $Links*

```
<links xmlns="http://schemas.microsoft.com/ado/2007/08/dataservices">
                  <uri>http://host/NorthwindService
                  /Northwind.svc/Order_Details(OrderID=10248,ProductID=11)</uri>
                  <uri>http://host/NorthwindService
                  /Northwind.svc/Order_Details(OrderID=10248,ProductID=42)</uri>
                  <uri>http://host/NorthwindService
                  /Northwind.svc/Order_Details(OrderID=10248,ProductID=72)</uri>
</links>
```

If you want to change one of the associations between Order and Order_Details, all that would be required is to send a HTTP DELETE request along with the URL link <uri>http://host/NorthwindService/Northwind.svc/Order_Details(OrderID=10248,ProductID=11)</uri>; no request body would need to be specified in this request.

Service Description

In traditional SOAP-based RPC web services, the Web Services Description Language (WSDL) is the de facto standard method of how to explain your service to interested parties. WSDL defines an XML-based grammar for describing network services as a set of endpoints, which are SOAP endpoints. The operations and messages are described abstractly, which provides a level of extensibility.

In the RESTful world, there is no equivalent to WSDL. Advocates of the REST programming model are working together to create this standard. The name that they have used for the body of this work is the Web Application Description Language (WADL). The idea is that WADL would provide a simpler alternative to WSDL for use with XML/HTTP web sites. The WADL file is described using a combination of textual description and XML. It essentially provides an XML vocabulary that is machine readable, which client applications can then consume and use to generate proxies to interface with the service. The file outlines the complete XML vocabulary that is used in the service. It also supports URL templates and the HTTP methods that are used and tells the client which HTTP header to employ when making a request. WADL can also list the data representation formats that are supported, the format of the XML representation that might be exchanged, as well as the HTTP fault codes that may be expected.

■Note Dr. Marc Hadley, of Sun Microsystems, is the primary author of the WADL standard.

At the time of writing, the WADL format hasn't been adopted by the industry and also isn't rich enough to accommodate ADO.NET Data Services, so Microsoft decided to create its own standard. To retrieve the metadata from a data service, the $metadata query string operator needs to be appended to the base service (i.e., /Northwind.svc/$metadata). The CSDL file that is generated can be used to create the client proxy layer and is used by the DataSvcUtil to autogenerate this proxy layer. The CSDL describes the entity container, entity sets, entity type, associations, and function import. A cut-down version of the metadata for the Northwind service is shown in Listing 2-9.

Listing 2-9. *Example Metadata*

```
<edmx:DataServices>
    <Schema Namespace="NorthwindModel" ...>
        <EntityContainer Name="NorthwindEntities">
            <FunctionImport Name="SuppliersByCountry"
                EntitySet="Suppliers"
                ReturnType="Collection(NorthwindModel.Suppliers)"
                m:HttpMethod="GET">
                <Parameter Name="country" Type="Edm.String" Mode="In"/>
            </FunctionImport>

            <EntitySet Name="Categories"
                EntityType="NorthwindModel.Categories"/>
                <AssociationSet>
                ...
                </AssociationSet>
                <Entity Type Name="Categories">
                    <Key>
                    <PropertyRef Name="CategoryID" />
                    </Key>
                <Property Name="CategoryID" Type="Edm.Int32" Nullable="false" />
                <Property Name="CategoryName" Type="Edm.String"
                        Nullable="false" MaxLength="15" Unicode="true"
                    FixedLength="false" />
```

```
                <Property>
                    ...
                </Property>
            </EntityType>
        </EntitySet>
    </EntityContainer>
  </Schema>
</edmx:DataServices>
```

Data Representations

Whenever you exchange data, a particular representation is used: this can be a flat file representation, an XML representation, feed data, and so on. Typically, the same piece of information can be represented variously for different applications or usage scenarios. ADO.NET Data Services supports the notation of multiple data representations of the same data and even on the same server based upon the needs of the client. Instead of reinventing a new set of data representations for the data, ADO.NET Data Services keeps within web standards and reuses what is currently available. The best representation depends on the application using a particular data service and its runtime environment. For example, AJAX-based applications that run inside web browsers may find the JavaScript Object Notation (JSON) format is the easiest to use because JSON can be consumed as JavaScript objects. Client applications that are written in an environment with a built-in XML parser would use the Atom format. As mentioned previously, the different formats supported in this release are Atom and JSON.

The mechanism used to represent the format sent to the server is the HTTP Content-Type header. The default mechanism to control the format is returned by the system through the HTTP Accept header. Listing 2-10 presents an example of a typical HTTP GET request showing these headers.

Listing 2-10. *Example HTTP GET Request Header*

```
GET /Northwind.svc/Products
User-Agent: Microsoft ADO.NET Data Services
Content-Type: application/atom+xml
Accept: application/atom+xml
Host: adonet-data-poc
```

Table 2-5 lists the data representations that are supported in this release along with their typical clients and HTTP headers.

Table 2-5. *Supported Data Representations*

Data Representation	Content Type	Typical Clients
JSON	application/json	ASP.NET, AJAX, Silverlight
Atom	application/atom+xml	.NET Clients, Silverlight, ASP.NET mashups

■**Tip** In the current version of ADO.NET Data Services, there isn't a feature to switch between representations, as this is set by the client when making the request. A workaround is to not to use the data service client assemblies and just manually set the HTTP Accept headers in code as shown here:

```
WebRequest request = WebRequest.Create(DataServicesUrl);
//JSON
request.Headers["Accept"] = "application/json";
//Atom
request.Headers["Accept"] = "application/atom+xml";
```

Formulating Queries

The URL provides a uniform way of addressing data and can be used to retrieve data shapes from data services that can be navigated by their keys and the links that form their relationships. Following is the format of the URL in data services (note that the brackets—[ ]—indicate optional components):

```
http://host/<service>[/<EntitySet>][(<EntityKey>)][/<NavigationProperty>
[(<EntityKey>)/...]]] [?$expand] & [?$filter] & [?$orderby] & [?$top] & [?$skip]
```

In most user interfaces, you need to be able to present this data to the user using various options. ADO.NET Data Services provides presentation options that enable you to cut down the lines of code required on the client to manipulate this data. This can be achieved by specifying additional query options parameters in the URL. These parameters are similar to query string parameters in normal web pages, and they can be used as presentation options to page, filter, sort, and expand data on the server as shown in Table 2-6.

Table 2-6. *Query Operations*

Function	Operation	Overview
Sorting	$orderby	This operation allows sorting of multiple columns in ascending or descending order by defined data type (e.g., date, integer, or string).
Paging	$skip, $top	Paging is achieved with a combination of both query operations $skip and $top.
Expanding	$expand	This operation is used to expand the data that is returned from the data service. This is achieved by passing one or more entity set names into the URL; for example, you could return a Customer along with its Orders in one server round-trip.
Filtering	$filter	Filtering of data can be achieved using greater than, less than, and equal to syntax as well as an extensive list of query expressions.

Let's take a closer look at each of these query operations.

Sorting Data

This operation is used to order data returned by the data service. The data is by default returned in ascending order according to the key that has been established on the entity. In most cases this is sufficient because client-side code can be used at the presentation layer to display data differently. However, there are situations when data needs to be ordered on the server. Take the Northwind `Orders` entity as an example: suppose you want to retrieve `Orders` by `ShipCountry` sorted in alphabetical order. To achieve this you could use the URL `/Northwind.svc/Orders?$orderby=ShipCountry`. If these results are required in reverse order, the `desc` keyword can be placed at the end of the query string. The `$orderby` query operator also accepts a comma-delimited list of conditions so that you can build a sort clause that contains more than one column, for example, `/Northwind.svc/Orders?$orderby=ShipCountry desc, City desc`.

Syntax:

```
<service>/<EntitySet>[(<EntityKey>)][/<NavigationProperty>
[(<EntityKey>)/...]]] ?$orderby = propertyId [ desc | asc ] , [..]
```

Examples to try:

Sort customers in alphabetical order by city:

```
/Northwind.svc/Customers?$orderby=City
```

Sort customers in reverse alphabetical order by city:

```
/Northwind.svc/Customers?$orderby=City desc
```

Sort customers in ascending order by country, and then descending by city:

```
/Northwind.svc/Customers?$orderby=Country, City desc
```

Page Operations

Due to the massive amounts of data stored in most real-world systems, paging of some sort has to be implemented. In ADO.NET Data Services, this is achieved with two query string operators: `$skip` and `$top`. The `$skip` operator provides the ability to skip a certain number of items and then get all the items after that. If you were to request `/Northwind.svc/Customers?$skip=10`, you would not receive the first ten items from the Customers entity set, but you would get all the items after that. When the `$skip` operator is specified, this is performed on the default sort order of the data, so if the data needs to be skipped in a different sort order, the `$orderby` query string operator needs to be added to the query (e.g., `/Northwind.svc/Customers?$orderby=City desc&$skip=10`).

Note The `$skip` query operator only makes sense when used with sorted data and should be used with the `$orderby` parameter. If the `$orderby` parameter is omitted, ADO.NET Data Services uses the primary key for the entity set to order the data before using the `$skip` option.

The $top operator works by only returning a limited number of rows from a data source. For example, if you want to just return the top ten customers from a query, you could use /Northwind.svc/Customers?$top=10. Similar to the $skip operator, this works in combination with the default sort order based upon the entity key; so if you wanted to retrieve the bottom set of results, the data needs to be sorted into descending order by the key or by another a property of the entity set (e.g., /Northwind.svc/Customers?$orderby=City desc&$top=10).

The $skip and $top and $orderby parameters are used together to handle paging requirements. If you want to page through customers ten at a time, you could use /Northwind.svc/Customers?$top=10 for the first page, /Customers?$skip=10$top=10 for the second page, and so on. When using query string parameters, keep in mind that multiple parameters can be added together separated by an ampersand (&).

Syntax:

```
<service>/<EntitySet>[(<EntityKey>)][/<NavigationProperty>
[(<EntityKey>)/...]]]?$skip = integer & $top = integer
```

Examples to try:

Return the top five sales orders with the highest total due:

```
/Orders?$orderby=TotalDue&$top=5
```

Return the fourth page, in a ten-row page:

```
/Customers?$skip=30&$top=10
```

■**Tip** Paging in ADO.NET Data Services is a pretty straight forward. The only limitation is the ability to determine the total number of records that are available. This can be achieved by implementing a service operator to return a scalar value containing the total number of rows for a certain query.

Expanding Related Data

When querying data, related data is returned in the form of <link> elements for Atom and _Deferred for the JSON format. These links by default are not populated with data and are great for situations when you are not certain you require this data. There are two ways to load this data: lazy loading and eager loading. **Lazy loading** is performed from the client and is demonstrated in Chapter 3. **Eager loading**, which is performed by a query string operator, enables you to retrieve all related data in one hit instead of going back to the server. This is useful when you want to return a customer and their related orders to populate a screen.

To use the $expand operator in the query string, you must specify the relationship property that you want to be automatically retrieved. For example, you could use the following URL to return the ALKFI customer and related orders: /Northwind.svc/Customers ('ALFKI')?$expand=Orders. This would return the content in Atom feed format as shown in Listing 2-11 and JSON format as shown in Listing 2-12.

Listing 2-11. *Expanded Orders for ALKFI in Atom Format*

```
<entry>
    <link href="Customers('ALFKI')/Orders">
        <m:inline>
            <feed>
                <entry>
                <link rel="edit" title="Orders" href="Orders(10643)" />
                <link rel="../Order_Details" title="Order_Details"
                        href="Orders(10643)/Order_Details" />
                    <content type="application/xml">
                        <m:properties>
                            <d:Freight m:type="Edm.Decimal">29.4600</d:Freight>
                            <d:OrderDate m:type="Edm.DateTime">
                                1997-08-25T00:00:00</d:OrderDate>
                            <d:OrderID m:type="Edm.Int32">10643</d:OrderID>
                            <d:RequiredDate m:type="Edm.DateTime">
                                1997-09-22T00:00:00</d:RequiredDate>
                            <d:ShipAddress>Obere Str. 57</d:ShipAddress>
                            <d:ShipCity>Berlin</d:ShipCity>
                            <d:ShipCountry>Germany</d:ShipCountry>
                            <d:ShipName>Alfreds Futterkiste</d:ShipName>
                            <d:ShippedDate m:type="Edm.DateTime">
                                1997-09-02T00:00:00</d:ShippedDate>
                            <d:ShipPostalCode>12209</d:ShipPostalCode>
                            <d:ShipRegion m:null="true" />
                        </m:properties>
                    </content>
                </entry>
                  ...
                <entry>
                <link rel="edit" title="Orders" href="Orders(10692)" />
                <link rel="../Order_Details" title="Order_Details"
                        href="Orders(10692)/Order_Details" />
                    <content type="application/xml">
                        <m:properties>
                            <d:Freight m:type="Edm.Decimal">61.0200</d:Freight>
                            <d:OrderDate m:type="Edm.DateTime">
                                1997-10-03T00:00:00</d:OrderDate>
                            <d:OrderID m:type="Edm.Int32">10692</d:OrderID>
                            <d:RequiredDate m:type="Edm.DateTime">
                                1997-10-31T00:00:00</d:RequiredDate>
                            <d:ShipAddress>Obere Str. 57</d:ShipAddress>
                            <d:ShipCity>Berlin</d:ShipCity>
                            <d:ShipCountry>Germany</d:ShipCountry>
                            <d:ShipName>Alfred's Futterkiste</d:ShipName>
```

```
                <d:ShippedDate m:type="Edm.DateTime">
                    1997-10-13T00:00:00</d:ShippedDate>
                <d:ShipPostalCode>12209</d:ShipPostalCode>
                <d:ShipRegion m:null="true" />
            </m:properties>
        </content>
    </entry>

        <content type="application/xml">
            <m:properties>
                <d:CustomerID>ALFKI</d:CustomerID>
                <d:CompanyName>Alfreds Futterkiste</d:CompanyName>
                <d:ContactName>Maria Anders</d:ContactName>
                <d:ContactTitle>Sales Representative</d:ContactTitle>
                <d:Address>Obere Str. 57</d:Address>
                    ...
            </m:properties>
        </content>
    </entry>
    </feed>
        </m:inline>
    </link>
</entry>
```

Listing 2-12. *Expanded Orders for ALKFI in JSON format*

```
{
    "d" : {
        "__metadata":
            {
                    "uri":"http://localhost:1131➡
                    /Northwind.svc/Customers(\'➡
                    ALFKI\')",
                    "type": "NorthwindModel.Customers"
            },
            "Address": "Obere Str. 57",
            "City": "Berlin",
            "CompanyName": "Alfreds Futterkiste",
            "ContactName": "Maria Anders",
            "ContactTitle": "Sales Representative",
            "Country": "Germany",
            "CustomerID": "ALFKI",
            "Fax": "030-0076545",
            "Phone": "030-0074321",
            "PostalCode": "12209",
```

```
                        "Region": null,
                        "Orders": [
                        {
                            "__metadata":
                            {
                                    "uri": "http://localhost:1131➥
                                    /Northwind.svc/Orders(10643)",
                                    "type": "NorthwindModel.Orders"
                            },
                            "Freight": "29.4600",
                            "OrderDate": "\/Date(872467200000)\/",
                            "OrderID": 10643,
                            "RequiredDate": "\/Date(874886400000)\/",
                            "ShipAddress": "Obere Str. 57",
                            "ShipCity": "Berlin",
                            "ShipCountry": "Germany",
                            "ShipName": "Alfreds Futterkiste",
                            "ShippedDate": "\/Date(873158400000)\/",
                            "ShipPostalCode": "12209",
                            "ShipRegion": null,...
                        },
                        {
                            "__metadata":
                            {
                                    "uri": "http://localhost:1131➥
                                    /Northwind.svc/Orders(10692)",
                                    "type": "NorthwindModel.Orders"
                            },
                            "Freight": "61.0200",
                            "OrderDate": "\/Date(875836800000)\/",
                            "OrderID": 10692,
                            "RequiredDate": "\/Date(878256000000)\/",
                            "ShipAddress": "Obere Str. 57",
                            "ShipCity": "Berlin",
                            "ShipCountry": "Germany",
                            "ShipName": "Alfred\'s Futterkiste",
                            "ShippedDate": "\/Date(876700800000)\/",
                            "ShipPostalCode": "12209",
                            "ShipRegion": null,
                            ...
                        },
                        {
                            ...
                        }
                    }
                }
```

The expanded orders for the customer have been successfully returned in a single hit to the service, but notice the Atom feed still has empty <link> elements. If you want to expand multiple related entities, you pass in a comma-delimited list of relationships to include; for example, to get the orders and their details plus the customer's demographics, you would use /Customers ('ALFKI')?$expand=Orders/Order_Details, CustomerDemographics. Notice the Orders/Order_Details parameter: this allows you to return both the order and the order details in a single round-trip!

It isn't always a good idea to allow clients to have the flexibility to perform this type of deep navigation. ADO.NET Data Services accommodates this concern by restricting the number of expand segments that can be specified and the depth of relationships that can be traversed on the service. This is configured in the InitializeService() method by the MaxExpandCount and MaxExpandDepth properties, respectively, on the IDataServiceConfiguration object. To demonstrate this, add two lines to the InitializeService() method and set the properties MaxExpandCount and MaxExpandDepth to 2. Now try URL /Northwind.svc/Orders (10248)?expand=Order_Details/Products, Customers. You will now receive an HTTP 400 Bad Request exception from the server. This is because the number of segments that ADO.NET Data Services has determined for this request is three, as it separately counts each segment of the relationship Order_Details/Products.

Syntax:

```
<service>/<EntitySet>[(<EntityKey>)][/<NavigationProperty>
[(<EntityKey>)/...]]] ?$expand=propertyid [/..]  [, propertyid [/..]]
```

Examples to try:

Return the customer with related sales orders and employees information:

```
/Customers('ALFKI')?$expand=Orders, Orders/Employees
```

Return the orders with related employees information and related shipper information:

```
/Orders(10248)?$expand=Employees, Shippers
```

■**Tip** If the MaxExpandCount and MaxExpandDepth properties are set on a service, they will apply to all URLs that are queried on the service. There is currently no ability to restrict this to certain relationships or entity sets. If a restriction on certain entity sets is required, you need to create separate data services.

Filtering

You are now able to retrieve entities and their related data as well as page and order them. The next step is to restrict the amount of data that is returned by filtering out the unwanted data. There are two methods to filter data that is returned. The first way is to specify an entity key against the entity sets; this would simply return a single specific entity (e.g., /Northwind. svc/Customers ('ALKFI')). However, if you want to return multiple entities based upon a query, this final query operator allows you to further filter out the data that you don't require. For example, you may want to filter suppliers for a country or orders within a date range. The $filter query string operator is used to meet these types of requests and can accept various combinations of operators and functions to handle the criteria. It can be used to filter data within an entity or even traverse the relationships of that entity to apply this filter. The `$filter` operator uses a simple expression language that can also be employed in the `$orderby` query string operator. The expression language is specified using a vast range of operators and functions against properties of an entity and ADO.NET Data Services data type literals. A **data type literal** could be a string that is enclosed in quotes, dates that are specified in a certain format, numbers with a +F literal to represent a float, and so on. Let's see how literals and properties work in an expression with a quick example. If you want to return just the customers in London for the Northwind service, you would use the following filter expression:

```
/Northwind.svc/Customers?$filter=City eq "London"
```

If we break this down into the expressions components, this would be

```
/Northwind.svc/Customers?
$filter=<Entity Property> <Logical Operator> <String Literal>
```

This is a simple example of an expression, but it demonstrates something important in that expressions need to use the correct syntax and case in order to work. This is because a key component of the ADO.NET Data Services engine is essentially string interpretation of URLs. The engine is not forgiving, and even logical operators such as the equals sign (=) must be specified as eq or the expression will stop at the second =. The other interesting part of the preceding example is the data type string literal London, which is enclosed in single quotes. The quotes indicate to data services that what they enclose is a string. Literals become more important when they are used against different types and must be specified with the correct literal syntax in order for an expression to operate as intended. In fact, to enable all data services types to be recognized, each type has a literal representation. Table 2-7 shows a subset of these types with a URL example of how they can be used in a filter expression.

Table 2-7. *Data Type Literals*

Literal	EDM Type	CLR Type	URL Example
null	null	null	/Northwind.svc/Customers ?$filter=Region ne null
true|false	Edm.Boolean	Bool	/Northwind.svc/Products ?$filter=Discontinued eq true
datetime'yyyy-mm-ddT hh:mm[:ss[.ffffff]]'	Edm.DateTime	DateTime	/Northwind.svc/Products ?$filter=OrderDate gt datetime'1996-01-01'
'[0-9]+'	Edm.Int32	Int32	/Northwind.svc/Order_Details ?$filter=Quantity gt 10
'char*'	Edm.String	String	/Northwind.svc/Customers ?$filter=City eq 'Berlin'

The operators, functions, and type promotion options that can be used in a filter expression are shown in Table 2-8. These options are case sensitive and must be specified in the correct case as shown.

Table 2-8. *Filter Criteria Options*

Category	Type	Parameter	Description
Logical	Operators	eq	Equal to
		ne	Not equal to
		gt	Greater than
		gteq	Greater than or equal to
		lt	Less than
		lteq	Less than or equal to
		and	Logical "and" operator
		or	Logical "or" operator
		not	Logical "not" operator
Arithmetic	Operators	add	Addition of two numeric values
		sub	Subtraction of two numeric values
		mul	Multiplication of two numeric values
		div	Division of two numeric values
		mod	Modulo of two numeric values
Grouping	Operators	( )	Precedence grouping
String	Functions	substringof	Specified string argument p1 is contained within string argument p0
		endswith	String argument ends with
		startswith	String argument starts with
		length	Length of string
		indexof	Position of string argument
		insert	Insert string at specified position
		remove	Remove string from specified position
		replace	Replace string based on search criteria
		tolower	Convert string to lowercase
		toupper	Convert string to uppercase
		trim	Trim string argument
		concat	Concatenate string
Date	Functions	second	Second portion of date
		minute	Minute portion of date
		hour	Hour portion of date
		day	Day portion of date
		month	Month portion of date
		year	Year portion of date
Math	Functions	round	Round-up value
		floor	Floor of value
		ceiling	Ceiling of value
Type promotion	Type	IsOf	Check whether the type is of a certain type
		Cast	Cast a type into another type

■**Note** Due to a limitation of how relationships are traversed with /, aggregate functions such as sum, min, max, avg, and count are not allowed in this release of ADO.NET Data Services. Additionally, IsNull and Coalesce are not allowed; instead, these expressions are supported using the null literal. Bitwise operators are also not supported.

If you scan Table 2-8, you will realize that filter expressions are mostly self-explanatory and map to regular programming concepts. In a similar vein, when programming you often want to group together multiple expressions to form complex logical statements. This is also possible using filter expressions that group multiple operators together using parentheses. These are then executed in a defined operator precedence: add, sub, div, mul, mod, and finally ( ).

Syntax:

```
<service>/<EntitySet>[(<EntityKey>)][/<NavigationProperty>
[(<EntityKey>)/...]]]?$filter=[Filter Expression]
```

Examples to try:

Return customers in London:

```
/Northwind.svc/Customers?$filter=City eq 'London'
```

Retrieve customer orders for 1997 using greater and less than:

```
/Northwind.svc/Orders?$filter=(OrderDate gteq '1997-01-01')
and (OrderDate lt '1998-01-01')
```

Retrieve customer orders for 1997 using year portion of date:

```
/Northwind.svc/Orders?$filter=(year(OrderDate) eq 1997)
```

Retrieve customers who lived in UK and have a postal code (ZIP code) that contains WA:

```
/Northwind.svc/Customers?$filter=(Country eq 'UK')
and (substringof(PostalCode,'WA'))
```

Hosting Data Services

When developing data services, typically you will perform all development on your local machine using the Visual Studio Web Development Server. In a production environment, you will need to deploy the data service to IIS 6.0 to enable it to be accessed over the Internet. To ensure that the server works in IIS, you will need to set the database permissions for any data source that the data service works on. If you're using SQL roles, this will typically be the database reader and writer roles on the tables. Most SQL database administrators will not allow direct permissions on tables, so it is good practice to use the mapping functionality in the Entity Framework to use views and stored procedures with data services instead of the tables directly. This will give the ability to create a separate SQL database role that can then be granted permissions to only the views and stored procedures and not the underlying tables.

In addition you will also need to configure IIS to allow additional HTTP to pass through, because by default IIS will not allow HTTP verbs DELETE, PUT, and MERGE. The reason is that this would be a security risk, as you are effectively giving the ability to delete or replace items directly on the server. To get this security issue past web administrators, you will need to sit them down and go through the architecture of ADO.NET Data Services and why allowing these verbs will actually give them better visibility on resources that are being accessed within the Internet. Also, tell them that these verbs will only be granted to the ADO.NET Data Services virtual directory, which will provide a level of isolation.

EXERCISE 2-3: HOSTING A DATA SERVICE IN IIS

This exercise outlines how to host the Northwind data service in IIS 6.0. The key purpose of this exercise is to demonstrate that you must change the default IIS behavior for web sites by allowing HTTP verbs DELETE, PUT, and MERGE to put the service into production. This exercise assumes that IIS 6.0 has been installed on your local development machine. If it hasn't been installed, please refer to Microsoft MSDN documentation on how to install IIS on your local machine.

1. Open the Visual Studio 2008 Northwind Web Site project that was created in Exercise 2-1.

2. Create a new virtual directory to host the data service: in Solution Explorer, right-click the Northwind project and select Properties from the context menu. Click the Web tab and change the Visual Studio development server to the local IIS server. Click Create Visual Directory, which will put the service into IIS, as shown in Figure 2-10.

Figure 2-10. *Creating a new virtual directory*

3. Modify the .svc application extension to allow the additional HTTP verbs to be used by first going to the Start Menu and selecting Administration Tools ➤ Internet Information Services (IIS) Manager to open IIS 6.0. Expand the (local) server node, expand the Web Sites node, and then expand Default Web Site. Right-click the NorthwindDataService virtual directory and select Properties. The Virtual Directory Properties dialog will appear. From this dialog, click the Configuration button located on the Virtual Directory tab. The Application Configuration dialog will appear. Scroll down the application extensions to locate the .svc extension (if the .svc extension doesn't exist, follow step 4 to create it). Click edit, and add the DELETE, PUT, and MERGE verbs to this dialog, as shown in Figure 2-11. Check the Script Engine option is enabled and click OK.

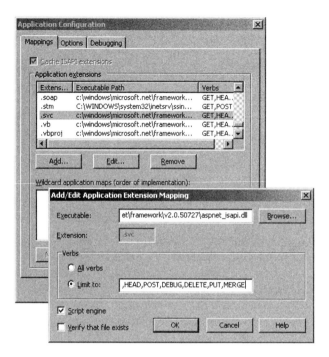

Figure 2-11. *Allowing HTTP DELETE, PUT, and MERGE*

4. If the .svc extension doesn't exist, it needs to be created by clicking the Add button in the Application Configuration dialog. Enter **c:\windows\microsoft.net\framework\v2.0.50727\aspnet_isapi.dll** in the Executable text box, and enter **.svc** in the Extension text box. In the Verbs area, set the Limit to option to DELETE, PUT, GET, HEAD, POST, DEBUG, and MERGE. Check that the Script Engine option is enabled and click OK.

■**Note** If you need to run the data service in debug mode from Visual Studio 2008, you will need to ensure that the virtual directory has anonymous switched off and Windows Authentication switched on. To do this, open IIS 6.0 and navigate to the NorthwindDataService virtual directory. Right-click and select Properties. Select the Directory Security tab and click Edit. Uncheck the Enable anonymous access option and check the Integrated Windows authentication option.

Surfacing Custom Data Sources Using CLR Classes

If we need to access a data source that is something other than a supported database, we must create a CLR class that interacts with this source and then returns a collection of objects that support the IQueryable<T> interface. Examples of these custom sources are

- Custom .NET collection

- Excel spreadsheet

- XML document

- Custom database

In the following exercise, we'll walk you through the steps to set up a custom data source.

EXERCISE 2-4: CREATING A .NET CLR DATA SOURCE

In this exercise you'll create a custom data source. To start, you need to create a new Visual Studio 2008 Web Site project called CustomDataSource.

1. In Visual Studio 2008, create a new C# ASP.NET Web Site project by selecting File ➤ New ➤ Project. Select the ASP.NET Web Site Visual Studio project template and enter CustomDataSource as the project name.

Next you need to create the data source that you want to expose. The data source will contain collection of entities that represent inductees to the Rock and Roll Hall of Fame. First you must create a CLR class that represents the inductee entity by following this step:

2. In your new project, create a new class called Inductee by right-clicking the Web Site project in Solution Explorer and selecting Add New Item. Select the class template from the Visual Studio templates dialog and name the class **Inductee**. A prompt will appear suggesting to place the class in the AppCode folder' click Yes.

3. Overwrite the code in the Inductee class by using the code in Listing 2-13.

Listing 2-13. *Inductee Class*

```
using System;
using System.Collections.Generic;
using System.Linq;
using System.Web;
using System.Data.Services.Common;

public class Inductee
{
    public string Name { get; set; }
    public bool Group { get; set; }
    public int YearInducted { get; set; }
}
```

Whenever you manually create classes in ADO.NET Data Services, you need to back up each of these with a static method that is used to populate a collection of entities. The primary reason for this is that there isn't a way of accessing the query expression that is being used by the caller. Therefore, there is no way to determine exactly which entities are required.

4. Use the static method in Listing 2-14 to populate a collection of inductees.

Listing 2-14. *Populate Inductee's static Method*

```
public static List<Inductee> MakeInducteeList()

{
   return (new List<Inductee>()
   {
      new Inductee()
      {
          Name = "Rolling Stones",
          Group = false,
          YearInducted = 1990,
      },
      new Inductee()
      {
          Name = "Beatles",
          Group = false,
          YearInducted = 1986,
      }
   });
}
```

To return a query a list of entities that is surfaced to the data service, you must create a class that contains an IQueryable<T> property for each entity exposed.

5. Create the new class by right-clicking the Web Site project in Solution Explorer and selecting Add New Item. Select the class template from the Visual Studio template dialog and name the class **DataModel**.

6. Overwrite the code in the DataModel class by using the code in Listing 2-15.

Listing 2-15. *DataModel Class*

```
using System;
using System.Collections.Generic;
using System.Linq;
using System.Web;
using System.Data.Services;

public class MyDataModel
{
    static List<Inductee> inductee;
```

```
    static MyDataModel()
    {
        inductee = Inductee.MakeInducteeList();
    }

    public IQueryable<Inductee> Inductees
    {
        get
        {
            return inductee.AsQueryable();
        }
    }
}
```

Now you'll create the data service that will query our new data source. The data source will use the MyDataModel class as the DataService<T> class that is exposed.

7. Create the data service by right-clicking the Web Site project in Solution Explorer and selecting Add New Item. Select the ADO.NET Data Service template from the Visual Studio template dialog and name it **CustomSource**.

8. Navigate to the CustomSource.cs file and overwrite the /* TODO: put your data source class name here */ with MyDataModel.

9. The data service only supports the IQueryable<T> interface. Add this rule to the InitializeService method on the data service using the following code:

```
config.SetEntitySetAccessRule("*", EntitySetRights.AllRead);
```

You must add the references to the ADO.NET Data Services assemblies that will be used in this project.

10. Create the references by right-clicking the Web Site project in Solution Explorer and selecting Add Reference. Highlight System.Data.Services, System.Data.Services.Common, and System.Data.Services. Design in the .NET tab in the Add Reference dialog, and then click OK.

Now that you have created the class, data model, and the data service, you should just be able to press Ctrl+F5 and modify the web.config to run it. When you do this you will notice that a request error is returned from the browser. The reason for this error is because you need to make sure that entity instance that is returned from the service is uniquely addressable. This is achieved by adding the DataServiceKey[] attribute to your Inductee class. This attribute points to one or more properties that make up a unique instance.

11. Open up the Inductee class and add the [DataServiceKey("Name")] attribute at the top of the Inductee class as shown in Listing 2-17.

Listing 2-17. *Updated Inductee Class*

```
using System;
using System.Collections.Generic;
using System.Linq;
using System.Web;
using System.Data.Services.Common;
```

```
[DataServiceKey("Name")]
public class Inductee
{
    ...
}
```

If you now test the service again, similar to the Northwind service, you will be presented the service home page that lists the entities that appear on the service. The service is pretty boring because only one entity set is exposed.

Summary

Microsoft conceived the ADO.NET Data Services project in the summer of 2007 and christened it Astoria, named after the cloudiest region of the States. The reason why Microsoft chose this name is unclear, as at the time the company didn't have a database cloud solution (at least not one that we knew of). We now know that this has changed with Microsoft's SQL Server Data Services (SSDS) offering, or what we like to call hosted SQL Server, which will challenge other hosted data solutions such as Amazon S3 and Google Base. ADO.NET Data Services will be at the core of SSDS.

ADO.NET Data Services is unique in many ways and was the first technology to employ a transparent design approach within Microsoft. This essentially means that all design decisions were made public, and active feedback helped shape how the services would ultimately be shipped. This process was very successful, and it has been announced that the next version of Astoria and the Entity Framework will use this approach.

This chapter gave a rundown of some of the many features of ADO.NET Data Services with code examples. The platform is a combination of a runtime and a RESTful addressable interface through which its services are exposed. A data service can be queried from many different environments using different APIs and has extensive support for traditional .NET, Silverlight, and AJAX clients. We will demonstrate how to use ADO.NET Data Services with these clients in the following chapters.

CHAPTER 3

■■■

ADO.NET Data Services Development

In the last chapter we focused on providing an introduction to how to query data services. However, you probably want to have more than just querying capabilities for your service. ADO.NET Data Services provides support to enable Create, Update, and Delete (CUD) operations. Also, often complex data services require business logic to be executed against resources. Instead of writing this logic directly into the underlying data source, developers can transfer this to the ADO.NET Data Services layer, which is then executed whenever a CUD operation is performed. This can be used to restrict data that is exposed by the service and to ensure data integrity.

Business logic is achieved by intercepting queries and updates before execution is made against the underlying data source. RESTful interfaces are always conceptually very easy to understand, but often there are cases where a query or update doesn't map directly to the resource. In these cases it is often easier to write a functional call; to rapidly achieve this goal, Microsoft provides service operations that are similar to traditional RPC calls.

The following topics will be discussed in this chapter:

- **ADO.NET Data Services assemblies**: We provide a list of the WCF 3.5 assemblies that make up ADO.NET Data Services and how they conceptually fit into ADO.NET Data Services.

- **Debugging using Fiddler**: Fiddler is an essential debugging tool that is used to capture HTTP requests and responses to a data service. We provide a quick start guide to using this tool with the Northwind data service you created in the last chapter.

- **Client support**: We show how client support is provided in traditional .NET applications as well as Silverlight- and AJAX-style Rich Interactive Applications (RIAs). The assemblies support a rich set of LINQ features that enable querying, inserting, updating, and deleting against the data source.

- **Scalar values**: Scalar values can be returned to the client interface by appending a standard query operation to the URL.

- **Data interceptors**: The interception of queries and updates are captured on the server side before the operation is executed against the underlying data source. This allows developers to inject business logic that can then be used to perform validation and security before the request is executed.

- **Service operations**: These operations go against a traditional RESTful interface because they allow direct RPC function calls. The primary reason to include these features is that sometimes a RESTful interface just won't fit the functional requirement.

- **Batching**: Keeping within HTTP 1.1, data services handle batching by using multipart MIME types that are processed as batches of requests by the server.

- **Concurrency**: Similar to batching, concurrency support conforms to the HTTP 1.1 standard by using Entity Tags (ETags), which provide a method of performing concurrency on HTTP operations. An ETag is basically a token that is placed in the response header from the web server. This token is then checked for consistency on every update operation.

- **Securing services**: There are four means of using secure services in ADO.NET Data Services: using the host's built-in authentication model, restricting the resources' visibility, intercepting data before execution, and service operations.

- **Error handling support**: Error handling in ADO.NET Data Services involves mapping custom exceptions to HTTP status codes that are returned from a data service. We provide best practices on how to surface exceptions from your data services.

ADO.NET Data Services Assemblies

The ADO.NET Data Services framework provides the capability to create data-centric services over the Web. The technical features are split into two aspects: server and client. Recall from Chapter 1 that the key server-side classes `DataService<T>`, `DataServiceHost`, and `DataServiceHostFactory` are implemented on top of WCF 3.5, which uses the WCF syndication layer to deliver data through open formats such as JSON and Atom. Due to data services working differently from traditional WCF services, consumers do not need to understand the contracts, addressing, and binding of the service. Clients can just operate with the service using an HTTP assembly that provides the ability to construct HTTP requests to an endpoint. If this option is chosen, the client would then be put in charge of creating the HTTP request and then converting the result into client-side objects. To simplify this interaction an extensive ADO.NET Data Services client-side assembly can be used. The `System.Data.Services.Client.*`

assembly provides support for clients such as Windows Forms, Windows Presentation Framework, Silverlight, and web sites and allows typed resources to be seamlessly sent and received from a data service. In addition the client-side assembly also has the ability to perform basic LINQ querying against data service resources. Table 3-1 lists the assemblies that make up ADO.NET Data Services.

Table 3-1. *ADO.NET Data Services Assemblies*

Assembly	Description
System.Data.Services.*	Contains core assemblies that are used to develop data services on the server. The key classes are **DataService<T>**, **DataServiceHost**, and **DataServiceHostFactory**, which are used to instantiate data services and provide support for URL and data translation.
System.Data.Services.Client.*	Provides the capability to perform standard query operations against data services from the client using both URL and LINQ queries. Maintains client-side representation of the state using the DataContext<T> class.
System.Data.Services.Common.*	Provides shared classes that are used on both the client and server. The current RTM release has only the [DataServiceKey] attribute class, which is shared.
System.Data.Services.Design.*	Contains assemblies that are used by code generation libraries to create strongly typed classes on clients. The DataSvcUtil executable and the Add Service Reference Wizard use these libraries.
System.Data.Services.Internal.*	Contains internal classes that are used to implement support for queries with eager loading of related entities.
Sys.Data.DataService.*	Provides data service query execution and JSON support in AJAX applications. This assembly is provided on CodePlex (dataservices.js and dataservicesDebug.js libraries).

A conceptual overview of how these assemblies fit within ADO.NET Data Services is shown in Figure 3-1.

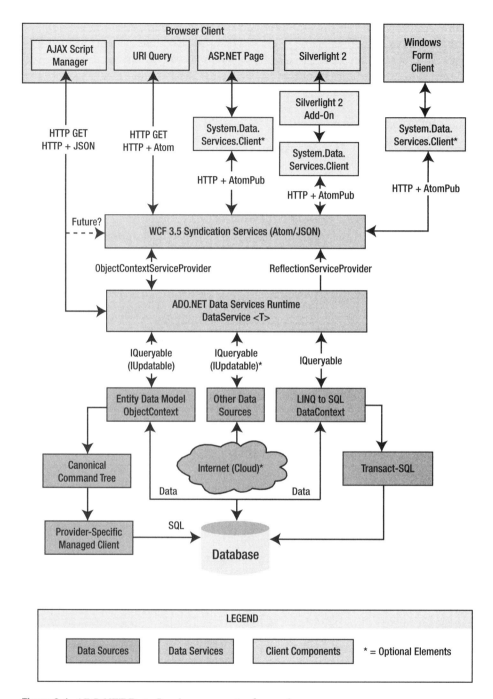

Figure 3-1. *ADO.NET Data Services conceptual overview*

■**Note** In the ADO.NET Data Services documentation, you will see the Atom Publishing Protocol (AtomPub) and Atom format mentioned in the same breath. The difference between Atom and AtomPub is that Atom is the format of the data, and AtomPub is the application-level protocol or the rules for interacting with the data. The AtomPub standard describes the publishing and editing of web resources through HTTP using Atom-formatted representations as documented in the Atom syndication format. The Atom and AtomPub standards were submitted as separate RFCs (Internet protocol standards). RFC 4287 was submitted in December 2005 for the Atom format, and RFC 5023 was submitted in October 2007 for the Atom Publishing Protocol. For further information on these standards, please go to `http://www.rfc-editor.org/rfc/rfc5023.txt` or `http://www.rfc-editor.org/rfc/rfc4287.txt`.

Debugging Data Services Using Fiddler

The query string is the fundamental part of ADO.NET Data Services and the REST programming model. It dictates the shape of the data that is returned and how it is represented. When you first learn how to use ADO.NET Data Services, you may want to test the various permutations and discover how easy it is to manipulate data. To do this you will probably use a browser because you can easily point to a URL and start playing. However, there are limitations on using browsers; for instance, you cannot change the default representations, access to query operations is limited, and you won't be able to perform PUT, POST, or DELETE operations against the data. To get around these limitations, we'll introduce a tool that is invaluable in REST programming: Fiddler.

Fiddler, created by Microsoft, is a web debugging proxy that logs all HTTP(S) traffic between your computer and the Internet. It allows you to inspect all HTTP(S) traffic, set breakpoints, and "fiddle" with incoming or outgoing data. Fiddler also includes a powerful event-based scripting subsystem that can be extended using any .NET language. If you're having issues with your application and not sure if it's ADO.NET Data Services or something else that's causing them, then Fiddler is the resource you should turn to; it will capture all the data services' HTTP traffic between the client application and the server. Additionally, as you will see, Fiddler allows you to test the various concepts in ADO.NET Data Services without having to create a client, so it is helpful when you want to replay test scenarios.

EXERCISE 3-1: USING FIDDLER WITH ADO.NET DATA SERVICES

The steps in this exercise provide details on how to set up Fiddler and then how you can use it to test your data service through HTTP requests.

1. Download Fiddler from `http://fiddler2.com/fiddler2/version.asp`.

2. Perform a default installation of the tool.

3. Read the MSDN article on the tool at `http://msdn.microsoft.com/en-us/library/bb250446.aspx` and watch the "getting started" video on the Fiddler web site: `http://www.fiddlertool.com/fiddler`.

Now that you have Fiddler installed, you can start to do some Fiddling! You'll start with submitting a simple query string against the Northwind data service and viewing the HTTP result in the Atom format. Then by changing the HTTP headers, you will see how easy it is to change the HTTP result's data representation to JSON format. Finally, you'll update a value on a resource returned by the data service.

Performing an HTTP GET Query in Fiddler

1. Open the NorthwindDataService Visual Studio 2008 project that you created in the last chapter. The data service should be run using the Visual Studio Development Web Server. To do this, from Solution Explorer right-click NorthwindDataService and select Properties from the context menu. Click the Web tab and ensure that the Visual Studio Web Development Server option is set. Click the Specific port option and enter **1101** in the Specific port text box.

2. Run the Northwind data service by pressing Ctrl+F5 in Visual Studio 2008.

3. Perform an HTTP GET request. Start by opening Fiddler and clicking Request Builder. Select the GET verb from the drop-down list. Specify `http://localhost:1101/Northwind.svc/Products(1)` as the HTTP request URL.

4. Review the HTTP response by clicking the last web session in the left-hand pane. Select the Session Inspector tab and click the TextView tab as shown in Figure 3-2.

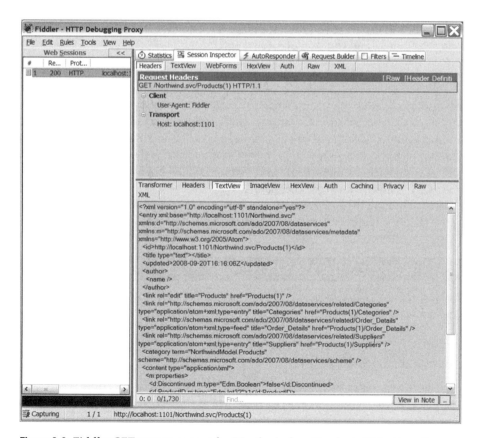

Figure 3-2. *Fiddler GET request output for /Northwind.svc/Products(1) in Atom format*

5. Change the data representation to the JSON format by clicking Request Builder. Type the HTTP headers **Content-Type: application/json** and **Accept: application/json** into the Request Headers area as shown in Figure 3-3 and click Execute.

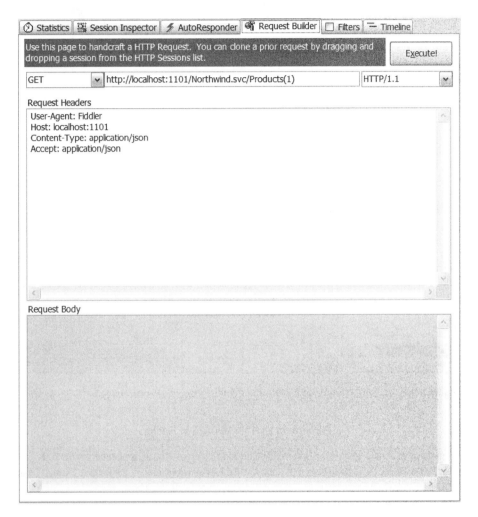

Figure 3-3. *Modifying content headers in Fiddler*

6. Click the Session Inspector tab to review the HTTP response output as shown in Figure 3-4.

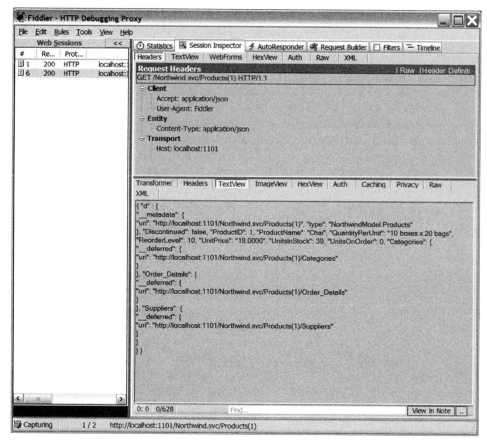

Figure 3-4. *Fiddler GET request output for /Northwind.svc/Products(1) in JSON format*

Performing an HTTP UPDATE in Fiddler

1. To perform an update against the Northwind data service, increase the units on order for the first product to 1: in Fiddler, enter the code in Listing 3-1 and into the Request Body area in the Request Builder. Change the HTTP verb to PUT and click Execute.

Listing 3-1. *PUT Request*

```
{
"Discontinued": false,
"ProductID": 1,
"ProductName": "Chai",
"QuantityPerUnit": "10 boxes x 20 bags",
"ReorderLevel": 10,
"UnitPrice": "18.0000",
"UnitsInStock": 39,
"UnitsOnOrder": 1
}
```

2. This PUT request intentionally fails because of a permission issue in the service. To understand the issue, notice that the HTTP status code returned in Fiddler is HTTP 403 as shown in the left-hand pane. To see the actual JSON HTTP error response returned, click the HTTP 403 session, click the Session Inspector tab, and click the TextView tab to see the output as shown in Listing 3-2.

Listing 3-2. *JSON Error Returned*

```
{
   "error":
   {
   "code": "", "message": {
   "lang": "en-US", "value": "Forbidden"
      }}
}
```

■Tip To understand how ADO.NET Data Services handles errors, please see the "Error Handling Support" section of this chapter.

3. The error is due to the original data service being set up to only allow read access. To fix this issue, you must give the Northwind data service write permission. Start by opening `Northwind.svc.cs`. Navigate to the `InitializeService()` method and change `SetEntitySetAccessRule` to the `EntitySetRights.All` enum as shown in Listing 3-3.

Listing 3-3. *Allowing Full Entity Set Permissions*

```
public static void InitializeService(IDataServiceConfiguration config)
{
    config.SetEntitySetAccessRule("*", EntitySetRights.All);
    ...
}
```

4. Retry the HTTP PUT request in Fiddler. The HTTP response should now be HTTP 204, which indicates the PUT request was successful.

■Note If you are running your service using Visual Studio Web Development Server, Fiddler will not capture these requests by default. If the data service is run in IIS, the HTTP requests will be captured by the tool as long as the machine's host name is used instead of localhost.

Client Support

To start working with a data service, all that is required is the ability to send HTTP requests to an endpoint. This enables interoperability with multiple development platforms such as Java, Ruby, and so forth because all that is required is an HTTP library and the endpoint to retrieve the string-based results. Most development platforms worth their salt will have an HTTP library to enable this interaction. In .NET this library resides in the System.Net assembly, and specifically the HttpWebRequest object can be used. To see how to use the HTTP library, create a simple console application, add a reference to the System.Net, System.IO, and System.Xml libraries, and copy the code in Listing 3-4 into the main method of the default Program.cs class.

Listing 3-4. *Example HTTP GET Request Using the .NET HTTP Library*

```
HttpWebRequest request = (HttpWebRequest)WebRequest.Create(
            "http://localhost:1101/Northwind.svc/Customers('ALFKI')");
request.Method = "GET";
HttpWebResponse response = (HttpWebResponse)request.GetResponse();
StreamReader reader = new StreamReader(response.GetResponseStream());
XmlDocument xmlResult = new XmlDocument();
xmlResult.Load(reader);
response.Close();

Console.WriteLine(xmlResult.OuterXml);
Console.ReadLine();
```

This code shows how to initialize an HttpWebRequest object and set the HTTP method to GET. Finally, the request.GetResponse stream is used to read the results into an XML document named xmlResult. The client can then choose to perform XPath querying of the XML document to retrieve the properties of the request. Obviously, to operate with data services in this way is both time consuming and error prone. To create a richer client experience in .NET environments, a set of client assemblies are provided that support Silverlight and traditional .NET clients. Additionally, there is also a third-party CodePlex JavaScript library that enables AJAX support. This third-party library will be discussed in Chapter 5.

The client library assembly System.Data.Services.Client.*, provided from Microsoft, is for Windows Forms, Windows Presentation Foundation, Silverlight, and web applications. This assembly has low footprint that enables natural object-based interaction with data services such as traversal of entity associations, for example, a collection of orders for a customer. A limitation of using this assembly is that by default it will only use the Atom format to send and receive requests from a data service; this format cannot be changed. This is the reason why there is a separate library for AJAX applications where the data that is exchanged is minimal.

The two main constructs in this assembly are the DataServiceContext and DataServiceQuery objects. These objects mirror the Entity Framework's ObjectContext and ObjectQuery types. The DataServiceContext and DataServiceQuery constructs work with client-side .NET objects that represent the entities that define the data service. These objects can be either manually hand-crafted or generated automatically by one of the tools provided with ADO.NET Data Services.

When these are defined manually, ADO.NET Data Services allows these objects to be created using Plain Old CLR Types (POCO). This means that the object doesn't need to contain other attributes or code around the class that is normally required in many client-side proxies. Thus, a simple class as shown in Listing 3-5 could be used. This has advantages because these types are very clean and simple to work with.

Listing 3-5. *Plain Old CLR Class*

```
public class Customer
{
     public int ID
     {
         get{;}
         set{;}
     }

public int CompanyName
{
     get {;}
     set {;}
}
```

The only class decoration that needs to be considered when using POCO classes is the [DataServiceKey] attribute. This attribute is used to mark which property is the identity key, which is required for identity and change management, as discussed next in the "DataServiceContext" section. Often the [DataServiceKey] attribute isn't always needed because if this attribute isn't applied, then ADO.NET Data Services will try to imply the key from any property named either <typename>ID or ID. In the example in Listing 3-5, the ID property would automatically be recognized as the key without having to apply the [DataServiceKey] attribute.

DataServiceContext

The client library supports identity resolution and optimistic concurrency tracking via the DataServiceContext object. The DataServiceContext is essentially used to hold state on the client. Even though data services themselves are stateless, this object will be used to store the state of each response, which is required to support change tracking and is achieved by tracking the identity of the entities in the DataServiceContext. To do this the client-side entity classes must be decorated with the [DataServiceKey] attribute (if not automatically taken care of by data services as described previously). The key is then used in ObjectStateManager of the DataServiceContext to uniquely identify which entities need to be updated or appended to from each data service response. The DataServiceContext MergeOption property has an important role to play in tracking entity changes. This property is used to synchronize the entities that are returned from a data service response to the context. It has four possible options, AppendOnly, NoTracking, OverwriteChanges, and PreserveChanges, as shown in Table 3-2.

Table 3-2. *Merge Options*

Member Name	Description
AppendOnly	Appends only new entities, and does not modify existing entities that were previously fetched. This is the default behavior.
NoTracking	Does not modify ObjectStateManager.
OverwriteChanges	Replaces the current values in the ObjectStateEntry with the values from the store. This will overwrite the changes that have been made locally with data from the server.
PreserveChanges	Replaces the original values without modifying the current values. This is useful for forcing the local values to save successfully after an optimistic concurrency exception.

As an example, if the context was set to AppendOnly and a request was made to the data service, only new entities that were not already available in the context would be added. If ObjectStateManager came across an entity that was already present in the context, then the client's state for this entity would be preserved. The OverwriteChanges option is similar to AppendOnly except that new and existing changes will be automatically overwritten. This is useful when you want a refresh of the object from the server. The PreserveChanges option can be useful when you want to ensure that any unchanged values from a previous call are updated from the server but any other values are left unchanged. To enable tracking of the DataServiceContext, the MergeOption property on the context must be set to something other than NoTracking.

DataServiceQuery

The DataServiceQuery object is used to query data services using URLs. When requesting data from the server, this object always has to be used in conjunction with the DataServiceContext. In fact the only way to query data services is to use one of the query methods on the DataServiceContext object. There are essentially two methods on the DataServiceContext that are used to perform execute synchronous URL queries: CreateQuery<T> and Execute<T>. The generic type <T> that is used in these methods is a local .NET object type that represents one of the entities in the server data model. When the data service query is executed, the DataServiceContext object services will attempt to serialize the query response from the server into this generic type <T>. The primary difference between CreateQuery<T> and Execute<T> is that the Execute<T> method accepts a full URL to be executed (e.g., /Customers$orderby=City), whereas the CreateQuery<T> method will only accept an entity set name (e.g., /Customers). Even with this limitation, the CreateQuery<T> method can still be used to construct Execute<T> type queries. This is achieved by appending multiple AddQueryOption instances onto the end of the query. Additionally, as shown in Listing 3-7, the CreateQuery<T> method is used extensively in the client-side code output generated by the DataSvcUtil tool or the Add Service Reference Wizard.

The code shown in Listing 3-6 demonstrates both of these methods using a query that will return a list of suppliers ordered by country. The difference between the CreateQuery<T> and the Execute<T> methods is very small as they both establish the DataServiceContext that points to the Northwind data service endpoint. The main difference as discussed is that the CreateQuery<T> method appends the query options whereas the Execute <T> method includes these in the URL string. Once the data service query (DataServiceQuery) is executed by either of the two methods, the object services of the DataServiceContext will then serialize the Suppliers objects from the server into local .NET client types. These entities will be added to the DataServiceContext based upon the default AppendOnly tracking behavior. This means only new entities that are retrieved will then be appending to the local DataServiceContext.

Listing 3-6. *Querying Using URL*

CreateQuery<T> Option

```
DataServiceContext service = new DataServiceContext( new Uri("http://localhost:1101/
Northwind.svc"));

DataServiceQuery<Suppliers> query = service.CreateQuery<Suppliers>("/Suppliers")
.AddQueryOption("$orderby", "Country");
```

Execute<T> Option

```
DataServiceContext service = new DataServiceContext( new Uri("http://localhost:1101/
Northwind.svc"));

IEnumerable<Suppliers> suppliers = service.Execute<Suppliers>
(new Uri("Suppliers?$orderby=Country", UriKind.Relative));
```

Creating Local Client Types

When the data service grows, the processing of manually creating client types becomes complex and time consuming. To assist developers in generating these client types, ADO.NET Data Services integrates with the Add Service Reference Wizard in Visual Studio 2008 SP1. In Exercise 3-2 you'll see how to use this wizard to generate the client types. If more control is required on how client types are generated, you would want to use a tool called DataSvcUtil. This tool is located in the .NET Framework 3.5 directory, so it can be used from the Visual Studio command prompt. The tool provides the ability to generate client types from either a physical URL of the service or from a Conceptual Schema Definition Language (CSDL) file. In any case the output that is generated is the same as that of the Add Service Reference Wizard. The tool's options are shown in Figure 3-5.

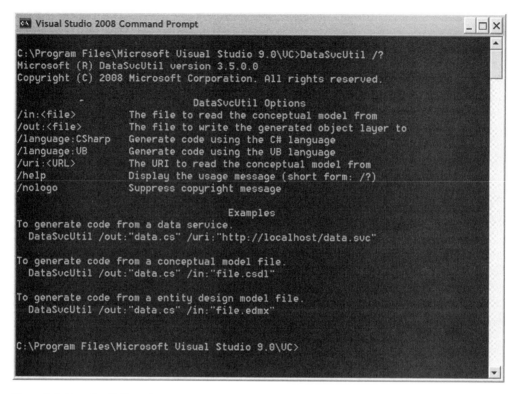

Figure 3-5. *DataSvcUtil options*

One of two key options of the DataSvcUtil tool must be specified from the command line: either /in: to indicate the input CSDL file, or /uri: to indicate the URI to the service. Let's examine the generated output using the command-line tool that will use the physical URL of our Northwind data service. To do this, first run the Northwind Data Service Visual Studio 2008 project by pressing Ctrl+F5. Load the Visual Studio 2008 command prompt by selecting Start ➤ Program Files ➤ Visual Studio 2008 ➤ Visual Studio 2008 Command Prompt. Type the following into the command prompt:

```
DataSvcUtil /out: "C:\output.cs" /uri: "http://localhost:1101/Northwind.svc"
```

This will now generate the client types in the c:\output.cs file. If you open up this file, you will notice that the client types such as Customers and Suppliers are similar to the POCO class that you created earlier. The main difference is that these types also contain static helper methods that can be used create an instance of an object. If you move focus to the NorthwindEntities class, this inherits the DataServiceContext object and has DataServiceQuery properties for each entity. This means that it's possible to reference an entity directly from the context without concerning yourself about how to get this entity in the context first, because behind the scenes a DataServiceQuery is automatically executed for you. The NorthwindEntities class has also methods for adding entities to the context via an AddTo[Entity] method as shown in Listing 3-7. These methods and properties provide a richer client experience because these entities can be interacted with using typed names.

Listing 3-7. *Client-Generated Proxy*

```
public partial class NorthwindEntities :
      global::System.Data.Services.Client.DataServiceContext
{

    /// <summary>
    /// Initialize a new NorthwindEntities object.
    /// </summary>
    public NorthwindEntities(global::System.Uri serviceRoot) :
         base(serviceRoot)
    {
        ...
    }

    public System.Data.Services.Client.DataServiceQuery<Customers> Customers
    {
        get
        {
            if ((this._Customers == null))
            {
                this.Customers =base.CreateQuery<Customers>("Customers");
            }
            return this.Customers;
        }
    }

    ...

    public void AddToCustomers(Customers customers)
    {
        base.AddObject("Customers", customers);
    }
    ...
}
```

If you now return back to the types that have been generated, you will notice in the
RTM version of data services that the types don't support INotifyPropertyChanged or
INotifyPropertyCollectionChanged. These interfaces are important in .NET because they are
used to notify clients, typically binding clients that a property value has changed. The reason why these interfaces were left out of the autogeneration is because the ADO.NET Data
Services team wanted these classes to be as clean as possible. If you have clients that require
these binding interfaces, you can add these interfaces manually to the client types; an example
of doing this for the Customers type is shown in Listing 3-8.

Listing 3-8. *Implementation of INotifyPropertyChanged Interface*

```
public partial class Customers :
    System.ComponentModel.INotifyPropertyChanged
{
    public event System.ComponentModel.PropertyChangedEventHandler
    PropertyChanged;

    protected virtual void OnPropertyChanged(string propertyName)
    {
        if (PropertyChanged != null)
        {
            PropertyChanged(this, new
            System.ComponentModel.PropertyChangedEvent
            Args(propertyName));
        }
    }

    ...

    public string Address
    {
        get
        {
            return this._Address;
        }
        set
        {
            if (value != this._Address)
            {
                this.OnAddressChanging(value);
                this._Address = value;
                this.OnAddressChanged();
                this.OnPropertyChanged("Address");
            }
        }
    }
    private string _Address;
    partial void OnAddressChanging(string value);
    partial void OnAddressChanged();

    ...
}
```

Now that we have examined some of the high-level features of the client assembly, let's consume the Northwind data service using one of many .NET clients. To keep this exercise straightforward, you will consume the service using a Windows console application.

EXERCISE 3-2: CONSUMING DATA SERVICES USING A .NET CLIENT

The steps in this exercise outline how to consume data services using a simple .NET client console application.

1. Create a new Console project in Visual Studio 2008 by selecting File ➤ New ➤ Project. Select the Console project type, enter **ClientConsoleApp** as the project name, and click OK.

2. You must run the Northwind data service in order to add a service reference. Open the Northwind Data Service Visual Studio 2008 project and press Ctrl+F5 to run the service in debug mode. This should run the service in the browser as URL `http://localhost:1101/Northwind.svc/`.

3. Generate the .NET client proxy classes that will interact with the Northwind data service by right-clicking the ClientConsoleApp project and selecting Service Reference. In the dialog that appears, enter `http://localhost:1101/Northwind.svc/` in the Address text box and click Go. The Northwind data service should be shown in the left-hand pane of the dialog as you can see in Figure 3-6. Enter **NorthwindDataService** in the Namespace text box and click OK.

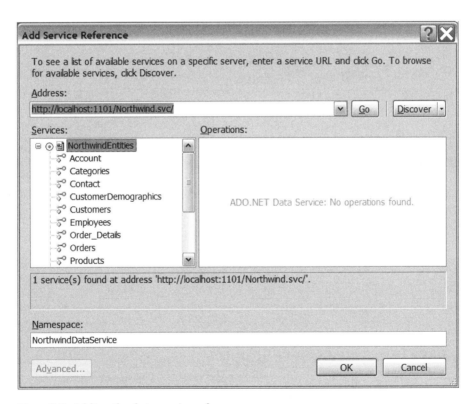

Figure 3-6. *Adding the data service reference*

4. Add the code in Listing 3-9 to the existing `Program.cs` class in the console application to retrieve a complete list of customers from the data service. This is the same as entering `http://localhost:1101/Northwind.svc/Customers` in a web browser.

Listing 3-9. *Retrieving a List of Customers*

```
using System;
using System.Collections.Generic;
using System.Linq;
using System.Text;
using System.Data.Services.Client;
using ClientConsoleApp.NorthwindDataService;

namespace ClientConsoleApp
{
    class Program
    {
        static void Main(string[] args)
        {
            NorthwindEntities northwindDataCtx = new
            NorthwindEntities(new
            Uri("http://localhost:1101/Northwind.svc/"));

            DataServiceQuery<Customers> customers =
            northwindDataCtx.CreateQuery<Customers>("/Customers");

            foreach (Customers customer in customers)
            {
                    Console.WriteLine(String.Format("Customer ID : {0},
Company
                    Name {1}", customer.CustomerID, customer.CompanyName));
            }

            Console.ReadLine();
        }
    }
}
```

Language Integrated Query Support

As outlined in Chapter 1, Language Integrated Query (LINQ) is a set of new features introduced in .NET Framework 3.0. At the heart of LINQ is a set of collection extension methods
called Standard Query Operators (SQOs). These methods represent a set of functions that
can be performed on any data source and are similar to SQL statements such as SELECT, JOIN,
WHERE, GROUPBY, and so forth. LINQ enables developers to perform a standard way of manipulating objects over multiple data sources such as LINQ to XML and LINQ to Dataset. Recently
the library has been extended to support LINQ to Entities operations as part of the Entity
Framework. This provides the same level of commonality while working with these disparate
sources.

ADO.NET Data Services comes with its own LINQ provider for data services that allows you to write LINQ queries that are then transformed into URL-based query strings. This is because the data sources are exposed using IEnumerable<T> and IQueryable<T> interfaces, which mean that these inherit the list of SQOs, which in turn allows LINQ statements to be written.

This is very helpful because it means that you don't need to become a URL query linguist to use ADO.NET Data Services. It also reduces the amount of code required to write URL queries—you can just imagine all the string append functions you'd have to include otherwise!

LINQ to REST, as we will call this LINQ provider, supports most LINQ SQOs and translates LINQ query expressions or method call syntax into URL requests. The primary LINQ semantics that LINQ to REST doesn't support are expanding, joining, and subquerying related data. Grouping or aggregate operations such as Any, and GroupBy, Count, Max, Min, and so forth are also disallowed. The issue with these expressions is that they cannot be mapped to the URL in the target service, because the LINQ language is richer than the URL. If you try one of these operations, put a breakpoint after the query to the incorrect data services URL constructed from the LINQ expression.

Listing 3-10 shows an example of a supported LINQ query, which is equivalent to the URL-based DataServicesQuery shown earlier in Listing 3-6. Notice that the result of the query uses an anonymous type to cast the result of the query into a new type, DataServiceQuery<Customer>.

Listing 3-10. *LINQ Query Example*

```
DataServiceContext service = new DataServiceContext(URL);

var query = from c in service.Suppliers
            orderby c.Country
            select c;
```

WHAT ARE ANONYMOUS TYPES?

Anonymous types provide a way of encapsulating a set of one or more public read-only properties. They are used by the compiler and avoid having to explicitly define the new type. They are typically used in LINQ select expressions as they allow the creation of a new type from some of the properties from another type. For example, the following query will produce a new anonymous type that contains two read-only properties, Color and Price:

```
var productQuery = from prod in products
    select new { prod.Color, prod.Price };
foreach (var v in productQuery)
{
    Console.WriteLine("Color={0}, Price={1}", v.Color, v.Price);
}
```

Creating, Updating, and Deleting Data (CUD Operations)

When performing Create, Read, Update, and Delete (CRUD) operations, three types of HTTP success status codes are returned by the server. The main distinction between these status codes, which are listed in Table 3-3, is that the update and delete operations do not return a response body, whereas GET and POST do. All status codes are surfaced to the client except for HTTP GET, which is insulated from the client when querying the data service using DataServiceQuery<T>. These status codes are useful to know when trying to debug issues with tools like Fiddler.

Table 3-3. *HTTP Operation Success Return Codes*

Operation	Success Code
GET	200 OK
POST	201 Created
PUT	204 No-Content
DELETE	204 No-Content
MERGE	204 No-Content

The client assembly System.Data.Services.Client.* contains base methods to handle CUD operations as listed in Table 3-4. The basic flow to update changes from a client would be to use one or more of these methods to add, update, and delete entities in the DataServiceContext. Once the changes have been made to the local context, these are then persisted using the SaveChanges() method on the DataServiceContext. The client's local DataServiceContext object contains all the entities that have been changed and sends these changes to the data service via the appropriate HTTP request (POST, PUT, DELETE, or UPDATE). The server will then attempt to update these changes to the data source using the IUpdatable interface and then return a DataServiceResponse object back to the client. We will discuss the DataServiceResponse object in the "Batching" section.

Table 3-4. *Client-Side CUD Methods*

Method	Description
AddLink	Marks a relationship link in the DataServiceContext to be created (Note that this is a redundant method; we recommend you use SetLink.)
AddObject	Marks the object in the DataServiceContext to be added to the entity set
AttachLink	Attaches the link to an entity set
AttachTo	Adds an entity to the DataServiceContext
DeleteLink	Deletes the link from the DataServiceContext
DeleteObject	Marks the object in the DataServiceContext to be deleted
Detach	Removes entity from the DataServiceContext
DetachLink	Removes the requested relationship from the DataServiceContext
SetLink	Marks a relationship link in the DataServiceContext to be created
UpdateObject	Marks the object in the DataServiceContext to be updated in the entity set

Each entity and link that is held within the context is tracked using an entity state that indicates whether the object has been added, updated, or deleted, or is unchanged. These states are then used by the ObjectStateManager to determine which entities are sent for updating on the server. The entity states are listed in Table 3-5.

Table 3-5. *Entity State Enumerations*

Enum Name	Description
Detached	The entity was detached since the last SaveChanges() call.
Unchanged	The entity is unchanged since the last SaveChanges() call.
Added	The entity was added since the last SaveChanges() call.
Deleted	The entity was deleted since the last SaveChanges() call.
Modified	The entity was deleted since the last SaveChanges() call.

To demonstrate how to use CUD operations, we have provided examples that show inserting, updating, and deleting entities along with an example that shows how to perform an insert of an entity and its associations.

Creating Entities

If you want to insert a new record into the data source, you must first add the object into the local context before initiating SaveChanges() to persist the change. There are two ways that this can be achieved: you can use either the overloaded method AddTo[Entity] or the AddObject method. When using the AddObject method, you avoid having to add the entity set string name to the method call. However you choose to do this, you must add the entity to the context before calling the SaveChanges() method as shown in Listing 3-11.

Listing 3-11. *Inserting Data Example*

```
NorthwindEntities entities = new NorthwindEntities(new Uri("http://localhost:1101
/Northwind.svc/"));

Customers customer = new Customers();
customer.CustomerID = "TEST1";
customer.CompanyName = "Testing Corp Inc";
customer.ContactName = "Joe Smith";
customer.ContactTitle = "President";
customer.Address = "4000 Telegraph Avenue, Suite 600";
customer.City = "Berkeley";
customer.Region = "CA";
customer.PostalCode = "94705 ";
customer.Country = "USA";

entities.AddObject("Customers", customer);
entities.SaveChanges();
```

Updating Entities

To successfully update an entity, you first need to load it into the DataServiceContext by either querying the service or by attaching it to the context as shown in the last example. If you now change the new customer entity contact name field and call the UpdateObject() method, this will mark the object to be updated before calling the SaveChanges() method as shown in Listing 3-12.

Listing 3-12. *Updating Data Example*

```
customer.ContactName = "Joe Bloggs";
entities.UpdateObject(testCustomer);
entities.SaveChanges();
```

Deleting Entities

If you want to delete an object from the server, use the DeleteObject() method to mark that the object is to be deleted; on the next persistence point the object will then be physically removed from the context. When deleting an object from the context, you need to load it into the context before calling the DeleteObject() method as shown in Listing 3-13. This example shows the customer object being materialized by LINQ and then returning the first object from the enumerable list via the FirstOrDefault() method. This method uses generics to cast this object into the customer entity object.

Listing 3-13. *Deleting Data Example*

```
Customers customer = entities.Execute<Customers>(new
        Uri("Customers('TEST1')", UriKind.Relative)).FirstOrDefault();
entities.DeleteObject(customer);
```

■Tip If you want to perform CUD operations against entities, they must be present in the context first. This can be achieved by loading the entity into the context. A round-trip to the server can be avoided if the object is created on the client, and then attached to the context via the AttachTo method. This could be useful when you just want to delete an entity. In this case, all that is required is an instance of an object that has the appropriate entity key values set. You can achieve this by first creating an entity using the static construction method of the entity type. The entity should then be attached to the context before calling the DeleteObject method and finally the SaveChanges() method to remove it from the data service, which only requires a single trip to the server.

Entity Associations

Along with the ability of adding, deleting, and updating entities, it's also possible to change the links of entities. The links essentially hold how the entities relate to one another; for example, a customer has one-to-many orders. Entity links have essentially three states, Added, Deleted, and Unchanged, as specified by the entity states enumeration.

To create links between entities, the `SetLink` method on the `DataServiceContext` is used. This method has the following signature:

```
SetLink(Object EntitySetSource, string SourceProperty, Object
        EntitySetTarget)
```

When the method is used, it notifies the context that a link now exists between source and target entities that is represented by the `SourceProperty` parameter. If `SourceProperty` is not null, then the link is added in an Added state that is then sent by `ObjectStateManager` on the next trip to the server. If `SourceProperty` is null, then the link is added in a Deleted state, which will then remove this link from the server; this works in a way similar to the `DeleteLink` method. Following is an example of using `SetLink`:

```
entities.SetLink(customer, "Orders", order);
```

To delete links, the method `DeleteLink` changes the state of the links that have been tracked to a Deleted state. It has a similar method signature to the `SetLink` method, but the difference is that it will set the state of the link to Deleted instead of Added. Following is an example of using `DeleteLink`:

```
entities.DeleteLink(customer, "Orders", order);
```

It's possible to detach a link that has been added incorrectly to the context using the `DetachLink` method. This removes the link from the list of links that have currently been tracked by the context. This is useful when constructing and linking entities that will be updated on the server in a single round-trip operation.

Merging Entities

When modifying certain properties on an entity, you can merge these to the server by performing an HTTP MERGE operation. This operation ensures that only the properties that have changed will be updated, and all other properties will be preserved on the server. This is different from an HTTP PUT, which will overwrite the full entity. This feature also means that the payload is reduced because only the changed properties need to be sent in the request.

Currently there is no support in the `System.Data.DataServices.Client.*` assembly for this type of operation. However, it is supported using calls from an HTTP library. A useful application of this feature is in an AJAX client where you only want to exchange a minimum amount of data with the server.

Lazy Loading

Lazy loading is a software design pattern that is used to defer the initialization of an object until it is needed. When data is requested from a data service, the entities-related data that is contained with its relationship links are not initially loaded, because loading this related data could involve a huge hit of potentially unneeded data. As explained in the last chapter, if related data is required in one hit, it can be loaded eagerly by using the $expand query string operator. There are two ways to handle the lazy loading of data: implicit and explicit. This distinction is very subtle but important. The implicit mode essentially means that the model handles the loading of related data and doesn't require extra code to get this data. Basically, if you perform a query on the client side that requests related data, the client would go to the server and get this data without any extra code to do so. The explicit method means that you need to explicitly load this related data by writing extra code.

ADO.NET Data Services reuses the Entity Framework V1 approach to loading data and by default employs the explicit model to load related data into the DataServiceContext by using a LoadProperty() method. This design decision was made by the ADO.NET Data Services development team because they wanted developers to be aware that every time they want related data they must explicitly use a method that would involve a round-trip to the data store. To implement the LoadProperty() call, you just need to pass the entity object and the name of the relationship that you want to be loaded. An example of this code is shown in Listing 3-14.

Listing 3-14. *LoadProperty Method Example*

```
var query = from c in entities.Customers
            where c.CustomerID == "ALFKI"
              select c;

//Force materialization of customer alfki entity
Customers alfki = query.AsEnumerable<Customers>().FirstOrDefault();

//Load related orders
entities.LoadProperty(alfki, "Orders");

//For each order
foreach (Orders o in alfki.Orders)
{
    sbResult.Append(String.Format("Order ID = {0}, Order Date = {1} \r\n",
    o.OrderID, o.OrderDate));

    //Load Order Details for each order
    entities.LoadProperty(o, "Order_Details");
    foreach (Order_Details od in o.Order_Details)
    {
        sbResult.Append(String.Format("Product ID = {0}, Quantity = {1},
            UnitPrice = {2} \r\n", od.ProductID, od.Quantity, od.UnitPrice));
    }
}
```

Personally, we like the LoadProperty() behavior because it makes programmers aware that the code will involve an extra round-trip. We can also see the point of view of the implicit lazy loading camp because of the extra code required to make these calls. Although the implicit method isn't available by default, client-side code could be written to implement this feature.

Asynchronous Actions

If we need to perform multiple HTTP operations in a single persistence request or load large sets of data, we may need to perform these actions asynchronously to avoid blocking the current thread. The ADO.NET Data Services client .NET assembly supports these types of actions by Begin/End method pairs (BeginExecute()/EndExecute(), BeginExecuteBatch()/ EndExecuteBatch(), BeginSaveChanges()/EndSaveChanges(), BeginLoadProperty()/ EndLoadProperty()) that are implemented using the IAsyncResult interface. An example of implementing the BeginExecute() method is shown in Listing 3-15. In this example, notice the implicit cast of the LINQ anonymous type into a DataServiceQuery object. The reason for this is we must explicitly use the BeginExecute method on the DataServiceQuery, which won't be possible unless we do this casting.

Listing 3-15. *Begin/End Execute Async Method Example*

```
private void SomeMethod()
{
    var qry = from c in entities.Customers
                orderby c.CompanyName
                select c;

    DataServiceQuery<Customers> customerQuery = (
        (DataServiceQuery<Customers>)qry;

    // Start the execution
    customerQuery.BeginExecute(new AsyncCallback(OnLoadComplete),
        customerQuery);
}
private void OnLoadComplete(IAsyncResult result)
{
    DataServiceQuery<Customers> customerQuery =
        (DataServiceQuery<Customers>)result.AsyncState;

    List<Customers> customers = customerQuery.EndExecute(result).ToList();

    //Update UI Thread
    this.Invoke
     ((MethodInvoker)delegate
     {
        ...update the controls
     });
}
```

■**Note** In Silverlight and AJAX all interactions with the server by default are asynchronous, so the Asynchronous pattern must always be used in these clients. This is shown in Chapters 5 and 7 which discuss AJAX and Silverlight, respectively.

Try Before You Buy

To reduce round-trips to the server and to help with the writing of code to prevent errors, two useful methods are provided in the DataServiceContext to check whether the entity already exists on the client:

- TryGetEntity(Uri identity out, out EntitySet)

- TryGetUri(object EntitySet, Uri identity out)

The TryGetEntity and TryGetUri methods are similar in that they will return either a reference to an entity set object or a URL that points to the entity set object. Listing 3-16 shows an example of the TryGetEntity method that checks whether the ALFKI customer is already loaded in the client's context. The reason why these methods are helpful for writing of preventative code is because if you try to add a link to an entity that doesn't exist in the context, an exception is thrown in the client, so it's helpful to check first.

Listing 3-16. *TryGetEntity Example*

```
//TryGetUri takes the absolute URI for a resource
Uri custUri = new Uri("/Customers('ALFKI')", UriKind.RelativeOrAbsolute);

if (entities.TryGetEntity<Customers>(custUri, out customer))
{
    Console.WriteLine("Customer exists");
}
else
{
    Console.WriteLine("Customer doesn't exists");
}
```

More Data Services Features

The features listed in Table 3-6 demonstrate that ADO.NET Data Services isn't just another data access layer. It has built-in features that support some of the most common issues faced in software development, such as batching and concurrency. It also has features that can simplify how to handle media data. The table shows the feature and the query string operation that the feature applies to. These query string operators work in a way similar to the standard query string operators $orderby, $expand, and so forth shown in Chapter 2.

Table 3-6. *More Data Services Features*

Feature	Operation	Description
Scalar values	$value	Return the scalar value from an entity column.
Data interceptors	N/A	Capture queries and change data requests before being executed.
Service operations	N/A	Provide additional RESTful methods on the interface.
Batching	$batch	Performs batch processing. Batch responses are always of type multipart/mixed that can contain a mixture of HTTP success and failures.
Concurrency	N/A	Implemented in data services using HTTP ETags.

Scalar Values

ADO.NET Data Services supports the notation of a scalar value that can be returned from a member property on an entity. This is achieved by appending a $value query string operator to the end of the query; for example, /Northwind.svc/Products(1)/ProductName/$value will return the raw product name. This is useful when you want to just show a raw value without the XML goo around it. The $value modifier is referred to as a **dereference operator** because you're asking for just the raw data of the requested property. This operator works solely on scalar properties and cannot be applied to a collection of entities or to an individual entity because there is no concept of a default value for these types. If you try to use /Northwind.svc/Products/$value, for example, you will receive an HTTP 400 "Bad Request" exception.

You're probably thinking, "Big deal. Why bother when I can just serialize the data service feed into a client-side object and then just reference one of the properties?" However, there is more to this than meets the eye, because the $value operator supports MIME types that can be returned from URL queries. In the previous example, by default the ProductName that is returned uses the text MIME type to output a string. If this value holds binary data for an image, using the $value operator will automatically convert the binary data to an image. This saves having to write code to handle image data. The $value operator supports MIME types by decorating the data service class with the [System.Data.Services.MimeType] attribute. This attribute enables developers to specify that when properties are accessed using the $value operator, they will be returned as the MimeType given in this attribute. Another feature of the $value operator is that it's possible to update individual properties of an entity directly without sending the full object to the server.

The following exercise gives an example of how the $value operator could be used to return a simple HTML page that displays a list of customer rankings. This example adds a service operation to your Northwind data service that returns a HTML page.

EXERCISE 3-3: EXPOSING HTML PAGES WITHIN A DATA SERVICE

In this exercise you will add a new service operation to the Northwind data service that you created in the last chapter. This operation will show how you can serve a raw HTML page via the $value operator.

1. Open up the *.cs code file for the Northwind data service.

2. Add the following MimeType attribute to the data service class definition:

   ```
   [System.Data.Services.MimeType("CustomerOrders", "text/html")]
   ```

3. Copy the code in Listing 3-17 into the data service class. This method performs LINQ query "projection" that will create a sorted list of anonymous objects that contains basic customer details and a count of their orders.

   Listing 3-17. *Serving the HTML Web Page*

   ```
   [SingleResult]
       [WebGet]
       public IQueryable<string> CustomerOrders()
       {
       var orderCounts =
           (from c in this.CurrentDataSource.Customers
   ```

```
        select new {c.CustomerID, c.CompanyName,
        c.ContactName, OrderCount = c.Orders.Count()})
        .OrderByDescending(o => o.OrderCount);

        string customerOrderRanking = "";

        foreach(var orderCount in orderCounts)
        {
            customerOrderRanking += String.Format("Customer ID : {0},
            Customer Name : {1}, Contact Name : {2}, Orders : {3} <br>",
            orderCount.CustomerID, orderCount.CompanyName,
            orderCount.ContactName, orderCount.OrderCount);
    }

        return new string[]
        {
        "<html>" +
        "<head><title>Customer Ranking</title></head>" +
        "<body><h1>Customer Ranking</h1>" +
                customerOrderRanking +
        "</body></html>"
        }.AsQueryable();
    }
```

4. Rebuild the service, press F5, and navigate to `http://localhost:1101/Northwind.svc/`
   `CustomerOrders/$value` to view the HTML output in a browser as shown in Figure 3-7.

Figure 3-7. *Customer Ranking page*

Another useful application that springs to mind is the manipulation of images. In the past it has been generally difficult to write code to access, insert, and update images to a database. Often you would need to chunk the data, handle binary streams, and so forth. Now in ADO.NET Data Services the client just needs to perform a simple HTTP PUT operation and the image is uploaded directly into the database. In addition we can use a simple data repeater control that points to our image data that will then render a collection of these images' $values directly in the browser in a single hit. This will be possible once the ADO.NET Data Services team has shipped an ASP.NET data source control called DataServiceDataSource. The capability to handle images has already been acted upon in the Windows Live Photo Atom API, which enables web sites to view and update Windows Live photo albums using the Atom Publishing Protocol (AtomPub). This API uses similar semantics to those of ADO.NET Data Services.

Data Interceptors

Data interceptors allow developers to add custom business logic on the server before queries or changes are executed. This logic runs within the processing request/response pipeline on the server, which is why the name "interceptor" is used. Data interceptors are typically used for custom validation and security logic to be executed on a per-request basis. There are two types of interceptors that can be created: query and change. Interceptors only work on the entity sets that are exposed by the data service. To create an interceptor, you need to create a custom method on the data service that is decorated with either the [QueryInterceptor] or the [ChangeInterceptor] attribute.

Query Interceptors

A **query interceptor** is essentially a lambda expression that is returned and added to a query provider before it is run. An example of an implementation of the query interceptor is shown in Listing 3-18. If we break down this query interceptor in parts, the expression we have, <Func>, takes an input value, the Customers entity set, and returns a Boolean value based on whether the Customers entity set passes the filter or not. The actual filter expression (true/false) is held in the lambda expression that is created: c => c.Country == "USA". This filter expression is actually passed on to the query provider (IQueryable<T>) which will execute this expression along with the URL query that has been specified; that is, /Customers?filter=City eq 'New York' will still be executed along with the extra filter on the Country. As you can see from the query interceptor in our example, this restricts users from querying anything other than customers in the USA, which is a simple security feature.

Listing 3-18. *Query Interceptors Example*

```
[QueryInterceptor("Customers")]
public Expression<Func<Customers,bool>> OnQueryingCustomers()
{
    //Only return customers from USA
    return c => c.Country == "USA";
}
```

The following points summarize the creation of a query interceptor and error handling:

- A public method is created in your data service that is decorated with
  `[QueryInterceptor("<EntitySet>")]`. The entity set literal given is the interceptor
  that is applied to that entity set.

- The method must return a lambda expression (`<Func<T,bool>>`) and cannot accept any
  parameters. The generic type `<T>` needs to be the base entity set that the interceptor
  applies.

- If an error is thrown, processing is complete and the error is returned in an HTTP
  response.

WHAT ARE LAMBDA EXPRESSIONS?

A **lambda expression** is an anonymous function that can contain both expressions and statements and can
be used to create delegates or expression tree types. All lambda expressions use the => operator, which
indicates that the left-hand side "goes to" the right-hand side. The left-hand side of the operator specifies
the input parameters, and the right-hand side has the expression or statement block. There are two types
of lambda functions: a lambda expression and a lambda statement. The main difference is that a lambda
expression is used to create expression trees whereas lambda statements are used to construct string output and cannot be used in expression trees.

```
(Input parameters) => (Expression Tree or Statement)
```

An **expression tree** is a tree-shaped structure with each node representing a different part of the
expression that is being used.

Lambda expressions and expression trees are extensive topics that are outside the scope of this book. For
more information, the following *MSDN Magazine* article gives a good overview: http://msdn.microsoft.
com/msdnmag/issues/07/09/BasicInstincts. Additionally, there are many books on the topic such
as *Pro LINQ: Language Integrated Query in C# 2008* by Joseph C. Rattz, Jr. (Apress, 2007).

Change Interceptors

A **change interceptor** is used to intercept changes to an underlying data source. This is useful when validation or security measures need to be applied before updates are allowed. The
change interceptor is a method that has a void result and accepts only two parameters: an
entity set and an `UpdateOperations` enumeration. The `UpdateOperations` of the enumeration is
automatically set by data services to the HTTP operation that is currently being executed; for
example, `Change` equals PUT, `Insert` equals POST, `Delete` equals DELETE, and `None` means no
operations are performed on resource. The change interceptor shown in Listing 3-19 performs
a validation check on an insert or update action.

Listing 3-19. *Change Interceptor Example*

```
[ChangeInterceptor("Suppliers")]
public void OnSuppliersChange(Suppliers supplier, UpdateOperations
    action)
{
    if (action == UpdateOperations.Change || action
                    ==UpdateOperations.Insert)
    {
    //Contact name must be alpha chars only
    if (!new Regex("[^a-zA-Z]").IsMatch(supplier.ContactName))
    {
        throw new DataServiceException(400, "Suppliers Contact name must
            contain alpha characters only");
    }
    }
}
```

The following points summarize the creation of a change interceptor and error handling:

- A public method is created in your data service that is decorated with `[ChangeInterceptor("<EntitySet>"]`. The entity set literal given is the interceptor that is applied to that entity set.

- The method should return a void and only have two arguments, the entity set and an enumeration that defines the action—update, delete, insert—that is being requested.

- The entity set is an object reference, so it can be changed or set to a completely different object.

- If an error is thrown, processing is complete and the error is returned in an HTTP response. Any changes to the underlying data source are rolled back.

Service Operations

Service operations provide another way of exposing additional resources from the URL and can be used to add additional business logic, validation, and security rules that might be required. This is useful when a situation arises to add something that doesn't quite fit the standard ADO.NET Data Services interface. Service operations are implemented by using either the [WebGet] attribute for addressable querying or the [WebInvoke] attribute for insert, update, and delete operations. To implement a service operation, a public instance method needs to be defined on the data service, which has to be decorated by one of these two attributes. Let's implement two service operations on the Northwind data service as shown in Listing 3-20.

Listing 3-20. *Service Operations Examples*

```
[WebGet]
public IQueryable<Suppliers> SuppliersByCountry(string country)
{
    return this.CurrentDataSource.Suppliers.Where(s => s.Country ==
    country);
}

[WebInvoke]
public void UpdateSupplierCountry(string supplierID, string country)
{
    Suppliers supplier = this.CurrentDataSource.Suppliers.Where("SupplierID",
        new ObjectParameter("@SupplierID", supplierID)).First();

    if (supplier != null)
    {
        supplier.Country = country;
        this.CurrentDataSource.SaveChanges();
    }

}
```

To access the [WebGet] service operation from the browser, you just need to enter /Northwind.svc/SuppliersByCountry?country='USA'. This will return all suppliers that reside in the USA. A nice feature of this service operation is that the return type is IQueryable<T> for GET requests. The IQueryable<T> interface allows further decomposition of the results, which basically allows further query operators to be appended to the URL. This means that the service operation can act in a RESTful way like any other resource and has access to the full range of ADO.NET Data Services features; for example, the following URL allows the results that are returned to be ordered: /Northwind.svc/SuppliersByCountry?country='USA'&$orderby=City.

To ensure that data services conform to a RESTful model, there are certain restrictions on how service operations can be represented:

- Only methods that are decorated with [WebGet] and [WebInvoke] attributes are classed as service operations.

- Service operations can only accept [in] parameters.

- If parameters are defined, the type of parameter must be primitive (strings, integers, Boolean, etc.).

- Methods can return only void, IEnumerable<T>, or IQueryable<T>. The generic type <T> must represent a resource type that is present in the data model. If IEnumerable<T> is used, no further decomposition is allowed (e.g., you cannot add more query strings onto the URL).

Batching

Two forms of batching are supported by ADO.NET Data Services: simple and advanced. The simple batching option isn't really an option because it is provided by default on the querying and update semantics on normal data services usage. Nevertheless, this is still batching because multiple results can be acted upon in one hit. For example, when querying entities you can perform a batch-like option when you use the $expand query string operator to retrieve multiple related entities. Similarly, you are doing a form of batching when you insert a resource (e.g., Customer) and attach related resources inline (e.g., Orders).

In most cases simple batching can be used to solve business requirements. However, in certain circumstances there could be a requirement to batch multiple HTTP requests on the client before submitting these in a single atomic HTTP POST to the server. This could occur when an application has a data source of related and unrelated entities. To query the unrelated entities would not be possible using the $expand option because there are no navigation links; also, to save these entities would involve multiple round-trips, which cannot guarantee the atomicity requirement.

The batching semantics that are implemented in ADO.NET Data Services use the $batch query operation that is appended to the URL. This is appended to the URL either when the SaveChangesOptions.Batch is used on the SaveChanges() method or when using the ExecuteBatch method.

We can demonstrate how advanced batching works by capturing HTTP requests in Fiddler. To enable us to do this, we must first swap from Visual Studio Web Development Server to IIS as outlined in the "Hosting Data Services" section in Chapter 2. Now we'll demonstrate what happens when batching isn't switched on. To do this, we'll make multiple changes to the context without using batching. In this example we will update the properties on two products before persisting these to the server, as shown in Listing 3-21.

Listing 3-21. *Saving Changes Without Batching*

```
NorthwindEntities entities = new
            NorthwindEntities("http://host/NorthwindDataService/Northwind.svc");

entities.MergeOption = MergeOption.OverwriteChanges;

List<Products> products = (from p in entities.Products
                        where p.ProductID == 1 || p.ProductID == 2
                        select p).ToList();

products[0].UnitPrice = 50;
products[1].UnitPrice = 10;

//Mark as Updated in entities
entities.UpdateObject(products[0]);
entities.UpdateObject(products[1]);

//Save changes without batching
entities.SaveChanges(SaveChangesOptions.None);
```

When the code is executed, two separate HTTP 204 responses are received for the two separate updates from the request. This is normal operation for the exchange of HTTP traffic for data services because the client communicates with the server by sending a single HTTP verb, header, and body request for each part of the request separately. The response returned from the server, which has a one-to-one relationship with the request, is shown in Listing 3-22.

Listing 3-22. *Normal HTTP Request and Response*

```
Request

GET /NorthwindDataService/Northwind.svc/Products HTTP/1.1
User-Agent: Microsoft ADO.NET Data Services
Accept: application/atom+xml,application/xml
Host: adonet-data-poc
Proxy-Connection: Keep-Alive
...

Response

HTTP/1.1 200 OK
Date: Sun, 15 Jun 2008 22:35:31 GMT
Server: Microsoft-IIS/6.0
X-Powered-By: ASP.NET
X-AspNet-Version: 2.0.50727
Cache-Control: no-cache
Content-Type: application/atom+xml;charset=utf-8
Content-Length: 121925

<?xml version="1.0" encoding="utf-8" standalone="yes"?>
<feed>
  <entry>
     <!-- Entity Content-->
  </entry>
</feed>
```

To demonstrate a batching request, we change the last line of our code to the following:

```
DataServiceResponse response =
    entities.SaveChanges(SaveChangesOptions.Batch);
```

Executing the query again will return a single HTTP 202 response as shown in Listing 3-23.

Listing 3-23. *Batching HTTP Request and Response*

```
Request

POST /dataservice.svc/$batch HTTP/1.1
Host: localhost
Content-Type: multipart/mixed; boundary=batch(36522ad7-fc75-4b56-8c71-56071383e77b)
```

```
--batch(36522ad7-fc75-4b56-8c71-56071383e77b)
Content-Type: multipart/mixed; boundary=
      changeset_8a612910-678c-4386-aa20-9eeedecd9707
Cache-Control: no-cache
```

Response

```
--batchresponse_03d94513-8485-4d69-8cc7-f63ea5b740f0
Content-Type: multipart/mixed; boundary=
      changesetresponse_27301eb2-fedb-4efc-b9c0-534ef0fe05fe
```

[Batched response 1]
```
--changesetresponse_27301eb2-fedb-4efc-b9c0-534ef0fe05fe

Content-Type: application/http
Content-Transfer-Encoding: binary

HTTP/1.1 204 No Content
Content-ID: 3
Cache-Control: no-cache
Content-Type: multipart/mixed; boundary=
      batchresponse_03d94513-8485-4d69-8cc7-f63ea5b740f0

DataServiceVersion: 1.0;
```

[Batched response 2]
```
--changesetresponse_27301eb2-fedb-4efc-b9c0-534ef0fe05fe

Content-Type: application/http
Content-Transfer-Encoding: binary

HTTP/1.1 204 No Content
Content-ID: 4
Cache-Control: no-cache
DataServiceVersion: 1.0;

--changesetresponse_27301eb2-fedb-4efc-b9c0-534ef0fe05fe—
--batchresponse_03d94513-8485-4d69-8cc7-f63ea5b740f0--
```

Batches consist of one or more QueryOperations and one or more ChangeSetOperations. The QueryOperation typically contains HTTP GET requests, whereas the ChangeSetOperation contains HTTP POST, PUT, and DELETE operations. Batch operations are sent over HTTP using multipart/mixed MIME messages. This approach enables physical separation between binary and text-based content both in the request and the response. The batch response contains one or more QueryResponses and ChangeSetResponses for each request received. This rule is broken if there is an exception with any of the ChangeSet operations in the batch. This is because ChangeSets are atomic, so if any fail, instead of having a separate failure for each request, a single HTTP response is returned. This will result in the complete batch transaction rolling back.

Implementing Concurrency

If you ever have taken a serious course on computer science, you know the concurrency topic always comes up. The lecturer would cover hours of theory about distributed computing, semaphore timeouts, mutual exclusion, race conditions, deadlocks, and starvation. This topic left me (John) uninspired as I personally couldn't find anything about it that really excited me—that was until I got into the working world and realized that it's actually quite important!

Concurrency is a property of several computational processes executed at the same time: it is essential for scaling large distributed systems because you want multiple servers to be able to interact with multiple resources at the same time. The problem occurs when data needs to be changed simultaneously. Suddenly, you must understand the state of the original request and compare it against the new request. Also, you need to make sure if you're going to change some data that you lock other users before your change has been executed. This is where the lecturer's words of semaphore timeouts, mutual exclusion, and other concepts start ringing in your ears.

To achieve atomic concurrency on resources, generally you need something to compare against to recognize whether the resource has changed. In legacy applications a version number would be used to increment every time you did a change. If your version number didn't match, a concurrency exception would occur. In modern applications, well-architected database structures contain timestamps that can be used to determine whether an individual row has changed from the last request. This mechanism is also used in replication when you want to sync multiple offline databases.

In practice, different types of applications have different requirements for concurrency, and essentially you either care about concurrency or you don't! If you don't care about concurrency, by default ADO.NET Data Services uses a "last change wins" model, which means that every change will be overwritten with the last without any checks. If concurrency is something that concerns you, you'll be glad to know ADO.NET Data Services implements a concise way of handling the situation and stays within HTTP standards.

This concept is called the Entity Tag (ETag), which is described in the HTTP 1.1 Specification. The ETag is essentially an HTTP response header that is placed in responses from the web server. The ETag can be any field that is suitable for concurrency checking, such as a timestamp or a version number. When you modify any entities, the ETag value is sent in an HTTP If-Match request header, which is then checked against the value stored on the server. If the ETag doesn't match, an HTTP 412 "Precondition Failed" status response is returned from the server. This status response indicates that the request was unsuccessful because one of the client's conditions has not been met, which in our case occurred because the value in the If-Match header didn't match the server. The flow of a concurrency request is illustrated in Figure 3-8.

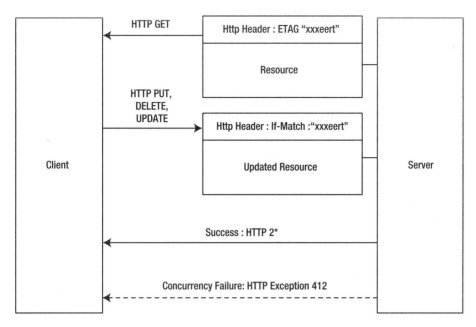

Figure 3-8. *Concurrency request/response*

To implement concurrency tokens using ETags, the framework has to have a consistent view of a resource at a given point in time. The ADO.NET Data Services framework only performs concurrency checking on resources that have been explicitly marked by the developer. This is achieved by the development team first identifying a set of properties that will always change on each update to the resource. A timestamp property is the perfect candidate for an ETag because it has the consistency that is required for ETag semantics. Therefore, the first step to achieve concurrency checking is to add the timestamp property to each entity in the underlying physical data structure. If the data source is served by another application or is owned by a third party, these changes are not possible, so other concurrency properties must be found. The ADO.NET Data Services framework accommodates this problem and provides the ability to mark one or more properties on the data model that will make up the ETag "concurrency token." The ETag is implemented by using a [ETag] attribute on classes as shown in Listing 3-24 or as an annotation in the EDM.

Listing 3-24. *ETag Attribute on CLR Class*

```
[DataServiceKey("RockStarInducteeID")]
[ETag("DateModified")]
public class Inductee
{
        public int RockStarInducteeID { get; set; }
        public string FirstName { get; set; }
        public string LastName { get; set; }
        public bool Group {get; set;}
```

```
        public string PerformerCategory { get; set; }
        public int YearInducted { get; set; }
        public DateTime DateModified { get; set; }
}
```

To set concurrency checking for entities in the Entity Framework Model, the concurrency mode for each property needs to be set to Fixed, which will assign the [ETag] attribute to these properties. If the ADO.NET Data Services framework encounters a class that has properties that have been tagged with the [ETag] attribute, it will use the ETag rules; otherwise, it will refer back to the default persistence of "last change wins."

According to the HTTP specification, the ETag property should be applied to the HTTP header when resources are returned from the server. This perfectly fits into the Atom Publishing Protocol rules when working with individual resources, but when there is a collection of resources, this doesn't work at all. This is because now we have a single ETag in the HTTP header for multiple resources. The ADO.NET Data Services framework solves this issue by applying the ETag to individual resources as part of the collection that is returned. In JSON the ETag is applied to the __metadata property for JSON. Essentially, this means that the ETag header that is returned in the header for collections is ignored. Listing 3-25 gives an example of a returned collection showing these ETag values.

Listing 3-25. *ETag in Data Feeds*

```
Atom Format with ETag

<feed>
    <entry m:type="NorthwindModel.Customers"
    m:etag="""'Alfreds%20Futterkiste','Maria%20Anders'""">
    <!-- Entity Contents -->
    ...
</entry>

<entry m:type="NorthwindModel.Customers"
    m:etag="""'Ana%20Trujillo%20Emparedados
    %20y%20helados','Ana%20Trujillo'""">
    <!-- Entity Contents -->
    ...
</entry>

</feed>

JSON Format with ETag
```

```
{ "d" :
    [
    {
    "__metadata":
    {
        "URL": "http://localhost:1101/Northwind.svc/Customers(\'ALFKI\')",
         "etag": "\"\'Alfreds%20Futterkiste\',\'Maria%20Anders\'\"",
        "type": "NorthwindModel.Customers"
    },
    <!-- Entity Contents -->
    ...
    },
    {
    "__metadata":
    {
        "URL": "http://localhost:1101/Northwind.svc/Customers(\'ANATR\')",
        "etag": "\"\'Ana%20Trujillo%20Emparedados%20y%20ohelados\',
        \'Ana%20Trujillo\'\"", "type": "NorthwindModel.Customers"
    }
    <!-- Entity Contents -->
    ...
    }
}
```

The concurrency tokens are validated against the server every time an HTTP PUT, DELETE, or POST request is sent. Data services by default will do a concurrency comparison on the server whenever a concurrency attribute is defined on an entity. This puts an emphasis on the client to include the If-Match header with the correct values; and by default this must be included on concurrency resources. There are occasions when the client doesn't know this concurrency token, or when you might want to overwrite the resource even though there is a potential concurrency problem. ADO.NET Data Services uses the If-Match="*" header, which means "any value will match," to force the overwriting of resources. Following is an exercise that shows how to implement concurrency on the Northwind Entity Data Model that you created in the last chapter.

EXERCISE 3-4: IMPLEMENTING CONCURRENCY

This exercise uses the Northwind database to demonstrate how to add concurrency tokens to an Entity Data Model. It then demonstrates a concurrency violation by using Fiddler. You will include concurrency checking for the Address, City, and PostalCode properties of the Suppliers entity.

1. In the Northwind Entity Data Model, highlight the Address field property of the Suppliers entity. In the Properties area modify the Concurrency Mode setting to Fixed as shown in Figure 3-9. Repeat this process for the City and PostalCode fields. Once this has been done, close down the model and rebuild the Northwind project.

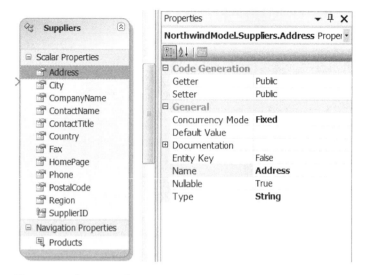

Figure 3-9. *Changing the concurrency option in the Entity Framework*

2. Run the Northwind Visual Studio project by pressing Ctrl +F5. Open up Fiddler, enter `http://localhost:1101/Northwind.svc/Suppliers(1)` into the Request Builder, and perform an HTTP GET of this data. If you review the response in the Session Inspector in Fiddler, you should see that the ETag HTTP header contains `ETag: W/"'49%20Gilbert%20St.1','LA','EC1%204SD'"`.

3. In Fiddler enter the header and request body shown in Listing 3-26, change the HTTP verb to PUT, and then click Execute. This will attempt to modify the `City` value to `London`, which will fail with an HTTP 412 status code with the error description "The etag value in the request header does not match with the current etag value of the object."

Listing 3-26. *Concurrency Request*

```
Request Header

User-Agent: Fiddler
Host: adonet-data-poc
Content-Type: application/json
Accept: application/json
Content-Length: 313
If-Match: W/"'49%20Gilbert%20St.1','LA','EC1%204SD'"
```

Request Body

```
{
        "SupplierID": 1,
        "CompanyName": "Exotic Liquids",
        "ContactName": "Charlotte Cooper",
        "ContactTitle": "Purchasing Manager",
        "Address": "49 Gilbert St.",
        "City": "London",
```

```
        "Region": null,
        "PostalCode": "EC1 4SD",
        "Country": "UK",
        "Phone": "(171) 555-2222",
        "Fax": null,
        "HomePage": null
    }
```

■**Note** This method of applying concurrency is error prone. To implement concurrency in an effective way, it is highly recommended you change the underlying data model and add a `Timestamp` field.

Securing Services

Security mechanisms in software applications broadly fall into two categories: authentication and authorization. In basic terms **authentication** is used to verify the user's supplied credentials against an authentication store. There are various examples of authentication methods such as Integrated Windows, Digest, Basic, and .NET Passport authentication. **Authorization** takes place after authentication and essentially determines the resources to which the user may gain access. Typical roles that are used in a system could be administrators, team leaders, managers, and data operators. Similar to authentication, there are also various authorization options available, such as the out-of-the-box ASP.NET Membership API or even a custom database store that simply associates users against roles.

Authorization and authentication in data services is spread across a collection of four features: inheritance of the host's authentication model, visibility of resources, interception of data before execution, and service operations. Also, wire-level protection can be made by using SSL. How these features are mapped to authentication and authorization mechanisms is shown in Table 3-7.

Table 3-7. *Data Services Security*

Feature	Security Area
Inheritance of host's authentication model	Authentication
Resource visibility	Authorization
Intercepting Data	Authorization
Service Operations	Authorization

Inheritance of Host Authentication

ADO.NET Data Services doesn't implement security authentication out of the box. The reason for this design decision was to simplify the model and not introduce yet another security mechanism. As a result, to provide security data services rely on the host provider to implement this effect—and this will always be true because a runtime host is always required. The types of hosts that a data service can run in are ASP.NET and an interface that can be used to create a custom WCF host. If the host is running in IIS, the service can utilize one of the authentication models provided such as Basic or Integrated Windows security. This is along with Forms Security, which can be used if the service is run only under the ASP.NET authentication model. When planning authentication, developers just need to look at how they currently authenticate web services and hook into the same methods. To achieve this, the client assembly exposes an ICredentials interface on the DataServiceContext that can be used to point to an object that implements security for the service.

Resource Visibility

The primary feature of ADO.NET Data Services is its ability to expose resources to applications using a RESTful interface. A key security feature that must be implemented is the ability to restrict how applications interact with these resources. For example, you may not want to allow applications to browse all the entities in the system. Similarly, you may want to stop applications from deleting reference data that is required by multiple related entities. To achieve this result, ADO.NET Data Services provides resource container–level security that restricts the ability to query, update, and write operations on each entity that is exposed. These rights are outlined in Table 3-8.

Table 3-8. *Entity Set–Wide Permissions*

Resource Container Permission	Description
EntitySetRights.All	HTTP GET single/multiple, PUT, DELETE, POST
EntitySetRights.AllRead	HTTP GET single/multiple
EntitySetRights.AllWrite	HTTP PUT, POST, DELETE
EntitySetRights.ReadMultiple	HTTP GET single/multiple
EntitySetRights.ReadSingle	HTTP GET single
EntitySetRights.WriteAppend	HTTP POST
EntitySetRights.WriteDelete	HTTP DELETE
EntitySetRights.WriteUpdate	HTTP PUT
EntitySetRights.None	No verb permissions allowed, and not visible in metadata

The entity rights are fairly self explanatory except for the ReadSingle permission. This permission provides the ability to stop users from performing browsing operations, which is useful when you have sensitive data that shouldn't only be returned singularly to an application.

When you first create a data service by default, all resources are locked down. The first action you must take is to grant security access control to your resources in the static InitializeService() method that is supplied to you. This is achieved by removing the comments in this static method and replacing them with the access rules. To reduce the number of lines of code, it's possible to grant generic permissions to all entities by specifying *, and then just applying individual permissions to entities that fall outside the norm. The code example in Listing 3-27 shows a service that by default allows full access to all resources. The entities that fall outside this are Product and Category. The Product entity allows full read access. The Category entity permissions show an example of multiple permissions that can be added together as a bitmask by adding each permission separated by a |. These restrictions are applied to not only the top container level, but also whenever the resources are addressed as part of a larger URL query, for example, when the entity is used as part of a query with an $expand operator.

Listing 3-27. *Resource Permissions Access Script*

```
namespace NorthWindService
{
public class NorthWindDataService : DataService<NorthWindEntities>
    {
public static void InitializeService(IDataServiceConfiguration config)
        {
                config.SetEntitySetAccessRule("*", EntitySetRights.All);
                config.SetEntitySetAccessRule("Product", EntitySetRights.AllRead);
                config.SetEntitySetAccessRule("Categories", EntitySetRights.ReadSingle
| EntitySetRights.WriteUpdate);

        }
    }
}
```

The main disadvantages of applying resource visibility in this way are that the visibility is hard-coded against the service and the security is set against a complete entity and not at row level. These deficiencies are addressed by a combination of interceptors and service operations.

Hiding Sensitive Data

The [IgnoreProperties] attribute is useful when you want to restrict properties that are shown on the public interface of the entity. This can be specified at the type level and can be used to ignore certain properties from the model altogether that are not to be surfaced. This can be used on a model where only a few properties need to be restricted, and is helpful when you don't want to super class an entity. An example of how to apply this property is shown in Listing 3-28.

Listing 3-28. *Applying the Ignore Propery Attribute*

```
[IgnoreProperties("Price")]
public class Automobile
{
      public int AutomobileId {get; set;}

      public double Price {get; set;}
      ...
}
```

Intercepting Data

As explained earlier in this chapter, there are two types of interceptors: change and query. Interceptors provide the ability to inject code before the query or update has been executed against the data model. This is useful when you want to implement either validation logic or row-level security permissions on a per-request basis. A typical security policy that is often required is the ability to restrict users to seeing only their own data. An example of this is on a social bookmarking application, for instance, when you want to restrict authenticated users to seeing only their bookmarks and associated data items.

To implement this restriction, a query interceptor predicate can be used to take the security principle of the HTTP request. Then you can add this principle to the query that is going to be executed. When the predicate has been defined against this resource, it will be executed against it regardless of how the application navigates to the resource, occurring either at the top level or as part of a larger query such as when using the $expand query string operator. The code in Listing 3-29 shows an example of how to do this by taking the security context of the request by adding this to the user's query. A similar change interceptor can be created to restrict a user's ability to only be capable of changing their own data.

Listing 3-29. *Restricting User Data Returned*

```
[QueryInterceptor("Users")]
public Expression<Func<User, bool>> OnQueryingUsers()
{

    return u => u.UserName == HttpContext.Current.User.Identity.Name;
}
```

Service Operations

The final part of the security features is service operations. As outlined earlier in this chapter, service operations provide the ability to run arbitrary logic that doesn't map in a one-one relationship to the model being surfaced. In the context of security, this feature is useful because it provides the client application with a way of running some security validation logic that might be required before making any requests. Also, a potentially useful security feature of the service operation is that you can decorate it with a *[SingleResult]* attribute. This means that the service operation will always return just one entity and not a collection or feed of entities. The effect is to essentially prevent users from "browsing" your data.

All service operations are treated like resources and are locked down by default. A permission must be given to the service so that it can be executed; available permissions are shown in Table 3-9.

Table 3-9. *Service Operation Security Restrictions*

Permission	Restriction
ServiceOperationRights.All	HTTP GET single/multiple, PUT, DELETE, POST
ServiceOperationRights.AllRead	HTTP GET single/multiple
ServiceOperationRights.ReadMultiple	HTTP GET multiple
ServiceOperationRights.ReadSingle	HTTP GET single
ServiceOperationRights.None	No verb permissions allowed, and not visible in metadata

The code in Listing 3-30 shows how to assign permissions to a service operation.

Listing 3-30. *Service Operations Access Permissions*

```
namespace NorthWindService
{
public class NorthWindDataService : DataService<NorthWindEntities>
    {
public static void InitializeService(IDataServiceConfiguration config)
        {
            config.SetServiceOperationAccessRule("SecurityValidation",
ServiceOperationRights.All);
        }
    }
}
```

Error Handling Support

ADO.NET Data Services provides error handling support that allows the capture and throwing of business errors back to the client. A data service could fail for a variety of reasons that generally fall into two categories: unhandled and handled errors. A handled error could be a validation rule failure on a change interceptor. In this case the error is captured and handled appropriately without throwing a nondescriptive error. Unhandled errors are something that happen unexpectedly, for example, a security error when accessing resources, a database key violation, code issue, and so forth. In this case the full error and stack are thrown back to the client.

When throwing exceptions back to the client, they should always be of type DataServiceException. The DataServiceException type allows the exception to be mapped to a HTTP status code along with a human-readable error description, which keeps the process within the RESTful programming world. In addition, using the DataServiceException type allows the data service host to serialize the public properties of this exception so that a structured error can appear back on the client.

Now follows advice on the best way to code your solution using the two categories of errors, handled and unhandled.

Handled Exception

In the case of an exception that you can handle, you must simply throw the appropriate exception as a DataServiceException. Listing 3-31 shows an example of a validation exception that is thrown back to the caller when a product category is incorrectly formatted. Typically, you would throw a validation exception when adding rules to a change interceptor.

Listing 3-31. *Validating a Product Category*

```
[ChangeInterceptor("Categories")]
public void OnChangeCategories(Categories c, UpdateOperations ops)
{
        if(ops == ReceiveEntityOperation.Insert ||
           ops == ReceiveEntityOperation.Update)
        {
          // single word, no spaces
          if(c.CategoryName.Substring( c.CategoryName.Length,1) =="S")
          {
              throw new DataServiceException(400,
                        "Category names must not end with s");
          }
        }
}
```

Unhandled Exception

There are two types of unhandled exceptions that must be caught: unhandled exceptions occurring before the service is initialized and afterward. To handle exceptions that happen after the service is initialized, you must override the HandleException method in the data service class. Within this method you must test the args exception parameter for a type of exception and then replace this with the DataServiceException, which is then thrown to the caller. This method is always called regardless of whether there is a handled or unhandled exception, so it's also a useful place to put tracing code. Listing 3-32 shows the HandleException method handling a SQL exception that has been surfaced.

Listing 3-32. *Overriding the HandleException Method*

```
public override void HandleException(HandleExceptionArgs args)
{
        if(args.Exception is SqlException)
        {
                SqlException e = (SqlException) args.Exception;

                if (e.Number == 547)
                {
                        args.Exception = new DataServiceException(400,
                            "Primary Key SQL Error",
                            "Duplicate Primary Keys are not allowed"
                            "en-US",
                            e);
                }
                else
```

```
        {
                args.Exception = new DataServiceException(400,
                    "SQL Error Code:" + e.Number,
                    "Data source error",
                    "en-US",
                    e);
        }
    }
}
```

The second type of unhandled exception occurs when the service hasn't been initialized. These types of exceptions normally happen during development. Unfortunately, because data services don't show any of the stack trace when this happens, you will only be faced with a request error with no further information. This is OK in a production environment, but in a development environment you need to see more. To enable these errors to surface, we must add a service behavior to WCF that allows exceptions to be thrown with the full trace. This is achieved by adding the [ServiceBehavior] attribute to the data service class as shown in Listing 3-33 or by adding this to the web.config file as shown in Listing 3-34.

Listing 3-33. *Enabling IncludeExceptionDetailsInFaults from Code*

```
[System.ServiceModel.ServiceBehavior(IncludeExceptionDetailInFaults = true)]
public class Northwind : DataService<NorthwindEntities>
```

Listing 3-34. *Enabling IncludeExceptionDetailsInFaults from the Config File*

```
<system.serviceModel>
    <services>
      <service name="ServiceNamespace.ServiceClassName"  behaviorConfiguration
="DebugEnabled">
        </service>
    </services>
    <behaviors>
      <serviceBehaviors >
        <behavior name="DebugEnabled">
          <serviceDebug includeExceptionDetailInFaults="true"/>
        </behavior>
      </serviceBehaviors>
    </behaviors>
    <serviceHostingEnvironment aspNetCompatibilityEnabled="true"/>
</system.serviceModel>
```

During development we can also switch the service on to throw detailed errors by including config.useVerboseErrors = true in the InitializeService() static method. For further advice on some debugging best practices, please read the MSDN forum post at http://forums. microsoft.com/MSDN/ShowPost.aspx?PostID=3720883&SiteID=1, which outlines ways to debug a data service by checking the WebException.Response to detect errors in the client and also using Fiddler to capture the errors from the data service.

HTTP Status Code Mapping

Table 3-10 lists some of the most common HTTP client error status codes and a suggestion of when these should be used. The HTTP status code should convey the exception without looking at the exception text.

Table 3-10. *HTTP Status Code Exception Mapping*

Status Code	Description	Type of Exception
400	Bad request	This indicates a validation error or business rule failure.
401	Unauthorized	The request is made on a resource that exists but fails security permissions. This could be for role-based security type permissions.
404	Not found	This is returned when a entity is requested but doesn't exist on the service.
405	Method not allowed	This is returned if a request is made on an entity and isn't allowed (e.g., a POST is made when the entity is read-only).
413	Request entity too large	This is returned when a request is posted that exceeds the maximum message size allowed.

Summary

This chapter provides a practical overview of the additional features of ADO.NET Data Services and how easy it is for a client to consume these services. The client library shown in this chapter provides a layer of abstraction on top of RESTful queries. This enables developers to work with data service endpoints using .NET objects, properties, and methods that they are used to. In later chapters, we will dive further into these features and how they can be used on both greenfield and existing projects.

PART 2

ADO.NET Data Services in the Real World

When a new technology arrives, developers spend time getting to grips with what the technology is for. After the technology is understood to some degree, the next big question the gets asked is "How does this affect my world?"

What does your enterprise look like? The vast majority of enterprises will contain a certain amount of legacy software. The term "legacy" does not necessarily mean old software, but software tends to "go off" a little like food, as business needs evolve. Therefore, unless the architecture of the enterprise is continually monitored and maintained, it is easy to end up with a maintenance headache, or worse still development paralysis, as the business begins to fear changing the legacy it has created.

Not everything about having a brown field enterprise with legacy software is bad. Legacy systems may be built on older technology, but that does not mean they are poorly designed. And a well-designed legacy system can have valuable assets that you may well want to evolve rather than replace. This way, you keep what is good about your investment, but you are not locked into the limitations of an aging technology.

To evolve a brown field enterprise to get the benefits of a new technology such as ADO. NET Data Services, you must step beyond understanding how to apply the new technology and think about how your existing assets can be integrated with it. This evolution in your enterprise will ensure that your enterprise architecture remains lean, and that the legacy never becomes a dictator to your business.

CHAPTER 4

■■■

Exposing Existing WCF SOAP Services and .NET APIs Through ADO.NET Data Services

The reality many enterprises will face when considering adopting ADO.NET Data Services is how to implement this new technology alongside their existing services and components. Unless important reasons exist to start from scratch, many will need to make use of their current investments in the .NET technology stack and the SOAP-based services they have built over the last few years. There can be little business justification in tearing down a working set of existing services just to create RESTful APIs. Indeed, many enterprises will have external clients who consume their SOAP services and cannot be forced to change to a RESTful world. Alternatively, such enterprises may need to expose some or all of their existing services to some clients through SOAP because they rely on WS-* policies for measures such as security. This chapter will cover one such scenario and discuss the measures that architects could take in order to preserve existing investments while benefiting from adding RESTful services to their enterprises. The current architecture in any enterprise is unique and is unlikely to match this example exactly, but some of the patterns used here are commonplace, and the chapter provides commentary throughout to describe some alternative scenarios.

The Legacy Customer Service

The example service used throughout the rest of this chapter is a customer service. This service has been prebuilt to represent a legacy SOAP service that will then be adapted through exercises to add an ADO.NET data service endpoint to the service offering. The legacy customer service would be used in a typical enterprise to manage customer information. This chapter will describe some example drivers for adding a REST endpoint to the existing service using ADO.NET Data Services.

■**Note** In reality, a customer service would be quite a complex undertaking, possibly incorporating integration into a CRM. This example service has been extremely simplified to include only four service operations with a simple customer entity. However, this example shows many common patterns associated with a request-reply-based SOAP service.

The customer service was built on top of the customer application. When the customer application was designed, the architect chose to store the customer data using SQL Server 2005. He built a strongly typed data access layer (DAL) using ADO.NET, executing stored procedures against the DbCommand object for all methods (using parameters that match those of the stored procedures) and additionally using the DbDataReader object for methods that needed to read multiple rows from a SQL result set. The architect chose to encapsulate all the business logic (such as validation) of the application in a business logic layer. He used a Data Transfer Object (DTO) pattern to pass strongly typed entity objects from the presentation layer, through the business layer, and into the data access layer and vice versa.

■**Note** The Data Transfer Object pattern separates out entities from business logic. Entity objects provide an object-oriented representation of the information with no business logic encapsulated. Entity objects are therefore the common currency in the application between the data access layer, business layer, and presentation layer.

The resulting architecture of the application is shown in Figure 4-1.

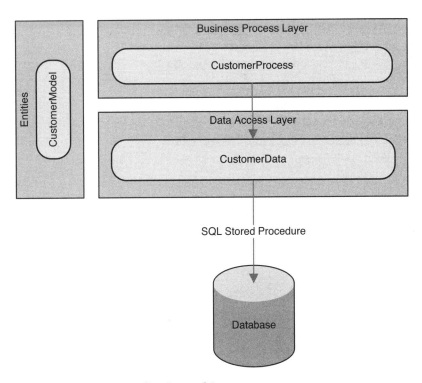

Figure 4-1. *Customer application architecture*

As the company grew, it realized that it needed to expose some functionality from the customer application as a service to third-party businesses, enabling the company to directly register new customers and retrieve this customer information. To do this, the architect chose to wrap the application's business logic layer with a service layer using WCF hosted in IIS 6.0.

■**Note** IIS is the host of choice for most web services because it provides process resilience to a service host, meaning that the host will recycle after a failure (such as an exception). In addition, IIS provides security for the host, as well as enabling access to features within ASP.NET (if enabled). While the production service would normally be hosted in IIS, it is common practice for WCF services to use other hosts during development for convenience. Visual Studio provides a built-in Web Development Server to host web sites under development. This provides a lightweight web server with access to all the features of ASP.NET like IIS.

They designed data contracts to communicate data through the service contract and translated data contracts to Data Transfer Objects in the service implementation (to enable the business logic layer of the application to be reused). They used a SOAP-based BasicHttpBinding because they did not foresee at that point a need to apply any WS-* policies to the service. The resulting architecture of the service is shown in Figure 4-2.

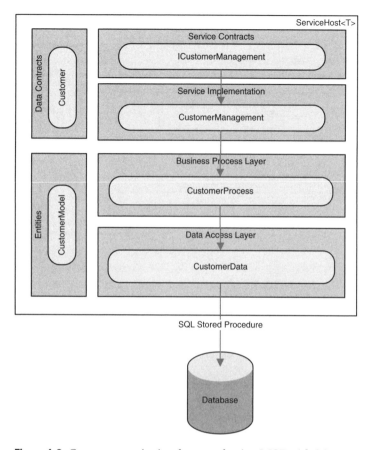

Figure 4-2. *Customer service implemented using WCF with SOAP*

■**Note** This service is a typical WCF SOAP-based service that follows the architectural guidance of Microsoft's Patterns & Practices group. You could create a SOAP service quickly using the Service Factory pattern,
available at http://msdn.microsoft.com/en-us/library/bb931187.aspx.

EXERCISE 4-1: EXAMINING THE LEGACY CUSTOMER SERVICE SOLUTION

The steps in this exercise take you through the legacy customer service solution, implemented as a WCF SOAP service using the architecture detailed previously. The code for this exercise can be downloaded from the Apress web
site (http://www.apress.com/book/sourcecode), and the solution targets .NET Framework 3.5 and Visual
Studio 2008. In reality, a legacy solution such as this would most likely have been built .NET 3.0, but to save time
in future exercises and for clarity, this solution is built using C# 3.0 and employs features such as LINQ to simplify
the code as much as possible.

1. Using Visual Studio 2008, open the solution named `Apress.Data.Services.CustomerService.sln` from the folder named `CustomerServiceExercise41`. This folder contains all the code and the database for the customer service solution before ADO.NET Data Services is applied to create a REST-based endpoint.

2. When the solution opens, examine Solution Explorer to see how the solution has been structured, as shown in Figure 4-3. The application layers are contained in the `Business Components` and `Data Access Layer` folders. The WCF service (including the service's host) is contained in the `Service` folder, and a test client console application is contained in the `Client` folder.

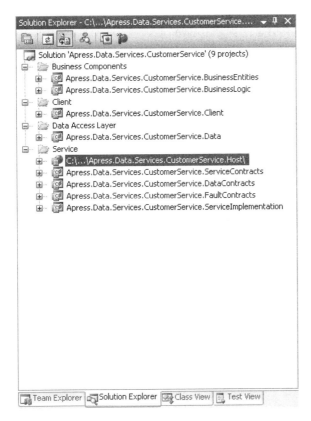

Figure 4-3. *Structure of the customer service solution*

3. Expand the service host web site (`Apress.Data.Services.CustomerService.Host`). The host project contains the service host file named `Customer.svc` and a `web.config` file. It also contains the customer database in the `App_Data` folder (implemented as a SQL Server 2005 Express database). Open the `App_Data` folder, right-click the `Customers.mdf` database file, and select Open. The `Customers` database will open in Visual Studio's Server Explorer window. Right-click the `Customer` table and choose Show Table Data. The `Customer` table data returned is shown in Figure 4-4.

	CustomerId	FirstName	LastName	DateOfBirth	SalutationId	GenderId
▶	1	Simon	Evans	20/06/1976 00:...	1	M
	2	John	Shaw	15/08/1970 00:...	1	M
	3	Jane	Smith	01/03/1982 00:...	3	F
	4	Angharad	Barton	17/07/1976 00:...	3	F
	5	John	Smith	09/09/1963 00:...	1	M
✳	NULL	NULL	NULL	NULL	NULL	NULL

Figure 4-4. *Customer information stored in the Customer table*

4. From the host web site, open the `web.config` file and scroll down to the section of the file called `system.serviceModel` to see how the WCF service has been configured using `BasicHttpBinding` (basic profile SOAP service). Open the `Customer.svc` file to see the `<%@ ServiceHost %>` page declaration, which points to the `Apress.Data.Services.CustomerService.ServiceImplementation.CustomerManagement` class to implement the service contract's functionality. Right-click the `Customer.svc` file and choose View In Browser. Because service metadata is enabled, when the browser window opens you should see the web page shown in Figure 4-5.

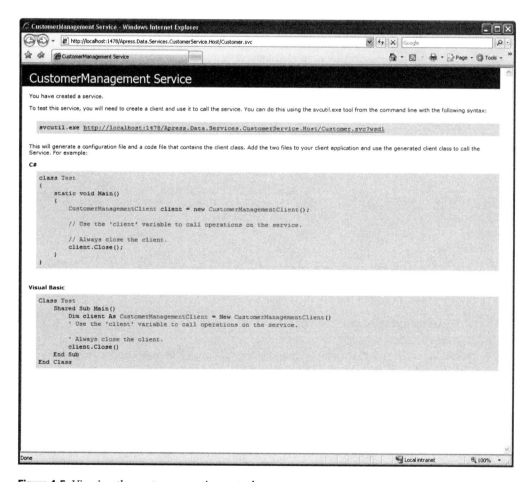

Figure 4-5. *Viewing the customer service metadata*

5. Note the port number that your localhost is using (the port number in Figure 4-5 is 1478), as the client will need to call the service endpoint at this address (we will build a client in Exercise 4-3). In Solution Explorer, select the client project and view the client's app.config file to check that the endpoint's address matches the service's address you browsed to previously and change it if necessary. With the client project selected, from the Debug menu choose Start without debugging. The application will run, and you should see the output from the console shown in Figure 4-6.

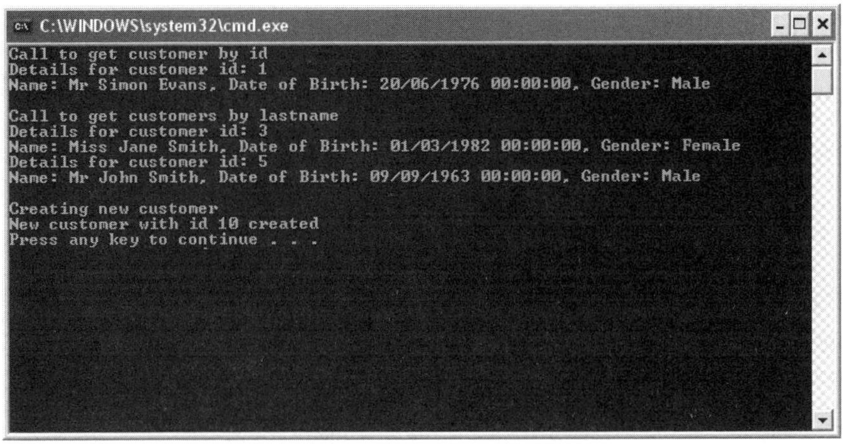

Figure 4-6. *Output from the test client making several calls to the SOAP customer service*

6. The test client makes three calls against the customer service. The first service call executes the GetCustomerById service operation for customer id 1, returning the customer Simon Evans. The second service call executes the GetCustomersByLastname service operation for last names containing the text Smith (two results are returned). The final service call executes the PersistCustomer service operation, inserting a new customer into the Customer table through the application's business logic. Check the Customer table in the database to see the new customer record inserted.

Drivers for REST Support in the Customer Service

After the successful implementation of the SOAP-based customer service for third-party businesses, the company decided it wanted to provide its customers with self-service functionality over the Internet. The architect looked at the existing service and realized that it currently did not provide all the functionality needed for the self-service web site. Upon further investigation, the architect decided that ADO.NET Data Services best suited the new functionality: the self-service web site would enable users to search for their customer records using a wide array of query parameters, and the web site being developed could then more easily support a richer user experience because the new service endpoint could use JSON-formatted messages, which are more suited to AJAX development scenarios.

■**Note** JSON was described in Chapter 1, and for more information on developing AJAX-enabled web sites to consume ADO.NET Data Services, please refer to Chapter 5.

This new service endpoint could also be exploited in the future for third parties who would prefer to communicate using a RESTful API instead of the existing SOAP-based service. However, adding REST support would need to be done without duplicating data access or business rules to ensure that the architecture remained maintainable to support both service endpoints and the client web site.

Refactoring the Customer Service for ADO.NET Data Services

SOAP-based services expose service operations, which are the "verbs" of what a service can do; this is a fundamentally different architectural approach to the "noun" based design of RESTful services. This means the ability to reuse large parts of any existing SOAP service stack will be limited, and so it is with our legacy customer service.

The first place to look at reuse is the database and data access layer. Clearly, the database itself is fit for our new data service, but the legacy service's use of stored procedures does not fit with making the data queryable via the service URI, because stored procedures normally encapsulate the specific SQL to be executed against a database. Therefore, each stored procedure executes a single set-based operation. Dynamic SQL, which executes a string of SQL against the database, enables more flexible querying of the database. Replacing the stored procedures for dynamic SQL therefore means great changes will be needed to the existing data access layer to support the continued running of the SOAP service without duplicating code and creating a maintenance problem for future developers.

While it's not possible for a procedural-based data access layer to be used in an openly queryable service, it is possible for the procedural SOAP service to use a queryable data access layer under the covers. Thus the solution here is to create a new queryable data layer in the existing architecture that is **below** the existing procedural DAL. This means that the existing DAL can be refactored to consume the new queryable data layer instead of stored procedures.

THE CASE FOR DYNAMIC SQL OVER STORED PROCEDURES

Any move away from applications running stored procedures to dynamic SQL will likely concern database administrators, particularly when we are suggesting putting the client in more control over what SQL is executed against the server.

One common concern will be security. First, how can administrators protect against SQL injection attacks? These are handled by both LINQ to SQL and the Entity Framework, so they are not possible. Additionally, DBAs may use stored procedures as a method of securing access to the database tables. This issue can be solved by writing a view over each table in the database.

Another issue many administrators may raise when refactoring away from stored procedures is that if they have SQL encapsulated that works perfectly well, why throw away perfectly good code? The answer here is that these procedures do not meet the requirements of a queryable service, so if administrators are using dynamic SQL for these purposes, they may as well reuse it for all purposes for the sake of maintainability. Of course, the cost here will be in retesting the legacy application, but this may well be a price worth paying going forward.

The new queryable data layer could be implemented using either the ADO.NET Entity Framework or LINQ to SQL, as both implement the IQueryable<T> interface that data services need to consume. The main differences between the two implementations are as follows:

- The Entity Framework provides a conceptual model and mapping layer to transform the structural (database) model into entities, whereas LINQ to SQL exposes the structural model as entities.

- The Entity Framework implements the IUpdateable interface, whereas LINQ to SQL does not (although the IUpdateable interface can be implemented by hand). Without an implementation of the IUpdateable interface, it is not possible for ADO.NET Data Services to process inserts, updates, or deletes against the database.

For our service, the structural model exposed by the database is sufficient to be exposed by the service endpoint, although we still need insert and update functionality, which requires implementation of IUpdateable. Therefore, we would normally choose the Entity Framework for this scenario. However, to provide a single example of using LINQ to SQL in this book, and also describe how to implement the IUpdateable interface, this chapter will implement the new queryable data access layer using LINQ to SQL. Figure 4-7 illustrates the changes made to existing SOAP services architecture to accommodate a queryable data access layer.

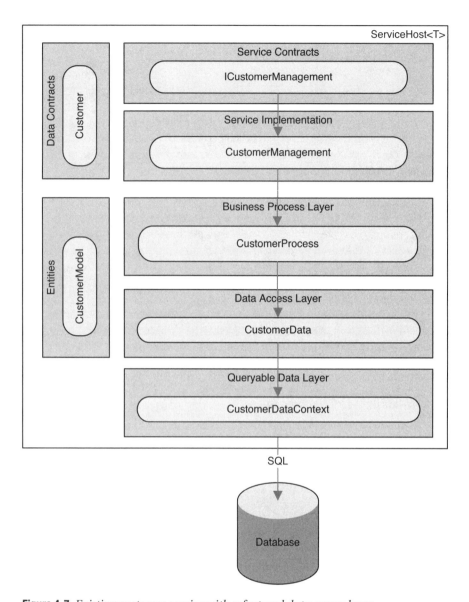

Figure 4-7. *Existing customer service with refactored data access layer*

EXERCISE 4-2: REFACTORING THE CUSTOMER SERVICE DATA ACCESS LAYER

In this exercise, we will take the legacy customer service and refactor the service's data access layer so that we can later on add a data service endpoint onto the customer service architecture. The resultant code for this exercise can be downloaded from the Apress site (http://www.apress.com/book/sourcecode). You'll find it within the folder named CustomerServiceDuring.

1. With the solution from Exercise 4-1 open, right-click the `Data Access Layer` folder and select Add ➤ New Project from the menu. Select the Class Library project template, name the project `Apress.Data.Services.CustomerService.Data.Linq`, and click OK. Delete the `Class1.cs` file within the newly created project.

2. Right-click the `References` folder and add a reference to the .NET component named `System.Data.Linq`. This is the component that contains the LINQ to SQL subsystem.

3. Right-click the project file and select Add ➤ New Item. Choose the LINQ to SQL Classes item template and name the file `CustomerDatabase.dbml`.

4. Open the Server Explorer window. If the `Customer.mdf` database does not already exist in your list of data connections, open the database contained within the `App_Data` folder of the service host web site.

5. Expand the `Tables` folder under the `Customer` database, select the `Customer`, `Salutation`, and `Gender` tables from the list, and drag them into the design surface. The designer autogenerates LINQ to SQL database classes as shown in Figure 4-8. In Solution Explorer, notice that two files are autogenerated under the `CustomerDatabase.dbml` file. If you open the `CustomerDatabase.designer.cs` file, you can read all the autogenerated code that has been created by adding the tables to the design surface.

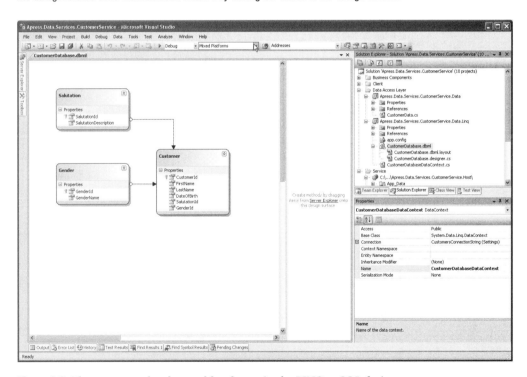

Figure 4-8. *The customer database tables shown in the LINQ to SQL designer*

6. Select the `GenderId` property from the `Customer` table. By default LINQ to SQL will set this property's type to `Char` (because the database table is typed as `Char`). Change this type to be of type `string`, which matches the type on the service's original entity model. By changing the type in the data context here, we don't need to cast the `Char` to a string in our own data access code.

7. Open the autogenerated `app.config` file from Solution Explorer and copy the connection string element (beginning with `<add...>`). Paste this connection string into the `<connectionStrings>` section of the `web.config` file of the service host web site.

8. Check the LINQ to SQL project builds and then add a project reference to it from the old `Apress.Data.Services.CustomerService.Data` project. Additionally, add a .NET component reference to the `System.Data.Linq` component to the old data access layer class library. Open the `CustomerData` class from this project. This class contains the legacy ADO.NET code to call the old database stored procedures.

9. In this class, add `using Apress.Data.Services.CustomerService.Data.Linq;` underneath the existing `using` declarations so that you can use your newly created LINQ to SQL classes from your old `CustomerData` class.

10. Refactor the four data access methods (`Get`, `GetByLastname`, `Add`, and `Update`) in the `CustomerData` class so they read as shown in Listing 4-1. These refactored methods now make LINQ to SQL calls through the new LINQ data layer, generating dynamic SQL on the fly.

Listing 4-1. *The Refactored Code for the CustomerData Class*

```
using System;
using System.Collections.Generic;
using System.Data;
using System.Data.Common;
using System.Linq;
using Apress.Data.Services.CustomerService.BusinessEntities;
using Apress.Data.Services.CustomerService.Data.Linq;

namespace Apress.Data.Services.CustomerService.Data
{
    /// <summary>
    /// The customer data access layer.
    /// </summary>
    public class CustomerData
    {
        private CustomerDatabaseDataContext database;

        public CustomerData()
        {
            database = new CustomerDatabaseDataContext();
        }

        /// <summary>
        /// Gets the specified customer id.
        /// </summary>
        /// <param name="customerId">The customer id.</param>
        /// <returns></returns>
        public CustomerModel Get(int customerId)
        {
            CustomerModel customer = (from c in database.Customers
                        where c.CustomerId == customerId
```

```
                            select new CustomerModel
                            {
                                Id = c.CustomerId,
                                FirstName = c.FirstName,
                                LastName = c.LastName,
                                DateOfBirth = c.DateOfBirth,
                                Gender = new GenderModel
                                {
                                    Id = c.Gender.GenderId.ToString(),
                                    Name = c.Gender.GenderName
                                },
                                Salutation = new SalutationModel
                                {
                                    Id = c.Salutation.SalutationId,
                                    Description = c.Salutation.
        SalutationDescription
                                }
                            }).FirstOrDefault();

                return customer;
            }


            /// <summary>
            /// Gets the customers by lastname.
            /// </summary>
            /// <param name="lastname">The lastname.</param>
            /// <returns></returns>
            public List<CustomerModel> GetByLastname(string lastname)
            {
                List<CustomerModel> customers = (from c in database.Customers
                                        where c.LastName.Contains(lastname)
                                        select new CustomerModel
                                        {
                                            Id = c.CustomerId,
                                            FirstName = c.FirstName,
                                            LastName = c.LastName,
                                            DateOfBirth = c.DateOfBirth,
                                            Gender = new GenderModel
                                            {
                                                Id = c.Gender.
        GenderId.ToString(),

                                                Name = c.Gender.GenderName
                                            },
                                            Salutation =
                                                new SalutationModel
                                            {
                                                Id = c.Salutation.
```

```
                                                                    SalutationId,
                                                    Description = c.Salutation.
        SalutationDescription
                                                }
                                        }).ToList();

            return customers;
        }

        /// <summary>
        /// Adds the specified customer.
        /// </summary>
        /// <param name="customer">The customer.</param>
        public void Add(CustomerModel customer)
        {
            Customer c = new Customer
            {
                FirstName = customer.FirstName,
                LastName = customer.LastName,
                DateOfBirth = customer.DateOfBirth,
                GenderId = customer.Gender.Id,
                SalutationId = customer.Salutation.Id
            };

            database.Customers.InsertOnSubmit(c);
            database.SubmitChanges();

            customer.Id = c.CustomerId;
        }

        /// <summary>
        /// Updates the specified customer.
        /// </summary>
        /// <param name="customer">The customer.</param>
        public void Update(CustomerModel customer)
        {
            Customer c = database.Customers.
    Where(cust => customer.Id == cust.CustomerId).FirstOrDefault();

            if (c != null)
            {
                c.FirstName = customer.FirstName;
                c.LastName = customer.LastName;
                c.DateOfBirth = customer.DateOfBirth;
                c.GenderId = customer.Gender.Id;
                c.SalutationId = customer.Salutation.Id;
            }
```

```
                    database.SubmitChanges();
                }
            }
        }
```

11. Build the project. Ensure that the service host is running in the Web Development Server by browsing to the `Customer.svc` file. Rerun the test console application. The application should run with the same results as before, proving the refactoring task has been successful.

12. Delete the old stored procedures (`GetCustomerById`, `GetCustomerByLastName`, `InsertCustomer`, and `UpdateCustomer`), and the `DataAccessBase.cs`, `DataHelper.cs`, and `EntityMapper.cs` classes, which are now redundant with the solution (these classes are helper classes for making ADO.NET calls).

Adding an ADO.NET Data Service Endpoint to the Refactored Service

With the SOAP endpoint now consuming a data layer that implements the `IQueryable<T>` interface, attention can now be focused on building the data service endpoint. Exposing a data service that consumes a LINQ to SQL `DataContext` is fairly trivial for the read (queryable) functionality, but requires additional work to implement the create, update, and delete functionality. This is because LINQ to SQL does not implement the `IUpdateable` interface out of the box. Therefore, implementing the data service will be split over two exercises: first, creating a read-only endpoint, and second, implementing the `IUpdatable` interface to provide write functionality.

To keep the component architecture for the new endpoint consistent with the existing SOAP endpoint, we will place the data service implementation (the `DataService<T>` class) in the same assembly as the SOAP service implementation class (the `CustomerManagement` class), and point the service host to the implementation in this assembly.

EXERCISE 4-3: ADDING AN ADO.NET DATA SERVICE ENDPOINT TO THE CUSTOMER SERVICE

In this exercise, you will add an ADO.NET data service endpoint to the refactored customer service completed in the previous exercise to expose the customer data as a queryable (read-only) data service. You will additionally create a new test client console application to make calls into the data service that mirror those made from the SOAP test client. The resulting code for this exercise can be downloaded from the Apress site (`http://www.apress.com/book/sourcecode`).

1. Open the solution created in Exercise 4-2. Right-click the service host web site (`Apress.Data.Services.CustomerService.Host`) and choose Add New Item. Select the ADO.NET Data Service item template and name the service file `CustomerDataService.svc`. Visual Studio will create two files, the host for the service (`CustomerDataService.svc`) and the service implementation, which is automatically generated in the `App_Code` folder of the service host.

2. For consistency in our architecture (and the fact that we need to reference the original business entities), we are going to place the service implementation of our data service into the existing service implementation project. Drag the `CustomerDataService.cs` file from the `App_Code` folder and drop it into the existing service implementation project (`Apress.Data.Services.CustomerService.ServiceImplementation`).

3. Add three .NET component references into the service implementation project for `System.Data.Linq`, `System.Data.Services`, and `System.ServiceModel.Web`. These references are for LINQ to SQL, ADO.NET Data Services, and the WCF web subsystem, respectively.

4. With the `CustomerDataService.cs` file open, select the entire `CustomerDataService` class, right-click, and choose Surround With ➤ namespace. A namespace code block will be created around the service implementation. Change the namespace to `Apress.Data.Services.CustomerService.ServiceImplementation`, which is the root namespace of the service implementation assembly.

5. Open the generated `CustomerDataService.svc` file and change the text in the `Service` attribute to `Apress.Data.Services.CustomerService.ServiceImplementation.CustomerDataService`. This points the service host file for our data service endpoint to the `CustomerDataService` in our service implementation project (already referenced by the web site).

6. Delete the `App_Code` directory as our service implementation is contained in a different project.

7. Add a project reference in the service implementation project to the `Apress.Data.Services.Customer.Data.Linq` project, which contains your queryable LINQ to SQL layer. At the top of the `CustomerDataService.cs` file, add `using Apress.Data.Services.CustomerService.Data.Linq;` to the list of declarations there.

8. Find the `TODO` comment at the top of the `CustomerDataService` class and replace this comment block with `CustomerDatabaseDataContext`. This points the data service to our LINQ to SQL queryable data context. At this point, check that the service implementation builds successfully.

9. Delete the comments in the `InitializeService` method and add the following two lines of code to the method to enable clients to query against all entities in the data service:

```
config.SetEntitySetAccessRule("*", EntitySetRights.All);
config.SetServiceOperationAccessRule("*", ServiceOperationRights.All);
```

10. Because we are using LINQ to SQL in our data access layer rather than LINQ to Entities, ADO.NET Data Services does not know what the keys of our entity sets are by default. To enable this, we must decorate the autogenerated `Table<T>` classes, identifying the primary and foreign keys in the data context. To achieve this, first add a .NET component reference in the `Apress.Data.Services.CustomerService.Data.Linq` project to the `System.Data.Services.Client` assembly. Then add a new class to this project named `CustomerDatabaseDataContext.cs`. This file will contain partial classes to the autogenerated `Table<T>` classes produced from the LINQ to SQL designer.

11. We are going to add some additional code into the newly created partial class, which will enable us to add data service key attributes to the LINQ to SQL–generated classes without amending the generated code. This approach also means we can regenerate the LINQ to SQL classes without losing our code. Change the code in the newly created `CustomerDatabaseDataContext.cs` so it resembles the code in Listing 4-2.

Listing 4-2. *LINQ to SQL Partial Class Code to Wire Keys for ADO.NET Data Services*

```
using System.Data.Services.Common;

namespace Apress.Data.Services.CustomerService.Data.Linq
{
    [DataServiceKey("CustomerId")]
    public partial class Customer
    {
    }

    [DataServiceKey("GenderId")]
    public partial class Gender
    {
    }

    [DataServiceKey("SalutationId")]
    public partial class Salutation
    {
    }
}
```

12. Open the `web.config` file in the service host. Note that adding the data service to the service host has automatically added an entry into the `<system.ServiceModel />` configuration section that reads `<serviceHostingEnvironment aspNetCompatibilityEnabled="true"/>`. This configuration setting enables the WCF service host to use features from ASP.NET such as membership and roles. While we are not going to implement any features from ASP.NET in this exercise, we are going to leave this setting turned on; however, this means we have to make a minor change to the original SOAP service implementation to enable ASP.NET compatibility, because both the SOAP and REST endpoints are being hosted in the same process. To enable this, navigate to the `CustomerManagement` class and add the following attribute to the top of the class definition:

    ```
    [AspNetCompatibilityRequirements(RequirementsMode =
    AspNetCompatibilityRequirementsMode.Allowed)]
    ```

13. Build the solution, make sure the service is running, and run the original test client, which calls the original SOAP service. This should produce the same results as it did in the previous exercise, proving that existing clients will not be broken by the SOAP service implementation change.

14. Select the `CustomerDataService.svc` file from the service host web site, right-click, and choose View In Browser. If the new data service endpoint is running successfully, you should see the output from the browser as shown in Figure 4-9. This displays the three entity sets surfaced by ADO.NET Data Services and LINQ to SQL.

Figure 4-9. *The customer service REST endpoint viewed from the browser*

15. Having built the data service, we now need to create a new test client to duplicate the results from the SOAP endpoint. Open a command prompt and execute the `DataSvcUtil` command from within the `C:\WINDOWS\Microsoft.NET\Framework\v3.5` folder. Execute the command as `DataSvcUtil.exe /out:CustomerDataService.cs /uri:http://localhost:1478/Apress.Data.Services.CustomerService.Host/CustomerDataService.svc`. This will generate a data service proxy for use in the test client console application.

16. In Solution Explorer, right-click the `Client` folder and select Add New Project. Select the console application template and name the project `Apress.Data.Services.CustomerService.DataClient`. Take the `CustomerDataService.cs`-generated file from the previous step and add the file into the newly created project by dragging the file from the folder it was created in and dropping it into the project. Add a .NET component reference to the `System.Data.Services.Client` assembly.

17. In the newly created test client, open the `Program.cs` file and change the code so that it reads the same as the code shown in Listing 4-3.

Listing 4-3. *The Code for the Data Service Test Client*

```
using System;
using System.Linq;
using System.Data.Services.Client;
using Apress.Data.Services.CustomerService.Data.Linq;

namespace Apress.Data.Services.CustomerService.DataClient
{
    class Program
    {
        static void Main(string[] args)
        {
            int id = 1;
            string lastname = "Smith";

            // note: the service URI is pointing to localhost:1478.
            // If your web development server opens on a different port
            // you will need to change this.
            CustomerDatabaseDataContext dataService =
                new CustomerDatabaseDataContext(new Uri("http://localhost:1478/
                Apress.Data.Services.CustomerService.Host/
                CustomerDataService.svc"));

            Console.WriteLine("Call to get customer by id");

            // get the first customer with id 1 or null if none returned.
            Customer customer = (from c in dataService.Customers.
Expand("Salutation").Expand("Gender")
                                where c.CustomerId == id
                                select c).FirstOrDefault();

            Console.WriteLine(
                string.Format("Details for customer id: {0}", id));
```

```
            if (customer != null)
            {
                Console.WriteLine(string.Format("Name: {0} {1} {2},
                Date of Birth: {3}, Gender: {4}",
                customer.Salutation.SalutationDescription,
                customer.FirstName, customer.LastName,
                customer.DateOfBirth, customer.Gender.GenderName));
            }

            Console.WriteLine();

            Console.WriteLine("Call to get customers by lastname");

            // get all customers where the lastname equals Smith
    and return the related salutation and gender entity sets
            var customers = from c in dataService.Customers.
    Expand("Salutation").Expand("Gender")
                            where c.LastName == lastname
                            select c;

            foreach (Customer c in customers)
            {
                Console.WriteLine(
                string.Format("Details for customer id: {0}", c.CustomerId));
                Console.WriteLine(
                string.Format("Name: {0} {1} {2}, Date of Birth: {3}, Gender:
    {4}",
    c.Salutation.SalutationDescription, c.FirstName, c.LastName, c.DateOfBirth,
    c.Gender.GenderName));
            }
        }
    }
}
```

18. Set the new test client project as the startup project, build the solution, and run the console application. The console application should run as shown in Figure 4-10, mirroring the read calls made by the SOAP test client.

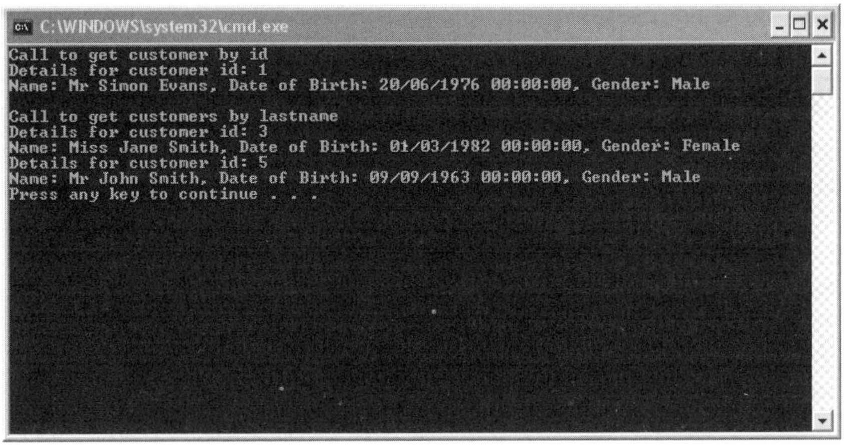

Figure 4-10. *The test client retrieving data from the new data service endpoint*

Implementing Write Operations in the Customer Data Service

Having created an ADO.NET data service endpoint that consumes the LINQ to SQL data access layer and surfaces read-only functionality, we now need to expose the write functionality for create, update, and delete operations. This requires the LINQ to SQL DataContext class to implement IUpdatable, which is used by ADO.NET Data Services to execute write operations.

To implement the IUpdatable interface on the LINQ to SQL data context (which is the IQueryable<T> implementation), the code needs to be placed inside a partial class for the generated data context so that regenerating the data context does not remove our code. ADO.NET Data Services will look for an implementation of this interface, and the implementation requires you to reflect over the objects being updated and make the required calls to the data context. Table 4-1 describes the methods in the IUpdatable interface, which are implemented in Exercise 4-4 using the LINQ to SQL data context.

Table 4-1. *IUpdatable Methods and Their Use*

Method Name	Description
AddReferenceToCollection	Adds a resource to the given collection navigation property
ClearChanges	Clears all changes made to entities in the underlying store
CreateResource	Called when a data service tries to add a resource by an HTTP POST
DeleteResource	Called when a data service tries to delete a resource by HTTP DELETE
GetResource	Get the resource as specified in the IQueryable<T> query (used for merge semantics)
ResetResource	Replaces the resource as specified in the IQueryable<T> query (used for replace semantics)
SetValue	Sets the value of the specified property with the given value
GetValue	Gets the value of the specified property
SaveChanges	Saves all the changes in the underlying store
SetReference	Sets the value of a navigation property
ResolveResource	Returns an instance of an object based on a resource
RemoveReferenceFromCollection	Removes a resource from a given collection navigation property

We will need to make calls into the existing business logic layer to ensure that important business rules are shared between the SOAP and REST endpoints for these write operations. This will be achieved in the ADO.NET Data Services implementation code by writing a change interceptor, which will call into the existing business logic layer.

■**Note** We would implement business logic for HTTP GET requests using a query interceptor in a similar way to how we will write our change interceptor.

The current customer application business logic layer encapsulates the business logic for specific business processes. In the customer service, the vast majority of business rules are contained when trying to persist (add or update) a customer entity. These business rules validate the customer entity being persisted. While in our example customer service these rules are fairly simple, they can be very complex in real-world scenarios. For example, persisting a customer might include a business process to authorize the new customer via a workflow.

In many business logic layers, business rules are tightly coupled to calls to the data access layer; in other words, a consumer of the customer business process would call into the Persist method and execute both the business rules and (if successful) the call to the data access layer to add or update the customer record. In order for the ADO.NET Data Services implementation to make use of the business rules, they need to be accessible to the client without making the data access calls, as the ADO.NET Data Services implementation has the ability to call the data source built in. Implementing an update interceptor allows us to execute business rules prior to this data access work being carried out, and stop the data access call if necessary.

The final customer service architecture, exposing both SOAP and REST endpoints, is shown in Figure 4-11.

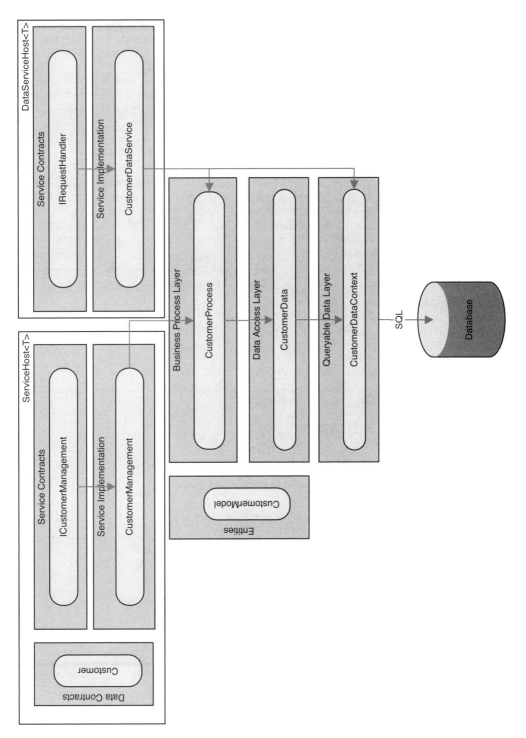

Figure 4-11. *The final customer service architecture*

EXERCISE 4-4: ADDING CREATE, UPDATE, AND DELETE FUNCTIONALITY TO THE DATA

In this exercise you will implement the `IUpdatable` interface on the LINQ to SQL `DataContext` so that write operations can be executed against the service. You will then write a change interceptor in the service implementation layer to reuse business logic from the service's existing business logic layer. The finished code from this exercise can be downloaded from the Apress site (http://www.apress.com/book/sourcecode).

1. With the solution created from Exercise 4-3, add a .NET component reference to the `System.Data.Services` assembly to both the `Apress.Data.Services.CustomerService.Data` and `Apress.Data.Services.CustomerService.Data.Linq` projects, respectively. This reference is required in order to implement the `IUpdatable` interface on the data context.

2. Open the `CustomerDatabaseDataContext.cs` file, which contains the LINQ to SQL partial classes that extend the classes generated by the LINQ to SQL designer. At the top of the file, add a `using` declaration to `System.Data.Services`. Add a partial class to this file for the `CustomerDatabaseDataContext` class implementing the `IUpdatable` interface. This implementation of the interface uses reflection to reference the loosely typed objects passed in and executes methods in the LINQ to SQL data context to tie the interface to the implementation. This code is shown in Listing 4-4.

Listing 4-4. *Implementing the IUpdatable Interface for LINQ to SQL*

```
public partial class CustomerDatabaseDataContext : IUpdatable
{
    #region IUpdatable Members

    public void AddReferenceToCollection(object targetResource,
 string propertyName, object resourceToBeAdded)
    {
        Type t = targetResource.GetType();

        PropertyInfo collectionProperty =
        GetPropertyInfoForType(t, propertyName, false);

        object collection = collectionProperty.GetValue(targetResource,
null);

        collection.GetType().InvokeMember("Add",
          BindingFlags.Public | BindingFlags.Instance |
          BindingFlags.InvokeMethod,
          null, collection, new object[] { resourceToBeAdded });
    }

    public void ClearChanges()
    {
        MethodInfo mi = this.GetType().GetMethod("ClearCache",
         BindingFlags.Instance | BindingFlags.NonPublic |
         BindingFlags.InvokeMethod);
```

```csharp
        mi.Invoke(this, null);
    }

    public object CreateResource(string containerName, string fullTypeName)
    {
        Type t = Type.GetType(fullTypeName);

        ITable table = GetTableForType(t);

        object value = Construct(t);

        table.InsertOnSubmit(value);

        return (value);
    }

    public void DeleteResource(object targetResource)
    {
        ITable table = this.GetTable(targetResource.GetType());

        if (table == null)
        {
            throw new
             DataServiceException("Failed to locate table for resource");
        }
        table.DeleteOnSubmit(targetResource);
    }

    public object GetResource(IQueryable query, string fullTypeName)
    {
        object result = null;

        foreach (object item in query)
        {
            if (result != null)
            {
                throw new
                 DataServiceException("A single resource is expected");
            }
            result = item;
        }
        if (result == null)
        {
            throw new DataServiceException(404, "Resource not found");
        }
        if (fullTypeName != null)
```

```
        {
            if (result.GetType().FullName != fullTypeName)
            {
                throw new DataServiceException("Resource type mismatch");
            }
        }
        return (result);
    }

    public object GetValue(object targetResource, string propertyName)
    {
        Type t = targetResource.GetType();

        PropertyInfo pi = GetPropertyInfoForType(t, propertyName, false);

        object value = null;

        try
        {
            value = pi.GetValue(targetResource, null);
        }
        catch (Exception ex)
        {
            throw new DataServiceException(string.Format(
                "Failed getting property {0} value", propertyName), ex);
        }
        return (value);
    }

    public void RemoveReferenceFromCollection(object targetResource,
      string propertyName, object resourceToBeRemoved)
    {
        Type t = targetResource.GetType();

        PropertyInfo collectionProperty =
        GetPropertyInfoForType(t, propertyName, false);

        object collection = collectionProperty.GetValue(targetResource,
null);

        collection.GetType().InvokeMember("Remove",
          BindingFlags.Public | BindingFlags.Instance |
          BindingFlags.InvokeMethod,
          null, collection, new object[] { resourceToBeRemoved });
    }

    public object ResetResource(object resource)
```

```csharp
{
    // Only required for replace semantics
    throw new NotImplementedException();
}

public object ResolveResource(object resource)
{
    return (resource);
}

public void SaveChanges()
{
    base.SubmitChanges();
}

public void SetReference(object targetResource,
string propertyName, object propertyValue)
{
    this.SetValue(targetResource, propertyName, propertyValue);
}

public void SetValue(object targetResource,
string propertyName, object propertyValue)
{
    Type t = targetResource.GetType();

    PropertyInfo pi = GetPropertyInfoForType(t, propertyName, true);

    try
    {
        pi.SetValue(targetResource, propertyValue, null);
    }
    catch (Exception ex)
    {
        throw new DataServiceException(
          string.Format("Error setting property {0} to {1}",
          propertyName, propertyValue),
          ex);
    }
}

private PropertyInfo GetPropertyInfoForType(Type t,
string propertyName, bool setter)
{
    PropertyInfo pi = null;

    try
```

```
        {
            BindingFlags flags = BindingFlags.Public |
BindingFlags.Instance;
            flags |= setter ? BindingFlags.SetProperty :
            BindingFlags.GetProperty;

            pi = t.GetProperty(propertyName, flags);

            if (pi == null)
            {
                throw new DataServiceException(
                string.Format("Failed to find property {0} on type {1}",
                  propertyName, t.Name));
            }
        }
        catch (Exception exception)
        {
            throw new DataServiceException(
              string.Format("Error finding property {0}", propertyName),
              exception);
        }
        return (pi);
    }

    private ITable GetTableForType(Type t)
    {
        ITable table = this.GetTable(t);

        if (table == null)
        {
            throw new DataServiceException(
              string.Format("No table found for type {0}", t.Name));
        }
        return (table);
    }

    private static object Construct(Type t)
    {
        ConstructorInfo ci = t.GetConstructor(Type.EmptyTypes);

        if (ci == null)
        {
            throw new DataServiceException(
              string.Format("No default ctor found for type {0}", t.Name));
        }
        return (ci.Invoke(null));
    }
    #endregion
```

```
    }
```

3. Open the CustomerDataService.cs file in the service implementation project. Add the following two
   using declarations to the top of file, required to call into the customer application business logic layer:

```
using Apress.Data.Services.CustomerService.BusinessLogic;
using Apress.Data.Services.CustomerService.BusinessEntities;
```

4. Add a change interceptor method to the CustomerDataService class that intercepts calls to change
   a Customer entity. The method will consume the CustomerProcess (business layer) class and call the
   IsPersistValid method to validate that a change can be made to the customer entity. In order to call this
   method, you need to create a CustomerModel entity class, which is an entity that the business layer uses
   to represent a customer. This entity can be created by assigning property values from the Customer entity
   exposed by LINQ to SQL. The code for this class is shown in Listing 4-5.

Listing 4-5. *The Change Interceptor, Consuming the Customer Business Logic Layer*

```
[ChangeInterceptor("Customers")]
public void OnCustomersChange(Customer c, UpdateOperations operations)
{
    CustomerModel customer = new CustomerModel
    {
        Id = c.CustomerId,
        FirstName = c.FirstName,
        LastName = c.LastName,
        DateOfBirth = c.DateOfBirth,
        Gender = new GenderModel
        {
            Id = c.GenderId
        },
        Salutation = new SalutationModel
        {
            Id = c.SalutationId
        }
    };

    CustomerProcess process = new CustomerProcess();

    if (!process.IsPersistValid(customer))
    {
        string message = "Customer entity is not valid.
                    Change operation failed";
        throw new DataServiceException(400, message);
```

```
        }
    }
```

5. Open the data service test client `Program.cs` file. In this class, add the code shown in Listing 4-6 to the bottom of the `Main` method to test adding a new customer to the service.

Listing 4-6. *Adding Customer Calls to the Test Client*

```
static void Main(string[] args)
{
    // add the following code to the bottom
        of the existing Main method....
    Customer newCustomer = new Customer
    {
        FirstName = "Jimmy",
        LastName = "Brown",
        DateOfBirth = new DateTime(1955, 10, 30),
        GenderId = "M",
        SalutationId = 1
    };

    dataService.AddToCustomers(newCustomer);

    DataServiceResponse response = dataService.SaveChanges();

    if (!response.HasErrors)
    {
        Console.WriteLine(
            string.Format("New customer with id {0} created",
            newCustomer.CustomerId));
    }
}
```

6. Build the solution and run the test harness to validate that the customer is being created successfully, as shown in Figure 4-12.

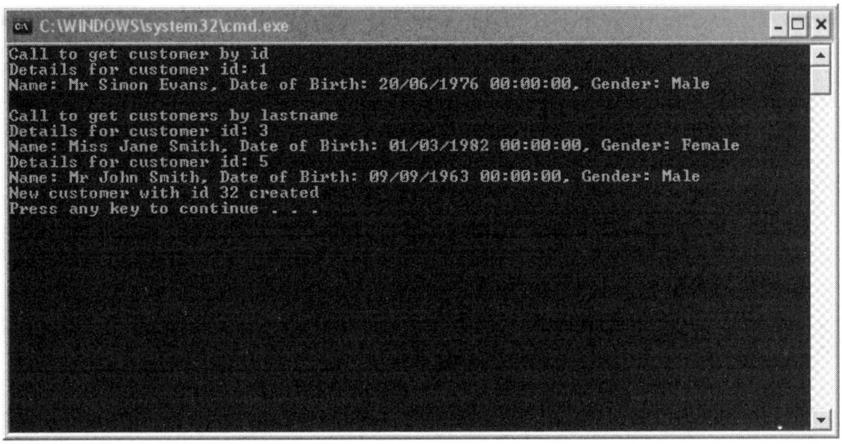

Figure 4-12. *The data services client inserting a new customer entity*

Summary

In this chapter, we have taken a typical (albeit simplified) legacy SOAP service implemented using WCF, refactored it to prepare it for adding an additional ADO.NET data service RESTful endpoint, reusing as much of the existing code base as possible.

It is unlikely that your existing applications and services exactly match the logical architecture described here. But the scenario described here is common to many existing solutions, and hopefully this chapter has helped you to start thinking about how and what you can reuse from your existing investment.

The key message of this chapter is that you should not consider ADO.NET Data Services to only be something of interest for green field projects; there are plenty of architectural strategies you can use to evolve your current applications to services to support REST endpoints while keeping your current investment live and maintainable.

PART 3

■■■

ADO.NET Data Services from the Outside

One of the great promises of service-oriented architecture is software reuse. Developers invest a significant amount of time designing a service in support of this goal. Software designed for reuse has a higher cost of development; therefore the worst outcome for such a development is to not reuse it, because there is no return on the additional investment.

When developers design services, they normally take time to consider the design of a service from the inside. The design of a service from the inside is important for performance, scalability, and maintainability. We employ techniques such as separating logic into discrete layers, using design patterns, and performing unit tests to ensure maintainability. We will pay attention to our database designs and object models to gain the optimum performance for our needs, and we'll endeavor to ensure that the architecture can scale out across a server farm without single points of failure that will impact resilience.

Yet for all the considerations of designing a service from the inside, many developers pay little attention to the design of a service from the outside, or in other words, how to design a service from the perspective of the consumer.

The impact of not designing a service that can be easily consumed is that it will put developers off of using your service. If your service is a public-facing service, this may discourage customers from your business. If your service is internal to your enterprise, it may encourage others to develop their own services that duplicate the functionality of your service. Thus, not giving due consideration to how your service can be consumed will impact its adoption, and therefore reduce the reuse of your service.

The best way to design a service from the outside is to consider how your service will be consumed in code. In the case of ADO.NET Data Services, this means considering whether the entity sets you surface have an elegant structure that is simple to understand and easy to work with. "Easy to work with" can mean having a logical URI structure, or it can mean it is easy to present in a user interface with a minimum of effort.

The other important aspect of designing services from the outside is to consider what mix of technologies your clients are likely to target. Increasingly, this is likely to be a broad set of technologies from web sites delivering rich user experiences through a technology like Silverlight to a business process needing to consume a service in middleware such as BizTalk Server.

Through the next four chapters of this book, we will explore the consumption of data services in several common scenarios: ASP.NET AJAX web sites, mashup sites, Silverlight applications, and BizTalk Server. These are some of the most common technologies that you are likely to consider when developing a data service for use in your enterprise.

CHAPTER 5

ASP.NET and AJAX Solutions

The majority of end users associate using the Internet with opening a browser to access web sites. While accessing web sites, users are connecting to web servers via HTTP using request-reply messaging to pull web pages down from different addresses (URLs). This statement has been true since the beginning of the Internet, but what continues to evolve is the format and type of content being returned in the response messages received by users.

The most common content type returned in response messages is Hypertext Markup Language (HTML), which is interpreted by browsers to present information with visual layout and styling. HTML is an example of a markup language. All markup languages share the separation of information and associated metadata. The metadata used in HTML describes how the information should be displayed to the user in the browser. The browser interprets the HTML metadata and presents the information back to the user in a browser window.

Typical content from web pages does not just contain HTML. The content can include richer content from plug-ins such as Flash or Silverlight. In addition to this, most web sites exploit the browser's capability to interpret JavaScript and Cascading Style Sheets (CSS). CSS is used to separate the HTML page's style and layout from the HTML itself. This level of separation provides cleaner markup and promotes reuse of styles across web pages within a site, making a site more maintainable. Additionally, CSS can be used to "skin" a site, providing different styles that can be personalized to a user's preferences. JavaScript is a procedural language, interpreted and executed by browsers to enrich web pages. Using JavaScript, it is possible to interact with the HTML content, CSS, and the browser itself. HTML content can be manipulated using the HTML Document Object Model (DOM), which gives you programmatic access to the HTML via JavaScript.

HTML is not the only markup language used in web development. Other markup languages are used for different purposes; indeed the Atom format used by ADO.NET Data Services is one such example, providing a specific implementation of XML to describe the data returned from an ADO.NET Data Services request. ASP.NET also has its own markup language, which describes how a web server will generate appropriate HTML content for return in a response message. This will be discussed in the section "The ASP.NET Server-Side Model" later in this chapter.

The Evolution of Web Applications

The richness of content provided by web sites on the Internet has evolved dramatically over the past ten years. The driving force behind this evolution has been competition between web sites for users, underpinned by competition and innovation between browsers. As innovations have become adopted by web sites, end-user expectations have in turn been raised, causing other web sites to follow suit in improving and updating their user experiences. Thus, HTML, CSS, and JavaScript "standards" have progressed and changed while the Internet matures. All Internet standards are prone to interpretation by browser vendors. A cynic will tell you that the differences in the way Firefox and Internet Explorer render content are down to great vendor conspiracy theories. But the reality is more likely to be a different interpretation of an unclear set of specifications for standards. What is clear though is that the evolution of browsers' use of standards has converged with every new version, while still enabling new features for developers to exploit.

What is the difference between the terms "web site" and "web application"? Loosely speaking, they are the same thing, but the term "web application" is more commonly used when referring to web pages that drive an application with a specific purpose. For example, an online banking site would be a web application that enables you to manage your finances, whereas the bank's corporate web site is more general information about the bank, with no specific application to use. Web applications normally contain much more business logic and are more data driven than web sites. Most data stored by web applications needs to be centrally stored on a database so that it can be shared between users. For example, product inventory on an e-commerce web site needs to be shared by all shoppers so that they know what the web site sells and how much stock the site has of a given product.

Centrally located databases for web applications introduce the need for running logic on the server; we must take data stored in our central database and present it to the user's browser in HTML. The logic we need to execute will contain some data access code to execute SQL against the database, but we may also need to execute complex business rules or workflow as part of a business process before ultimately rendering a page of HTML. ASP.NET forms the foundations for executing logic on a web server and rendering the content back to the browser in HTML.

Because of the need to locate data in one place on a secure server, executing server-side logic will always by necessary. The cost of executing server-side logic is the cost of a browser-to-server round-trip, which is a key consideration for web developers; the more logic that can run on the browser, the fewer server round-trips will be required. In the early days of web applications, almost all business logic would be run on the web server. Browser standards had not converged as much as they have today, and getting JavaScript code to execute business logic correctly across the most commonly used browsers was extremely difficult.

Another important reason why older web applications were very server centric is because the only HTTP requests sent from older browsers were for web pages containing HTML for presentation; so if you wanted to get a list of products from a database, execute some business logic, and return some HTML to a browser, you would have to execute this within a single HTTP request-and-response round-trip of a web page. This limitation meant that there was little opportunity for rich user experiences because any interaction with data on the web server would force a refresh on the entire web page.

Microsoft released a technology in Internet Explorer 5.0 called XMLHTTP. It was an ActiveX control that enabled an already downloaded web page to make an HTTP request from within JavaScript and then use the response content to manipulate the HTML DOM. Microsoft originally developed this technology to support a richer user experience in its Outlook web client, where HTTP requests were made to a web server fronting Exchange, and XML would be returned in response messages, which were used by JavaScript to manipulate the HTML DOM. Other browsers such as Firefox began to include support for XMLHTTP by around 2002. Common support across modern browsers opened up the widespread adoption of techniques using XMLHTTP commonly known as AJAX, or Asynchronous JavaScript and XML.

AJAX relies on the ability to use XMLHTTP to make background HTTP requests while a web page is already rendered in a browser. Calls to an XMLHTTP object are made from within JavaScript, usually retrieving data for display on a page of HTML. The key difference between a web page using AJAX and a traditional web page is that the initial web page of HTML will be requested from the web server, and then that page will in turn request the **data** to display in the web page. The XMLHTTP response is therefore not normally in HTML format, but is instead data manipulated client side by JavaScript. As the name implies, XMLHTTP was originally used to retrieve responses in XML format, but currently most AJAX web pages rely on responses in JSON format rather than XML. This is because by using JSON the JavaScript language does not have to deserialize the response data; the JSON format is native JavaScript, making it more efficient for the browser to handle.

AJAX requests for data are normally made against one or more services that execute server-side logic to work with data stored in databases. ADO.NET Data Services provides the ideal foundation for developing such services, because these services include the ability to serialize the response message into either Atom or JSON, meaning that they are easy to consume within an AJAX page using JavaScript. ASP.NET 3.5 now includes rich AJAX support, making it easier to develop AJAX web applications that consume services that support JSON such as those developed using ADO.NET Data Services.

ASP.NET 3.5 includes a `ScriptManager` control, which provides cross-browser plumbing to make XMLHTTP requests. It also provides a rich client-side framework, known as the Microsoft AJAX Library, for use within JavaScript. This library provides cross-browser APIs to manipulate the HTML DOM, as well as some language constructs such as inheritance and namespacing that supply structure and promote reuse within JavaScript.

Alongside the AJAX capabilities that ASP.NET 3.5 brings, Visual Studio 2008 provides the ideal development environment for developing web applications. It introduced support for JavaScript IntelliSense and enriched its support for JavaScript debugging, making development using JavaScript as easy as working with server-side code in C#. The environment also includes a much improved WYSIWYG designer for HTML and ASP.NET markup, which provides deep support for managing CSS files.

The existence of ADO.NET Data Services owes as much to the advance of web development techniques as it does to the evolution of services using REST. The remainder of this chapter will be devoted to describing ASP.NET in more detail, and how you can consume ADO.NET Data Services either server side using C# code or client side using AJAX techniques.

The ASP.NET Server-Side Model

Through each new version of the .NET Framework, ASP.NET has expanded upon its server-side capabilities to become an extremely powerful technology to develop web applications with.

An ASP.NET web page (commonly known as an ASPX file) is the same as any other web page except that it has some content that will execute logic on the web server (referred to as server side). Such content is made up of ASP.NET markup and C# code. The ASP.NET markup is contained within other HTML markup and normally separated from the C# code, which is contained in a separate file (commonly referred to as a code-behind or code-beside file).

ASP.NET markup is made up of ASP.NET controls that are interpreted by a web server to render HTML that the ASP.NET controls represent. Because the controls are rendered into HTML server side, it is possible to use information known to the web server to influence what HTML is rendered. For example, data from a database can be bound to an ASP.NET `GridView` control in markup to render repeating HTML for each item in a database.

The C# code that accompanies ASP.NET web page markup is contained within a class that represents the page being executed. This class inherits from the ASP.NET `Page` class, which provides a place for custom logic to be executed as part of the execution of the page itself. The `Page` class exposes events that can be handled at different points during the page's life cycle. The code written in these event handlers have complete access to the web page's control tree. The **control tree** is an object model built to access the controls contained in the page markup. This interaction between page markup and code-behind makes the model exposed by ASP. NET extremely powerful. The number of prebuilt controls provided by ASP.NET makes the building of the data-driven web applications much more productive than if you were to generate the required HTML by hand.

THE PITFALLS OF ASP.NET CONTROLS

For all the benefits of the ASP.NET model of using rich controls in markup that render HTML, one common complaint often cited is the lack of control this brings over the output HTML that the built-in controls render. As HTML standards have changed, some of the HTML emitted by controls such as the `GridView` is not very standards compliant. To resolve this issue, you can apply the CSS Control Adapters, which are freely downloadable from `http://www.asp.net/cssadapters/`. The CSS Control Adapters change how many of the most commonly used ASP.NET controls render the output HTML. This technique can be used for any other controls not covered by the adapters.

Commonly Used ASP.NET Controls

An ASP.NET web page mixes client-side HTML with server-side ASP.NET markup consisting of ASP.NET controls. Table 5-1 lists some example ASP.NET controls and describes their purpose.

Table 5-1. *Example ASP.NET Controls*

Control	Purpose
`<asp:Button />`	Renders an HTML input button with events to run sever-side code when the button is clicked.
`<asp:Label />`	Renders text inside a `<span />` HTML element.
`<asp:GridView />`	Renders a table-based view of multiple columns of data, with paging and sorting built in.
`<asp:ListView />`	Renders data into any templated HTML. This control is a flexible repeater control.
`<asp:Login />`	Enables a user to log in and then authenticate using a membership provider.
`<asp:TreeView />`	Renders a tree view based on hierarchical data.
`<asp:Menu />`	Renders a menu. This control can be used with a site map to manage navigation across the site.

Forms and Postbacks

ASP.NET web pages work using a page architecture that posts back HTML form data. A page is initially retrieved by a browser using an HTTP GET request (executing the web page once on the web server). Once the HTML page is returned to the browser, the user may submit the contents of the form (for example, by clicking an input button), which causes an HTTP POST request to the same page. This is commonly referred to as a **postback**. Data entered on the form is available server side. For example, a user may input user credentials and submit this data via a form, which can then be examined server side. If you need to interact with an ASP.NET control in the code-behind, you must place the ASP.NET control within the form. Checking whether a page is currently in a postback cycle can be easily examined by checking the value of the IsPostBack property of the Page object.

State Management

The HTTP protocol is a stateless protocol. This means that once a response is returned for a web page, none of the information submitted (state) is kept in memory on the web server. This is contrary to thicker client Windows applications, where you normally store application state in memory (on the client). The fact that HTTP is a stateless protocol helps web servers scale to large numbers of requests, because memory is not used up by unnecessary state. It does mean, however, that web developers have to apply strategies for managing state in web applications, because a truly stateless application would be useless.

ASP.NET provides several mechanisms for maintaining state from page request to page request. Table 5-2 lists the most commonly used methods for maintaining state.

Table 5-2. *ASP.NET Common Mechanisms for Maintaining State*

State Method	Description
ViewState	Serializes object state for a page into a hidden input element on the request form.
QueryString	Places text-based state into a page URL's query string.
Session	Stores object state into a Session collection on the web server that is either stored in memory or persisted to a database. Session state is stored per user session.
Profile	Stores object state into a Profile object persisted to a store configured by the ProfileProvider. Profile state is stored per user and persists beyond the user ending the session.
Cache	Stores objects based on a cache key in memory on the web server. The contents of the cache is accessible to all users, but is not maintained across web servers in a farm.
Cookie	Stores state on the user's browser, as long as the user has cookies enabled.

Each method of storing state has strengths and weaknesses and should be applied for different purposes. You should consider which methods of storing state to use before diving into writing code for a web page, based on how the page is used and by whom; for example, a page may be read-only or it may post back a lot of form information to the web server. You should not assume the same method for managing state best suits all the pages in your web application. It should also be recognized that all the state methods provided by ASP.NET are very generic, so you may opt to maintain all the data in a database instead. Following are examples of when to use these state methods:

- Use `Cache` when lots of different users would make exactly the same call to a database; the cost of the call is expensive, and the data in the database rarely changes.

- Use `Profile` when you are storing user preferences state that you want to persist between browser sessions.

- Use `Cookies` to store state that is not business critical if it is lost. A good example of this is remembering a logged-in user returning to web site, meaning that user does not need to log in again.

- Use `QueryString` when the data is something you want to be able to navigate to via a URL.

- Use `ViewState` on a data input form where there are postbacks to a server and you need to maintain the data that was entered before the page was submitted.

- Use `Session` to stored browser session state that will be lost once the browser is closed. Use `Session` when nothing else better fits.

IS VIEWSTATE THE WORK OF THE DEVIL?

Of all the state management tools in the ASP.NET box, `ViewState` is without a doubt the most abused, probably because it hides a multitude of web developer sins. The reason it is abused is because it is so easy to use and so helpful; just take an object from your code-behind, throw it into `ViewState`, and when you next post back the page, it is still there!

Nothing in life is free, and many web developers fail to look at the cost of `ViewState`, which is page bloat. The size of the data stored in the hidden input element created by `ViewState` grows as each object is saved in `ViewState`, which can add tens of kilobytes onto the page size.

Use of `ViewState` with ADO.NET Data Services clients is limited anyhow, because the generated types are not marked as `Serializable`, meaning that you cannot stored them in `ViewState` or `Session`.

`ViewState` is not evil; it is very useful. However, like all power, you must learn to use it carefully and considerately.

The Page Life Cycle

When an ASP.NET page is executed on a web server, the `Page` object runs through a page life cycle, where code is executed server side. Custom code that we write in a web page's code-behind is executed using event handlers during the page life cycle. Table 5-3 lists the main events that occur during a page life cycle (in order), and what you can use the events for.

Table 5-3. *ASP.NET Page Events Fired During the Page Life Cycle*

Event	Purpose
PreInit	Fires before the control tree is created. Used to change themes or master pages dynamically.
Init	Fires after the control tree is instantiated. At this point the controls are created but not fully set up.
InitComplete	Fires after the control tree has been completely created.
PreLoad	Fires before the load event and is the last point at which the page is accessed before loading ViewState.
Load	Fires after ViewState is loaded. Used to set properties on controls and bind data.
LoadComplete	Fires after all control events have fired (control events are not listed here).
PreRender	Fires before control HTML is rendered. Can be used to make final changes to controls before they are rendered.
Unload	Fires after all controls have been rendered. Can be used to perform any cleanup code.

Table 5-3 does not list events fired by each control in the control tree. Control events fire between Load and LoadComplete.

Data Binding

Data binding is the ability to take data returned from a database, API, or service (such as a data service) and render the data into some UI markup without the need to write lengthy code. Data binding support in ASP.NET controls comes in two parts: controls that expose properties that you can bind data to and controls that support collections of data to repeat markup for each item in any collection that implements IEnumerable.

Data binding against properties on an ASP.NET control is handled in markup using a binding expression. A binding expression syntax is <%# *Expression* %>, where the contents of this complete expression are replaced by the data contained in the expression.

All ASP.NET controls that can be bound to a collection of data inherit from DataBoundControl. Such example controls include the GridView control, the ListView control, and the DataList control. Controls that inherit from the DataBoundControl provide two different ways of binding a collection of data to the control: either programmatically or using ASP.NET markup.

To implement data binding using ASP.NET markup, the DataBoundControl exposes a property named DataSourceID, which should be set in markup to point to a control that inherits from DataSourceControl. Data source controls are nonvisual controls used to retrieve data from the underlying data source in ASP.NET markup. Example data source controls include the ObjectDataSource and the SqlDataSource.

The second method of implementing data binding using a DataBoundControl is to execute data binding programmatically. To achieve this, the DataBoundControl exposes a DataSource property and a DataBind method. The DataSource property is set to be the data returned from an API or service, and the DataBind method binds the data to the control.

WHICH DATA BINDING METHOD IS BEST?

The data source control model for data binding was introduced in ASP.NET 2.0, and when it first appeared, many thought that it superseded the older method of implementing data binding. However, many web developers hit the limitations of the data source control approach, and criticized the new model. The reality is that both models have strengths and weaknesses.

Using the data source control model gives clear separation of concerns between the view (the data bound control) and the data source. It also provides a reduced amount of code in the code-behind, and in simple scenarios, it can mean zero code. Additionally, developers get helpful design-time support for data source controls, making it easy to access data via a data source control.

While using data source controls provides some benefits over programmatically handling data binding, it does limit your control over the data binding mechanics. Typically, data source controls always rebind data regardless of whether the page is being retrieved for the first time or posted back. By applying data binding in code, you gain more control over when and how often your controls rebind data. This is particularly important on pages that post back to the server a lot, such as pages that require a lot of input fields.

Data bound controls also provide the ability to template the markup produced for each item in collection. Templating is a key concept of data bound controls, because it enables a developer to control exactly what contents to render for each item being displayed by a control. Controls such as the GridView provide the ability to create templates not only for read-only data, but also for editing data.

Partial Postbacks with the Update Panel

Every web form postback requires a server round-trip. Traditionally, this means refreshing the entire page when the response is received. The UpdatePanel control solves the problem of postback page flicker by executing an AJAX-style XMLHTTP request on the browser, submitting the form contents in what is known as a **partial postback**. ASP.NET is able to understand that the postback is partial by examining a special HTTP header on the form post. Server side, the ASP.NET page executes a full-page life cycle as normal, but the page only renders the HTML fragment needed by the partial postback. Once the response is received client side by XMLHTTP, the HTML DOM is manipulated automatically, swapping out the HTML fragment. The UpdatePanel control requires the creation of the ScriptManager control, discussed in more detail in the section "The ASP.NET AJAX Client-Side Model" later in this chapter.

HANDLE THE UPDATE PANEL WITH CARE

Update panels provide a quick-and-easy way to "AJAXify" server-side pages, but their cost should be properly understood before applying them. This cost is the need to execute a full server-side page life cycle on every page postback within the update panel.

The true problem of update panels is that they can hide a multitude of sins; it is all too easy to quick fix a usability issue caused by excessive post backs by simply wrapping an update panel around the offending markup. Indeed, it is not uncommon for lazy developers to just wrap an entire page in an update panel. But really, this is not solving the problem at all; it is merely hiding it.

The best way to treat update panels is to apply them to a server-side page after the fact. Forget about them right until you have developed a server-side page that you would be happy with releasing without update panels. Applying them at this point makes them a welcome free lunch. Also, be sure to apply update panels to the smallest possible region of markup on the page, because this greatly affects how big the size of the HTTP request is in partial postback scenarios.

Putting It All Together

Figure 5-1 shows a diagram that illustrates how an ASP.NET web page executes with a page life cycle using postbacks, and binding data.

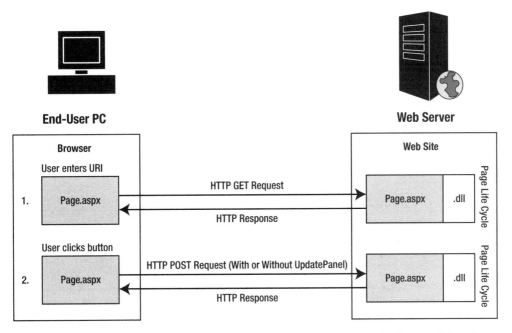

Figure 5-1. *ASP.NET server-side model executing code on the web server in the page life cycle*

Using ADO.NET Data Services with ASP.NET Server Side

In order for an ASP.NET web page to call a data service server side, ADO.NET Data Services proxy code needs to be executed from the code-behind in C#. Using the ASP.NET server-side model, the code-behind acts as a client to the data service. When the proxy calls the service from the web server, it will create an HTTP request message to the data service using the relevant URI. This model is shown in Figure 5-2.

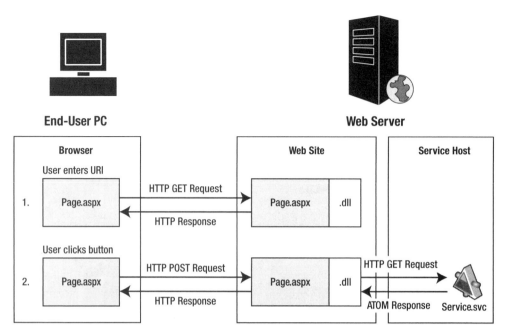

Figure 5-2. *Calling a data service from the ASP.NET server side*

It is possible to use the WebClient and WebRequest classes under the System.Net namespace to create HTTP requests against ADO.NET Data Services, but this method is a little crude and provides no specific support for ADO.NET Data Services features. ADO.NET Data Services provides a command-line tool called DataSvcUtil, which you can use to automatically generate a client library specifically tailored to your data service. This client library uses the System.Data.Services.Client assembly, which forms the backbone of the ADO.NET Data Services client stack.

To use the DataSvcUtil tool, open a Visual Studio 2008 command prompt and point the tool at your data service. For example, the command DataSvcUtil /out:Client.cs /uri: http://localhost/data.svc will point the tool at the given URI and generate a C# client library in a file named Client.cs for use by your ASP.NET web application.

■**Note** Visual Studio 2008 also supports the generation of client-side code using the Add Service Reference feature. This provides a more user-friendly way of generating client proxies without leaving the IDE.

Clients generated using DataSvcUtil provide many benefits over using the basic WebClient and WebRequest classes. The first and most obvious benefit is that data service clients generate client code to represent the entity sets exposed by your data service. Because they are aware of the entities used by your service, data service clients can construct URI queries to make HTTP requests with. This is extremely powerful because it means the client developer does not need to understand the syntax of ADO.NET Data Services queries. Moreover, the way the data service client is designed means that querying these entities is executed using LINQ, providing a strongly typed queryable API with IntelliSense support familiar to all developers.

Data service clients make calls under the covers using WebClient and WebRequest classes. They handle the construction of the correct URI and make HTTP requests asynchronously, ensuring that the client does not block threads unnecessarily. If the HTTP request causes the data service to throw an exception, the service will respond with the appropriate HTTP error number, and the client will throw a DataServiceException, which can then be handled in code.

EXERCISE 5-1: CONSUMING A DATA SERVICE USING ASP.NET SERVER CONTROLS

In this exercise, you will create a web page using ASP.NET that consumes a customer service built using ADO.NET Data Services. The starting point for this exercise can be downloaded from the Apress web site (http://www. apress.com/book/sourcecode); you'll find it under Exercise51Start. This solution is a refactored version of the customer service solution built in Chapter 4. The refactored service has been simplified; the architecture has been flattened, the SOAP endpoint removed, and the LINQ to SQL data layer swapped out for an ADO.NET Entity Framework data layer. The reason for these changes is to make the development of the client web pages clearer, and also to demonstrate a more fleshed out entity model for the client to consume. The Entity Framework data layer consumes a prebuilt customer SQL Server database contained in the App_Data folder of the web site. You will build on this solution throughout the exercises in the remainder of this chapter.

1. Open the starting customer service solution in Visual Studio. Navigate to the service implementation project, which contains the service implementation for the data service, including the Entity Data Model it consumes. Open the CustomerModel.edmx file to view the entity relationships exposed by the ADO.NET Entity Framework. These entities are shown in Figure 5-3.

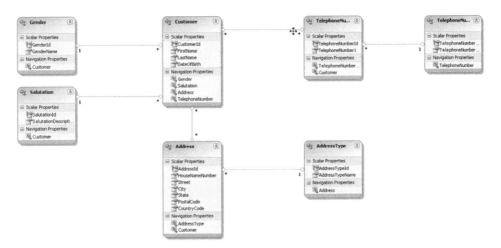

Figure 5-3. *Entity model for customer service*

2. Note the relationships between the `Customer` entity and the other entities: There is a one-to-many relationship between the `Gender` and `Customer` entities and a one-to-many relationship between the `Salutation` and `Customer` entities. There is a many-to-many relationship between the `Customer` and the `Address` entities, and likewise between the `Customer` and `TelephoneNumber` entities. For the many-to-many relationships, the conceptual model (shown in Figure 5-3) differs from the relational database model, where many-to-many relationships are normalized over several database tables. To view how the conceptual model is mapped to the data model, use the Model Browser and the Mapping Details windows.

3. Open the web site `web.config` file and locate the `<connectionStrings/>` configuration section of the file. Change the file path in the connection string to ensure that the web site is pointing to the location of the customer database located in the `App_Data` folder of the web site.

4. Right-click the `CustomerDataService.svc` host file in the web site, and select View In Browser to view the root URI of the data service. Copy this URI to the clipboard for the next step in this exercise. Try to query the service, retrieving all customers whose last name contains the text "smi" by appending `Customers?$filter=substringof('smi', LastName)` to the end of the address. The browser will respond by displaying an Atom feed of customers whose last name contains the letters "smi." This tests that the service is working correctly. Note the web site port number as you may need to change the URI code in step 9 to reflect this.

5. Right-click the `Client` folder and choose Add ➤ New Website. Select the ASP.NET Web Site template and change the folder location to point to a folder within the root of the solution folder named `Apress.Data.Services.CustomerService.ClientWeb`. This web site is separate from the data service host web site, because you are going to call the service as if it were remote from the client. This is a common scenario, but the additional reason why it makes sense for making server-side calls to data services is that you would not call into a local service server side; instead you would more likely make a direct call into the entities created using the ADO.NET Entity Framework.

6. On the newly created client web site, right-click the root of the project and select Add Service Reference. Paste the service root URI from step 4 into the dialog box and click Go. After a few seconds, Visual Studio should show the data service endpoint named `CustomerEntities` in the dialog box. Change the namespace to be `CustomerModel` and click OK. This will add the service reference to the web site under the `App_WebReferences` folder. Set the client web site as the startup project for the solution.

7. Open the `Default.aspx` web page created when the new web site was created. You are going to use this page to create a form that will search for customers by last name. Add an HTML heading element, a `TextBox` control, a `Button` control, and `GridView` control to the form as shown in the following listing:

```
<%@ Page Language="C#" AutoEventWireup="true" CodeFile="Default.aspx.cs"
Inherits="_Default" %>

<!DOCTYPE html PUBLIC "-//W3C//DTD XHTML 1.0 Transitional//EN"
 "http://www.w3.org/TR/xhtml1/DTD/xhtml1-transitional.dtd">

<html xmlns="http://www.w3.org/1999/xhtml">
<head runat="server">
    <title></title>
</head>
<body>
    <form id="form1" runat="server">
```

```
    <div>
        <h1>Search for customers by lastname</h1>
        <asp:TextBox ID="LastNameTextBox" runat="server"></asp:TextBox>
        <asp:Button ID="SearchButton" runat="server" Text="Go" />
        <asp:GridView ID="CustomersGridView" runat="server">
        </asp:GridView>
    </div>
    </form>
</body>
</html>
```

8. The text box will be used to enter search text, and when the user clicks the Go button, the search will be executed server side by calling the remote data service. To enable this, an event handler needs to be added to the `Button` control's `Click` event, where you will execute the search. Switch the page to design view, select the `Button` control, and switch the Properties window view to show events (if the Properties window is not shown, you can add it to the designer by navigating to the View menu and selecting Properties Window). Select the `Click` event in the Properties window and double-click the event to generate a click event handler in the page's code-behind class (the `Button`'s markup will also be changed to tie the markup to the event handler).

9. With the code bind class open, add a `using` statement to the top of the class for the `CustomerModel` and `System.Data.Services.Client` namespaces. Add a private variable to expose the customer entities from the data service, and a public read-only property to expose the `Customers` as a `List<Customer>` collection. Navigate to the click event handler and add a call to a method you will create called `BindData`. This method will contain the code to bind the data to `GridView` control using the `Customers` property to retrieve the collection of customers. Implement the `Customers` property by executing some LINQ code that will perform a search of customer entities where the text entered in the text box is contained in the customer's `lastname` property. Note that the LINQ query used in the sample code uses the `Expand` method to return the child `Salutation` and `Gender` properties. These are not returned by default because they are not POCO properties, and you will use their data later in this exercise. The completed code for the entire page is shown in the following listing:

```
using System;
using System.Collections.Generic;
using System.Linq;
using System.Web;
using System.Web.UI;
using System.Web.UI.WebControls;
using System.Data.Services.Client;
using CustomerModel;

public partial class _Default : System.Web.UI.Page
{
    // The following line of code points the data services proxy
    // to the root data service URI.
    // You may need to change the URI port number (1478)
    // to the port your data service is running on.
```

```csharp
    private CustomerEntities entities = new CustomerEntities(new Uri("http://
localhost:1478/Apress.Data.Services.CustomerService.Host/CustomerDataService.
svc"));
    private List<Customer> customers;

    protected void Page_Load(object sender, EventArgs e)
    {

    }

    protected void SearchButton_Click(object sender, EventArgs e)
    {
        BindData();
    }

    private void BindData()
    {
        // set the data source to the customers property
        // and bind the grid view to it
        CustomersGridView.DataSource = Customers;
        CustomersGridView.DataBind();
    }

    public List<Customer> Customers
    {
        get
        {
            // only populate this property from the data service once
            // in the life cycle of the page
            if (customers != null)
            {
                return customers;
            }

            if (!string.IsNullOrEmpty(LastNameTextBox.Text))
            {
                // retrieve the collection of customers complete with
                // Gender and Salutation reference properties populated
                customers = (from c in entities.Customers.Expand("Gender")
                                        .Expand("Salutation")
                                        where c.LastName
                                        .Contains(LastNameTextBox.Text)
                                        select c).ToList();
            }
```

```
            return customers;
        }
    }
}
```

10. Check the web site builds and view the Default.aspx page in the browser. Enter some text (for example, **smi**) in the text box, and click the Go button. The browser will perform a postback, executing the click event handler and binding the results to the GridView control. Figure 5-4 shows the results as displayed in the web browser.

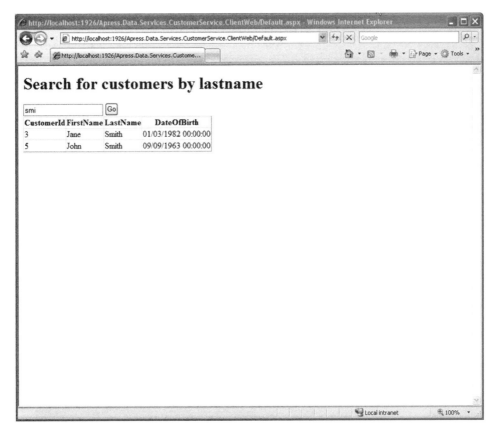

Figure 5-4. *Results from executing a customer search by last name*

11. Having gotten the search working, you are now going to focus on changing the markup on the GridView control to improve presentation, and also enable editing of returned results. Close the browser and open the Default.aspx page in design view. Select the GridView control and click the > arrow in the top-right corner to expand the tasks pane. Click the Edit Columns link to bring up the Fields dialog box. Uncheck the Auto Generated Fields box and add five BoundField columns, making the header text on each field Salutation, First Name, Last Name, Date Of Birth, and Gender, respectively. Set each DataField property to be Salutation.SalutationDescription, FirstName, LastName, DateOfBirth, and Gender. GenderName, respectively. Set the DataFormatString property of the DateOfBirth field to be {0:d}, representing a short date format.

12. Because you have removed the `CustomerId` column, you need to track the key in the `GridView` so that the key is known when that `GridView` performs a postback. To do this, select the `GridView` and navigate to the `DataKeyNames` property in the Properties window. Enter the text **CustomerId** to track the `CustomerId` property through postbacks.

13. Now you are going to enable editing in the `GridView` control. Switch back into design view in the `Default.aspx` page and again edit the columns from the task pane. Select each column in turn and click the "Convert this field into a TemplateField" link. This will turn each simple `BoundField` column into a `TemplateField` column, where you have much more control over formatting of the markup. In the `GridView` task pane, click the Edit Templates link to switch the designer view into template mode.

14. Within the ASP.NET markup, ensure the ID attributes of the `TextBox` controls used to edit the first name and last name are set to `FirstNameTextBox` and `LastNameTextBox`, respectively. You need to do this so that the controls can be identified in code later using meaningful names.

15. Once in template design view, select the `EditItemTemplate` for the `Date Of Birth` column from the Display drop-down. Delete the default `TextBox` control and add a `Calendar` from the toolbox pane. Change the ID of the control to be `DateOfBirthCalendar` in the Properties window. Select Edit DataBindings from the `Calendar` control's task pane and set the `SelectedDate` and `VisibleDate` property data binding expressions to be `Bind('DateOfBirth')`.

16. Select the `EditItemTemplate` for the `Salutation` and `Gender` columns. Delete the `TextBox` control and add a `Label` control. Again, edit the data bindings for this control, binding the `Text` property to a binding expression of `Eval("Salutation.SalutationDescription")` and `Eval("Gender.GenderName")`.

17. End template editing and set the `AutoGenerateEditButton` property to `true` from the Properties window. This adds an Edit button to each row on the `GridView` control.

18. Add a new `Label` control to the markup. Name this control `ErrorLabel` and delete the default text in the `Text` property. Set the `EnableViewState` property of this control to `false`. You will use this label in code to write out the contents on an exception from the data service when an update fails. You disable view state because you don't want the text of this label to persist from one postback to the next.

19. Use the events view of the Properties window to create event handlers on the `GridView` for `RowEditing`, `RowUpdating`, and `RowCancellingEdit` events. These control event handlers are needed to place code to handle what happens when the Edit button is clicked on a row, and then what happens when the Update and Cancel button are clicked once in edit mode. You need to write code for these handlers because you are handling your data binding in code rather than using a data source control.

20. Append the event handlers created in the previous point to handle making updates to the data service via the service reference. Change the event handlers to include the code listed here:

```
protected void CustomersGridView_RowEditing(object sender,
    GridViewEditEventArgs e)
{
    CustomersGridView.EditIndex = e.NewEditIndex;
    BindData();
}
```

```
protected void CustomersGridView_RowUpdating(object sender,
    GridViewUpdateEventArgs e)
{
    // get a reference to the edited row in the grid view
    GridViewRow row = CustomersGridView.Rows[CustomersGridView.EditIndex];

    if (row != null && row.RowType == DataControlRowType.DataRow)
    {
        // get the customerId for the edited row
        // out of the data keys collection
        int customerId = int.Parse(CustomersGridView
            .DataKeys[row.DataItemIndex].Value.ToString());

        // obtain references to edit template controls using find control
        TextBox firstNameTextBox = row
            .FindControl("FirstNameTextBox") as TextBox;
        TextBox lastNameTextBox = row
            .FindControl("LastNameTextBox") as TextBox;
        Calendar dateOfBirthCalendar = row
            .FindControl("DateOfBirthCalendar") as Calendar;

        if (firstNameTextBox != null && lastNameTextBox != null &&
            dateOfBirthCalendar != null)
        {
            // get the customer record being edited
            // from the data service by its customer id
            Customer customer = (from c in entities.Customers
                .Expand("Gender").Expand("Salutation")
                            where c.CustomerId == customerId
                            select c).FirstOrDefault();

            // update the properties locally using tracked changes
            customer.FirstName = firstNameTextBox.Text;
            customer.LastName = lastNameTextBox.Text;
            customer.DateOfBirth = dateOfBirthCalendar.SelectedDate;

            entities.UpdateObject(customer);

            try
            {
                // save the tracked changes back to the data service
                DataServiceResponse response = entities.SaveChanges();

                // switch the grid view out of edit mode
                // and rebind the data.
                CustomersGridView.EditIndex = -1;
                BindData();
```

```
                }
                catch (DataServiceRequestException ex)
                {
                    ErrorLabel.Text = string
                    .Format("Updating record failed with the following error {0}",
                    ex.Message);
                }
            }
        }
    }

    protected void CustomersGridView_RowCancelingEdit(object sender,
GridViewCancelEditEventArgs e)
    {
        CustomersGridView.EditIndex = -1;
        BindData();
    }
```

Take special note of the Updating event handler. The handler uses the GridView's event arguments passed into the event to obtain a reference to the row being edited. It uses the control's DataItemIndex property to retrieve the correct CustomerId from the DataKeys array. It uses the FindControl method (standard to all ASP.NET controls) to return a reference to the templated controls used to edit the data. A call to the data service is made to return the original customer entity that is being edited including its child Salutation and Gender entities. This is needed because the web page is stateless, and on postback the original call to the service is lost. Once the properties of the customer object are set to the edited data, the UpdateObject method is called to ensure that changes are tracked by the data service client. Finally, the SaveChanges method is called inside a try...catch block, so that a DataServiceRequestException can be caught if the update fails. The exception handler here writes the exception text to the ErrorLabel so that the user knows what the error is.

21. With the majority of the code now written, you can test that the application works and that updates are handled correctly by the service. You can debug the service while running the client by attaching the debugger to the web server that is running the service host while viewing the web site in the browser. This enables you to step through the business logic code that is contained in the change interceptor, called when inserts or updates are made to customer entities.

22. Assuming the application works, one final tweak to the user interface is to hide page flicker from the user by wrapping the main content that performs postbacks in an update panel. To do this, first add a ScriptManager control to the top of the form, setting its ID to ScriptManager. Cut all the original form content from the SearchTextBox control to the ErrorLabel control and paste it inside an UpdateDate panel control containing a ContentTemplate element. The final markup for the web page is shown here:

```
<%@ Page Language="C#" AutoEventWireup="true"  CodeFile="Default.aspx.cs"
Inherits="_Default" %>

<!DOCTYPE html PUBLIC "-//W3C//DTD XHTML 1.0 Transitional//EN"
"http://www.w3.org/TR/xhtml1/DTD/xhtml1-transitional.dtd">
```

```
<html xmlns="http://www.w3.org/1999/xhtml">
<head runat="server">
    <title></title>
</head>
<body>
    <form id="form1" runat="server">
    <div>
        <h1>Search for customers by lastname</h1>
        <asp:ScriptManager runat="server" ID="ScriptManager" />
        <asp:UpdatePanel runat="server" ID="CustomersUpdatePanel">
            <ContentTemplate>
                <asp:TextBox ID="LastNameTextBox" runat="server"></asp:TextBox>
                <asp:Button ID="SearchButton" runat="server" Text="Go"
                    onclick="SearchButton_Click" />
                <asp:GridView ID="CustomersGridView" runat="server"
                    AutoGenerateColumns="False"
                    AutoGenerateEditButton="True"
                    onrowcancelingedit="CustomersGridView_RowCancelingEdit"
                    onrowediting="CustomersGridView_RowEditing"
                    onrowupdating="CustomersGridView_RowUpdating"
                    DataKeyNames="CustomerId">
                    <Columns>
                        <asp:TemplateField HeaderText="Salutation">
                            <EditItemTemplate>
                                <asp:Label ID="Label6" runat="server"
                    Text='<%# Eval("Salutation.SalutationDescription") %>'>
                                </asp:Label>
                            </EditItemTemplate>
                            <ItemTemplate>
                                <asp:Label ID="Label1" runat="server"
                    Text='<%# Eval("Salutation.SalutationDescription") %>'>
                                </asp:Label>
                            </ItemTemplate>
                        </asp:TemplateField>
                        <asp:TemplateField HeaderText="First Name">
                            <EditItemTemplate>
                                <asp:TextBox ID="FirstNameTextBox"
runat="server" Text='<%# Bind("FirstName") %>'></asp:TextBox>
                            </EditItemTemplate>
                            <ItemTemplate>
                                <asp:Label ID="Label2" runat="server"
Text='<%# Bind("FirstName") %>'></asp:Label>
                            </ItemTemplate>
                        </asp:TemplateField>
```

```
                            <asp:TemplateField HeaderText="Last Name">
                                <EditItemTemplate>
                                    <asp:TextBox ID="LastNameTextBox"
    runat="server" Text='<%# Bind("LastName") %>'></asp:TextBox>
                                </EditItemTemplate>
                                <ItemTemplate>
                                    <asp:Label ID="Label3" runat="server"
    Text='<%# Bind("LastName") %>'></asp:Label>
                                </ItemTemplate>
                            </asp:TemplateField>
                            <asp:TemplateField HeaderText="Date Of Birth">
                                <EditItemTemplate>
                                    <asp:Calendar ID="DateOfBirthCalendar"
    runat="server" SelectedDate="<%# Bind('DateOfBirth') %>"
                                        VisibleDate="<%# Bind('DateOfBirth') %>">
                                    </asp:Calendar>
                                </EditItemTemplate>
                                <ItemTemplate>
                                    <asp:Label ID="Label4" runat="server"
                                        Text='<%# Bind("DateOfBirth", "{0:d}") %>'>
                                    </asp:Label>
                                </ItemTemplate>
                            </asp:TemplateField>
                            <asp:TemplateField HeaderText="Gender">
                                <EditItemTemplate>
                                    <asp:Label ID="Label7" runat="server"
    Text='<%# Eval("Gender.GenderName") %>'></asp:Label>
                                </EditItemTemplate>
                                <ItemTemplate>
                                    <asp:Label ID="Label5" runat="server"
    Text='<%# Eval("Gender.GenderName") %>'></asp:Label>
                                </ItemTemplate>
                            </asp:TemplateField>
                        </Columns>
                    </asp:GridView>
                    <br />
                    <asp:Label ID="ErrorLabel" runat="server"
    EnableViewState="false"></asp:Label>
                </ContentTemplate>
            </asp:UpdatePanel>
        </div>
        </form>
    </body>
    </html>
```

Through this exercise, you have created a web page that consumes a data service server side to perform read and update operations on the underlying data store. The page uses control events to handle edits to the data and an update panel to perform partial postbacks.

ASP.NET Security

ASP.NET provides security mechanisms for authentication and authorization. Authentication is the process of identifying who a user is, and authorization is the process of defining what a user can do. ADO.NET Data Services relies on ASP.NET authentication and authorization in both the client and the service.

Authentication

Authentication is the process of identifying who a user is. There are three possible mechanisms for authenticating users in ASP.NET web sites: Windows authentication, Forms authentication, and Passport authentication.

Windows authentication uses the credentials of the logged-in Windows account to authenticate a user. The credentials are handed to the web server by the user's browser if the browser is running the same domain as the web server. This enables certain integrated security scenarios, such as using the end user's account as a login against SQL Server, enabling all users to be fully audited against server resources. Windows authentication is the authentication method of choice in scenarios where the end user is identified, trusted, and part of a Windows domain. Such scenarios include intranets, and the benefits to the end user are a seamless authentication experience based singularly around their Windows login.

In Internet-facing web sites, it is impossible to safely identify the end user, and thus if authentication is needed, it must occur using a different mechanism from Windows authentication. There are two mechanisms to authenticate users on Internet-facing web sites: Forms authentication and Passport authentication.

Forms authentication is the most common mechanism to authenticate users on Internet-facing sites. It requires a user to log on to a web site via a web form and authenticate against a custom membership store. Such login pages require a user to enter his username and password credentials (normally handled using a Login control), which are then authenticated server side by ASP.NET. Once authenticated, ASP.NET returns a temporary cookie to the end user's browser, identifying the user for further requests made during the user's session.

During Forms authentication, the browser must authenticate a user against a membership store of known user accounts. This is achieved in ASP.NET by configuring a membership provider, accessible via the Membership API. The membership provider follows the ASP.NET provider pattern used for various configurable data stores. The pattern enables the developer to choose a pluggable provider to use for authentication. Out of the box, ASP.NET comes with a SqlMembershipProvider and an ActiveDirectoryMembershipProvider for storing user credentials in SQL Server or Active Directory. It is also possible to write your own membership provider should neither of these options suffice, or download one of the many freely available samples from the Internet.

The final mechanism that ASP.NET supports for authenticating users is Passport authentication, where the user is identified by their Windows Live ID account (formerly known as a .NET Passport). In this scenario, the entire membership store is handled externally to your web site by Windows Live, including the login page used to authenticate the user.

Authorization

Authorization is the process of checking whether the authenticated user is allowed to execute the requested operation. In ASP.NET, authorization is defined in the web site's configuration using a role-based security model. Roles enable you to specify actions that a user can fulfill, and then assign individual user accounts to one or more roles.

Similar to the `MembershipProvider`, ASP.NET also uses the provider pattern to store role-based data within the `RoleProvider`, accessible via the `Roles` API. ASP.NET provides a `SqlRoleProvider` implementation, where role-based data is stored in SQL Server, but again it is possible to write your own implementation if you do not want to store role-based data in SQL Server.

Authentication and Authorization in ADO.NET Data Services

ADO.NET Data Services utilize the ASP.NET service compatibility feature of WCF, which enables all the ASP.NET security features to be usable from within ADO.NET Data Services. Using the `Membership` and `Roles` APIs within query and change interceptors in a data service, you can use the same authentication and authorization semantics within your service as you would use within the rest of your web application.

The ASP.NET AJAX Client-Side Model

Using the server-side model in ASP.NET to make calls to ADO.NET Data Services through generated clients provides an easy-to-use method for calling data services, which supports server-centric web applications and remotely hosted web services. But for new web application developments designed with data services in mind, this is unlikely to be the most popular architecture for web application developers.

As mentioned at the beginning of this chapter, there will always be a need to execute logic server side in a web application that stores data in a database, because the database is a shared central data store that requires code to be executed against it. When you think about this statement with data services in mind, it becomes clear that there is little need for ASP.NET to execute server-side logic in addition to what a hosted data service will execute server side.

The advent of rich AJAX support within ASP.NET and Visual Studio provides web developers with an alternative architectural approach to developing web applications. This approach is much more client centric, relying heavily on the browser's capabilities to execute logic in JavaScript and make requests to services such as ADO.NET data services directly from the browser using XMLHTTP.

The backbone of ASP.NET AJAX support is a feature-rich JavaScript library called the Microsoft AJAX Library. This library is the core client-side framework used by ASP.NET web pages. The framework layers the following important features to standard JavaScript:

- A pseudo object-oriented model for JavaScript, including inheritance and namespaces to promote code reuse and organization

- An object creation and disposal system based around prototypes that provides a memory-efficient way to construct objects with event handlers on the browser

- A framework for creating client-side controls and behaviors to create richer user experiences in a maintainable fashion

- A browser-compatibility layer that abstracts the differences between modern browsers for common requirements

- A common method for making XMLHTTP requests to services such as ADO.NET Data Services

- An API for simplifying common JavaScript code issues, such as browser history

The Microsoft AJAX library supports modern versions of Internet Explorer, Firefox, and Safari across Windows XP SP2, Windows Vista, and Apple OSX (see Table 5-4).

Table 5-4. *Browsers Supported by the Microsoft AJAX Library*

Supported Browser
Microsoft Internet Explorer 6.0 and later
Mozilla Firefox 1.5 and later
Opera 9.0 and later
Apple Safari 2.0 and later

Common AJAX Library Namespaces

The Microsoft AJAX Library contains a rich client-side framework for working in JavaScript with the browser and the HTML DOM. Table 5-5 lists some of the most important classes in the framework and explains their purpose.

Table 5-5. *Common Microsoft AJAX Library Classes*

Class	Purpose
`Sys.Application`	Creates client-side controls and behaviors and manages their events
`Sys.StringBuilder`	Builds up a string by appending variables to the object
`Sys.Debug`	Provides client-side debugging information
`Sys.Component`	Represents the base class for `Control` and `Behavior` classes
`Sys.Net.WebRequest`	Encapsulates the call to make an XMLHTTP request
`Sys.Serialization.JavaScriptSerializer`	Serializes and deserializes JavaScript to JSON
`Sys.Services.AuthenticationService`	Provides AJAX support for Forms authentication
`Sys.Services.ProfileService`	Provides AJAX support for ASP.NET `Profile`
`Sys.UI.Behavior`	Creates a component that attaches behavior to an HTML element
`Sys.UI.Control`	Creates a control that encapsulates rendering HTML
`Sys.UI.DomElement`	Provides static methods to manipulate the HTML DOM

Working with the Microsoft AJAX library in JavaScript is straightforward. The library uses a default entry point for your code to run in a function called `pageLoad()`, which is similar in concept to the page load event in the ASP.NET server-side page life cycle. Objects are created using the namespaces listed previously.

The AJAX library also includes shortcuts to commonly used JavaScript methods. For example, $get is used as a shortcut to the getElementById() method. Another shortcut of note is $create, which is used to correctly instantiate objects that inherit Sys.Component. The $create function ensures that all event wiring is correctly created and disposed of once the component is finished with.

Introducing the Script Manager

ASP.NET provides a server-side control called the script manager. This is a nonvisual control that enables developers to wire up JavaScript libraries and service references to a web page using ASP.NET markup. The script manager is an important part of the ASP.NET client-side model, because it hides the complexities associated with loading scripts external to the page. Correct use of the script manager also ensures that downloaded scripts are cached by the browser, greatly improving the performance of your web application.

Listing 5-1 shows a web page with the script manager markup set to reference the ADO.NET Data Services script library.

Listing 5-1. *ASP.NET Script Manager Markup*

```
<asp:ScriptManager runat="server" ID="ScriptManager">
    <Scripts>
        <asp:ScriptReference Path="~/App_Scripts/DataService.debug.js" />
    </Scripts>
</asp:ScriptManager>
```

SCRIPT#

Script# is a project envisaged by Nikhil Kothari, freely available to download from http://projects.nikhilk.net/ScriptSharp/. The tool enables C# developers to write code using Visual Studio, but compile the code into JavaScript rather than MSIL. The main benefit of this approach is that developers gain all the normal benefits of a true object-oriented language like C#, and are therefore able to more productively produce JavaScript than if they were to manually write JavaScript. The JavaScript created is designed to work with ASP.NET AJAX, and the compiler produces both debug and release versions of the code, one with comments and whitespace and the other with the JavaScript stripped down to its smallest download size.

Script# proposes an interesting paradigm for web development, where JavaScript is considered to be the intermediate language of the browser. The tool is widely used by many web developers, and for complex AJAX applications it is a must to curtail the negative aspects of developing using JavaScript.

The Importance of Retail Mode

During development of AJAX solutions, debug script libraries are used to develop AJAX web pages so that the JavaScript is humanly readable. Debug versions of scripts are helpful during development because they enable developers to step through the code and diagnose problems. These debug scripts are therefore verbose, because they contain whitespace, which increases the file size downloaded by the browser. When in production, you should use the nondebug versions of script libraries, which have had all comments and whitespace removed. If you are developing your own script libraries, this is one benefit of developing your JavaScript using Script#.

In addition to using production versions of script libraries, you should also ensure that your production web servers are running using retail mode. **Retail mode** is a setting in the `machine.config` file (under the deployment element) that when set to `true` overrides various web config settings, such as tracing and debugging switches. More importantly for AJAX developers, it is the only way of ensuring that the JavaScript libraries used by your web application are cached by the browser. In other words, if you do not turn retail mode on in your production web servers, the JavaScript libraries used across multiple pages of your web site will be downloaded by every page request made to your web server. You have been warned!

Calling ADO.NET Data Services Using the Microsoft AJAX Library

Currently, the Microsoft AJAX library does not provide ADO.NET Data Services support out of the box with ASP.NET 3.5, but fear not, because support is available in the form of a JavaScript library freely available from CodePlex at `http://www.codeplex.com/aspnet/Release/ProjectReleases.aspx?ReleaseId=13357`. This client-side API lives under the `Sys.Data` namespace, enabling you to make AJAX calls to ADO.NET Data Services from within JavaScript. In order to make calls to ADO.NET Data Services, you must reference this script library using the script manager. The library works by wrapping the `Sys.Net.WebRequest` class, which handles calls to XMLHTTP for you in a cross-browser compatible fashion.

To call a data service, you need to instantiate a `Sys.Data.DataService` object that references the root URI of your service. Once created, you use this object to create queries against your data service using the `DataService.query` method.

The `query` method takes four arguments: The first is a string representing the suffix to the root URI of your service (this is your specific query). The second argument is a callback function that will be called on a successful response from your data service. The third argument is a callback function that will be called on an error response from your data service. The final optional argument is a user context object representing the user context state. Listing 5-2 shows an example of consuming a data service from JavaScript using the AJAX library (this code is used in Exercise 5-2 later in the chapter).

Listing 5-2. *Example Function in JavaScript Calling a Data Service*

```
function doSearch() {
    // get the element by id called SearchTextBox
    var searchTextBox = $get("SearchTextBox");

    var searchText = searchTextBox.value;

    if (searchText.length > 0) {
        // create a reference to the data service
        var svc = new Sys.Data.DataService("CustomerDataService.svc");
```

```
    // query the data service, returning customers whose last name contains the
search text, including gender and salutation reference properties in the results.
    svc.query(String.format("/Customers?$filter=substringof('{0}',LastName)&
$expand=Gender,Salutation", searchText), onsuccess, onfailure);
    }
    else {
        dataContainer.innerHTML = 'Please enter a lastname';
    }
}
```

The success callback function referenced by the DataService.query method consists of three arguments: the first is the result object, the second is the data service context, and the final argument is the service operation (this is a query string on the end of the URI). The result object contains the entities returned in the response from the data service request. The Sys.Data.DataService client library automatically sets the HTTP Accept header on the request to JSON, ensuring that the response is in JSON format native to JavaScript. This JSON object is the result object you are able to work with in the success callback. You can use the data contained in the result object in JavaScript to manipulate the HTML DOM and render data in markup (see Figure 5-5).

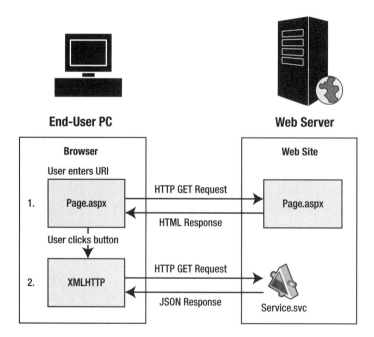

Figure 5-5. *ASP.NET AJAX client-side model using XMLHTTP*

Binding Data

The current version of the Microsoft AJAX library that comes out of box with ASP.NET 3.5 does not provide native support for data binding in the same vein that the server-side model does. This means that you need to manually write JavaScript code to render HTML elements into the DOM or rely on third-party solutions to the problem.

Fortunately, the ASP.NET team has provided a solution via an ASP.NET AJAX preview release available from CodePlex. At the time of writing the current version of the preview release is ASP.NET AJAX 4.0 Preview 2. This is likely to progress over the next 12 months, but you can get the latest information from the ASP.NET CodePlex site at `http://www.codeplex.com/aspnet`. While there are no guarantees on what features contained in this preview will make it into the next version of ASP.NET, it is likely that the data binding features demonstrated will evolve into native support over time.

Using this preview library, you are able to template HTML markup in a similar fashion to how you would treat server-side data bound controls. This creates much cleaner client-side JavaScript with a separation of concerns between markup and the data returned from the data service. Listing 5-3 shows the syntax of a template in HTML (this code is used in Exercise 5-2, which follows).

Listing 5-3. *Sample Template HTML*

```
<div id="DataTemplate" class="sys-template">
  <h3>Customer Id {{ CustomerId }}</h3>
  Name: <span>{{SalutationDescription + ' ' + FirstName + ' ' + LastName}}</span>
  <br />
  Date of Birth: <span>{{ DateOfBirth.format('MM/dd/yyyy') }}</span><br />
  Gender: <span>{{ GenderName }}</span><br />
</div>
```

This template HTML is used by the `Sys.UI.Template` class as a cookie cutter to generate HTML for each item in the collection. The key JavaScript to execute databinding against this template is shown in Listing 5-4 (this code is used in Exercise 5-2, which follows).

Listing 5-4. *JavaScript code to handle templating.*

```
// get the template element by id called DataTemplate using $get shortcut function
var template = new Sys.UI.Template($get("DataTemplate"));

...

// loop round search results, creating instances of the template in the
// data container element
for (var i = 0; i < result.length; i++) {
    template.createInstance(dataContainer,
    {
        CustomerId: result[i].CustomerId,
        FirstName: result[i].FirstName,
        LastName: result[i].LastName,
        GenderName: result[i].Gender.GenderName,
        SalutationDescription: result[i].Salutation.SalutationDescription,
        DateOfBirth: result[i].DateOfBirth
    });
```

EXERCISE 5-2: CONSUMING A DATA SERVICE USING ASP.NET AJAX

In this exercise, you will take the starting service used at the beginning of the previous exercise and employ the client-centric model in ASP.NET AJAX to consume a private data service. The page you will develop will enable you to call the data service to search for customers by their last name. You will call the service using the data service AJAX library and bind the JSON response to the HTML DOM in JavaScript, rendering HTML on the browser. The code for this exercise can be downloaded from the Apress web site (http://www.apress.com/book/sourcecode); you'll find it under exercise 5-2.

1. Open the starting solution in Visual Studio and check that it is running, much as you did at the beginning of Exercise 5-1.

2. Add a folder to the web site named App_Scripts. In this folder, place the scripts downloaded from CodePlex for both the data service library and the templates library (namely DataService.debug.js and MicrosoftAjaxTemplates.debug.js). Remember to include both the debug and release versions of these scripts in the folder.

3. Right-click the web site and select Add ➤ New Item from the menu. Choose Web Form from the templates list and name the page Default.aspx. Repeat the process, this time adding the Style Sheet template to the web site. Call the style sheet common.css.

4. Open the Default.aspx file. You will now add the core HTML markup to the page. Drag the common.css file into the header section on the HTML to create a link element pointing the page to the style sheet. Add a header element, two input elements (one text box and one button), and a div element. Add a ScriptManager server control to the page with two script references pointing to each of the two script libraries added to the App_Scripts folder. The resultant markup is as follows:

```
<%@ Page Language="C#" AutoEventWireup="true" CodeFile="Default.aspx.cs"
Inherits="_Default" %>

<!DOCTYPE html PUBLIC "-//W3C//DTD XHTML 1.0 Transitional//EN"
"http://www.w3.org/TR/xhtml1/DTD/xhtml1-transitional.dtd">

<html xmlns="http://www.w3.org/1999/xhtml">
<head runat="server">
    <title>Search customers by lastname</title>
    <link href="common.css" rel="stylesheet" type="text/css" />
</head>
<body>
    <form id="form1" runat="server">
    <h1>Search customers by lastname</h1>
    <div>
        <asp:ScriptManager runat="server" ID="ScriptManager">
            <Scripts>
                <asp:ScriptReference
Path="~/App_Scripts/DataService.debug.js" />
                <asp:ScriptReference
```

```
        Path="~/App_Scripts/MicrosoftAjaxTemplates.debug.js" />
                </Scripts>
            </asp:ScriptManager>
            <input id="SearchTextBox" type="text" />
            <input id="SearchButton" type="button" value="Go" />

            <div id="DataContainer">

            </div>
        </div>
        </form>
    </body>
    </html>
```

5. Now that you have created the core markup, you need to wire it up to the data service using JavaScript. On the button input element add an event handler to handle the `click` event, pointing the event to a JavaScript function called `onsearchclick()`. To do this, add the code `onclick="onsearchclick();"` to the input element. Below the end HTML element, create a script element, adding the `onsearchclick()` function. Point this function to another function named `doSearch()`. Add a `pageLoad` function, which will be called automatically by ASP.NET AJAX once the page has loaded. Create a variable here that gets a reference (using the `$get` function) to the div element named `DataContainer`. The JavaScript code so far should look as follows:

```
<script type="text/javascript">
    var dataContainer;

    function pageLoad() {
        // get the element by id called DataContainer
using $get shortcut function
        dataContainer = $get("DataContainer");
    }

    function onsearchclick() {
        doSearch();
    }

    function doSearch() {
    }
</script>
```

6. So far you have created the skeleton markup and JavaScript functions that will be called when the search button's `click` event is handled by the browser. Now you need to add code to the `doSearch` function to execute the search against the data service. You will get a reference to the text box input element to obtain the value of the text entered, and then call the data service using the `Sys.Data.DataService` object. Because the data service is private to the web site (it has to be because of security limitations using XMLHTTP), you reference the root URI using a relative path. Once you have a reference to the service, you can execute a query off of this root URI. You are going to execute a query against

/Customers?$filter=substringof('{0}',LastName)&$expand=Gender,Salutation. This URI queries all customers, where the customer last name contains the text entered in the text box. Notice the $expand argument; request that the Customer entity is also returned with the Gender and Salutation entities so that you can display this information to the user. The amended doSearch function is as follows:

```
function onsuccess(result, context, operation) {
}

function onfailure(error, context, operation) {
}

function doSearch() {
    // get the element by id called SearchTextBox
    var searchTextBox = $get("SearchTextBox");

    var searchText = searchTextBox.value;

    if (searchText.length > 0) {
        // create a reference to the data service
        var svc = new Sys.Data.DataService("CustomerDataService.svc");

        // query the data service, returning customers whose last name
        // contains the search text, including gender and salutation
        // reference properties in the results.
        svc.query(String.format("/Customers?$filter=substringof('{0}',
LastName)&$expand=Gender,Salutation", searchText), onsuccess, onfailure);
    }
    else {
        dataContainer.innerHTML = 'Please enter a lastname';
    }
}
```

7. Notice the preceding code includes two callback functions in the query method: onsuccess and onfailure. These functions handle the response from the data service, when the response is successful or an exception has occurred. To handle the success function, you are going to use the template library to template some HTML to repeat for each item returned in the result array. Before you write the JavaScript, you need to append your HTML template to the markup. Between the Search button input element and the div element, add a new div element named DataTempate. Set the element's class attribute to sys-template. This is the name of the CSS class you will use to hide the template markup in the browser. Make the DataTemplate div element contain the markup shown here:

```
<div id="DataTemplate" class="sys-template">
  <h3>Customer Id {{ CustomerId }}</h3>
  Name: <span>{{SalutationDescription + ' ' + FirstName + ' '
  + LastName}}</span><br />
  Date of Birth: <span>{{ DateOfBirth.format('MM/dd/yyyy') }}
  </span><br />
  Gender: <span>{{ GenderName }}</span><br />
</div>
```

8. The template HTML created in the previous step is used by the `Template` class in JavaScript to render the HTML layout repeatedly for each item of data returned by the service. The special syntax contained in this markup to identify where to bind the data is indicated by the variables contained in double brackets (for example, `{{ Variable }}`). These special tags are used by the template engine and are swapped out for data when the code runs.

9. You need to create the `sys-template` class that the template engine uses to hide the template from a user's view. Open the `common.css` class and add the following CSS class definition:

```
.sys-template
{
    visibility:hidden;
    display:none;
}
```

10. Now that you have fully defined the template in markup and CSS, you need to add some JavaScript code to the `onsuccess` function to use the template markup, rendering the output into the `DataContainer` div element. You instantiate the `Sys.UI.Template` class, giving it a reference to the template div element. You then iterate over the result array (the objects returned in the JSON response from the data service) and use the template object to bind the data in the result array to the template markup. You also need to add code to handle the `onfailure` callback from the data service in case the query fails. The final code for the `onsuccess` and `onfailure` functions is shown in the following code:

```
function onsuccess(result, context, operation) {
    // get the template element by id called DataTemplate
    // using $get shortcut function
    var template = new Sys.UI.Template($get("DataTemplate"));
    dataContainer.innerHTML = '';

    if (result.length > 0) {
        // loop round search results, creating instances of the
        // template in the data container element
        for (var i = 0; i < result.length; i++) {
            template.createInstance(dataContainer,
            {
                CustomerId: result[i].CustomerId,
                FirstName: result[i].FirstName,
                LastName: result[i].LastName,
                GenderName: result[i].Gender.GenderName,
                SalutationDescription: result[i]
                    .Salutation.SalutationDescription,
                DateOfBirth: result[i].DateOfBirth
            });
        }
    }
    else {
        dataContainer.innerHTML = 'No records returned';
    }
```

```
    }

    function onfailure(error, context, operation) {
        // handle data service failure
        var dataContainer = $get("DataContainer");
        dataContainer.innerHTML = 'Error retrieving customers';
    }
```

11. With the code to call the service and bind the response data complete, you can now view the web page in
     the browser. In the text box, enter **smi** and click the Go button. An AJAX call will be made to the data service,
     and the JSON response will be bound to the HTML template, rendering repeating customers in the browser.
     Figure 5-6 shows the result of executing this search in the browser.

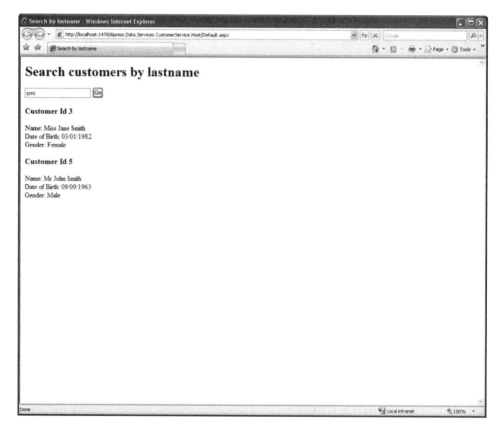

Figure 5-6. *Results of executing the customer search by last name using client-side AJAX*

12. Visual Studio 2008 treats JavaScript as a first-class language, providing debugging support for developing
     AJAX applications in a similar way to debugging server-side ASP.NET code. It is useful to try this out against
     this web page to see the response data from the data service. To enable this, you must first check the set-
     tings in Internet Explorer. Go to Tools ➤ Internet Options ➤ Advanced and ensure that the Disable Script
     Debugging options are unchecked. Place a breakpoint on the first line of code within the `onsuccess` func-
     tion on the page. Run the site (without debugging) normally and while the browser is open, switch to Visual
     Studio and go to Debug ➤ Attach to process. Attach to the `iexplorer.exe` process and then switch to the

browser and execute a customer search on the web page. Once the search has completed, Visual Studio will hit the breakpoint as normal. Visual Studio provides a `Script Documents` folder in Solution Explorer that contains the complete set of JavaScript libraries running on the page that you debug. Figure 5-7 shows a QuickWatch window on the `results` array with the object graph returned from JSON response.

Figure 5-7. *Evaluating the response from the data service in Visual Studio by debugging JavaScript*

In this exercise, you have created a web page that uses client-side AJAX techniques to call a data service and bind its response data to HTML markup.

Public and Private Services

One important concept to consider when developing web applications using a client-centric model is whether the services you plan to consume are private or public. If you are consuming third-party services, this decision is made for you; they are public services hosted elsewhere on the Internet using a different domain. This creates the need to make a **cross-domain** HTTP request to a service, where your web site is running under a different domain from the web service you want to call. For security reasons, XMLHTTP does not allow cross-domain HTTP requests.

Private services are services that cannot be called by other third parties across the Internet, because they have been secured to only be consumed by their intended client web application. In many scenarios, private services are very desirable; for example, if you are developing a web application in AJAX that will consume a data service containing personal information, you need to ensure that no third party can consume your service. The easiest way to solve this scenario is to host your data service in the same web site (and domain) as the front-end application and lock down the access permissions of the service using ASP.NET security.

Alternatively, you may want to intentionally expose your data service over the Internet for public consumption by third parties. Public-facing web services, such as those discussed in Chapter 6, enable mashup scenarios by third-party consumers. In these scenarios, you may choose to create a data service in a separate host web site to your consuming client, which is under a different domain. Such a scenario causes the same cross-domain issues encountered when calling any other public-facing web service.

The solution to calling a service outside the domain of your web site is to implement a cross-domain proxy service, otherwise known as a **bridge**. The bridge pattern involves your creating a private service under your web site's domain that acts as an intermediary to the endpoint you wish to call. The bridging service will make an HTTP request on the server to the service you wish to call. If you are developing the public facing service using ADO.NET Data Services, the bridge will use the same autogenerated .NET client library discussed during the server-side section of this chapter. This pattern is illustrated in Figure 5-8.

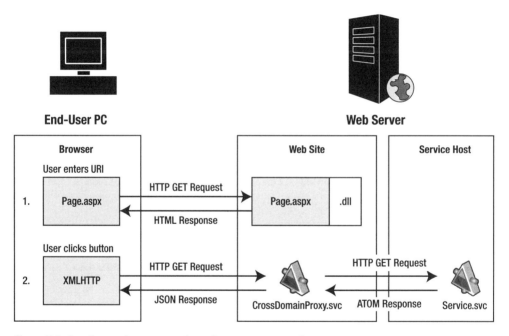

Figure 5-8. *Implementing a cross-domain proxy pattern for XMLHTTP requests to remote services*

ADO.NET Data Services does not support the creation of cross-domain bridges out of the box, so you will need to rely on WCF to create the bridge and then implement a data service client within the bridge's service implementation. In WCF you can create an ASP.NET AJAX–enabled endpoint using `WebHttpBinding` and JSON serialization.

Using WCF to create an AJAX-enabled endpoint for a bridge service involves creating service contracts and data contracts like any traditional SOAP-based WCF service. This means that your bridge will be verb based like a SOAP service rather than the noun-based approach of a data service endpoint. The service will be exposed through a `WebHttpBinding` and will use the `System.ServiceModel.Activation.WebScriptServiceHostFactory` in the `Bridge.svc` host file.

This host factory enables consumption of a WCF service using JavaScript in AJAX scenarios. The full host declaration in the host file reads as follows:

```
<%@ ServiceHost Language="C#" Debug="true" Service="BridgeService"
CodeBehind="~/App_Code/Bridge.cs"
Factory="System.ServiceModel.Activation.WebScriptServiceHostFactory" %>
```

The service operations of the bridge service need to apply the WebGet or WebInvoke attribute to specify the HTTP verb to use and set the message format to JSON for easy consumption in JavaScript.

Listing 5-5 shows an example service implementation for a WCF bridge service that exposes one service operation called GetCustomersByLastname. The code uses an ADO.NET Data Services proxy to forward the call on to a public data service.

Listing 5-5. *Example Bridge Service That Consumes an ADO.NET Data Service*

```csharp
using System;
using System.Linq;
using System.Net;
using System.Runtime.Serialization;
using System.ServiceModel;
using System.ServiceModel.Activation;
using System.ServiceModel.Web;
using System.Collections.Generic;
using System.Data.Services.Client;
using CustomerModel;

[DataContract]
public class CustomerModel
{
    [DataMember]
    public int Id { get; set; }
    [DataMember]
    public string FirstName { get; set; }
    [DataMember]
    public string LastName { get; set; }
    [DataMember]
    public DateTime DateOfBirth { get; set; }
    [DataMember]
    public SalutationModel Salutation { get; set; }
    [DataMember]
    public GenderModel Gender { get; set; }
}

[DataContract]
public class GenderModel
{
    [DataMember]
    public string Id { get; set; }
```

```
    [DataMember]
    public string Name { get; set; }
}

[DataContract]
public class SalutationModel
{
    [DataMember]
    public int Id { get; set; }
    [DataMember]
    public string Description { get; set; }
}

[ServiceContract(Namespace = "http://mywebsite.com.services/")]
[AspNetCompatibilityRequirements(RequirementsMode =
AspNetCompatibilityRequirementsMode.Allowed)]
public class BridgeService
{
    // The following line of code points the data services proxy
    // to the root data service URI.
    // You may need to change the URI port number (1478) to the port
    // your data service is running on.
    private CustomerEntities entities = new CustomerEntities(new
Uri("http://localhost:1478/Apress.Data.Services.CustomerService.Host/
CustomerDataService.svc"));

    [OperationContract]
    [WebGet(ResponseFormat = WebMessageFormat.Json)]
    public CustomerModel GetCustomersByLastName(string lastname)
    {
        // this service operation uses HTTP GET and formats the response into JSON
        List<CustomerModel> customers = new List<CustomerModel>();

        if (!string.IsNullOrEmpty(lastname))
        {
            // retrieve the collection of customers complete with Gender and
            // Salutation reference properties populated and cast into
            // CustomerModel data contract.
            customers = (from c in entities.Customers.Expand("Gender")
                .Expand("Salutation")
                         where c.LastName.Contains(lastname)
                         select new CustomerModel
                         {
                             Id = c.CustomerId,
                             FirstName = c.FirstName,
                             LastName = c.LastName,
                             DateOfBirth = c.DateOfBirth,
```

```
                        Gender = new GenderModel
                        {
                            Id = c.Gender.GenderId.ToString(),
                            Name = c.Gender.GenderName
                        },
                        Salutation = new SalutationModel
                        {
                            Id = c.Salutation.SalutationId,
                            Description = c.Salutation.SalutationDescription
                        }
                    }).ToList();
        }

        return customers;
    }
}
```

Listing 5-6 demonstrates how this bridge would be consumed in JavaScript.

Listing 5-6. *Consuming the Bridge Service from Within JavaScript*

```
<asp:ScriptManager runat="server" ID="ScriptManager">
    <Services>
        <asp:ServiceReference Path="~/Services/Bridge.svc" />
    </Services>
</asp:ScriptManager>

<div>
... page content would go here...
</div>

<script type="text/javascript">
var proxy;
var lastname = 'Smith';

function pageLoad()
{
    // the script manager service reference automatically generates a
    // JavaScript proxy to consume the Bridge service.
    proxy = new mywebsite.com.services.BridgeService();
    proxy.GetCustomersByLastName(lastname, OnComplete, OnError);
}

function OnComplete(result)
{
    // do data binding here...
}
```

```
function OnError(result)
{
    // handle errors here....
}
</script>
```

Mixing ASP.NET Client and Server Models

In reality, most web sites built using ASP.NET will want to mix both client and server models in order to get the benefits each model has to offer. For consuming your own data services from web pages, it is likely that the client-side model will be the weapon of choice, but you will still want to utilize the best features of ASP.NET server side to build parts of your web site.

Having a web site that contains some pages entirely using a server-centric model and some entirely using a client-centric model does not pose any real problems. However, mixing the client and server models on the same page is not as straightforward as it may first appear and should be approached with caution and planning. The reason that it is challenging is because ASP.NET server controls render their HTML ID attributes on the server, meaning that they are not known to the JavaScript developer at design time. Thus JavaScript that manipulates these rendered elements using the HTML DOM is not ensured to work, because the HTML IDs may change as the page evolves, or because the elements are rendered from repeating data.

So long as no client-side JavaScript acts on HTML rendered server side, there is no problem in mixing these two models together. Additionally, ASP.NET does provide a mechanism to augment server-side markup with ASP.NET AJAX components, through the use of extender controls. To develop extender controls, you need to download the AJAX Control Toolkit from CodePlex at http://www.codeplex.com/AjaxControlToolkit.

The AJAX control toolkit is an open source project led by Microsoft to develop rich AJAX controls for ASP.NET AJAX. The project contains controls that are client-side AJAX controls and behaviors, complete with extenders so that you can attach the components to server-side controls. Additionally, the download includes a Visual Studio template so that you can create ASP.NET AJAX extenders for your own client-side components. It is worth looking at the toolkit for both its prebuilt, highly valuable controls and its extender functionality.

Summary

ASP.NET is an extremely broad and deep technology that cannot be comprehensively covered in a single chapter; the aim of this chapter is to provide enough knowledge of ASP.NET to get you started in creating web sites that consume ADO.NET Data Services, so you can make informed decisions about whether to consume services using both the client and server model. To this extent, this chapter has described the following scenarios:

- Consuming a public-facing data service using C# code running on your ASP.NET web site's server

- Consuming your own private data service using JavaScript code running on the browser

- Consuming a bridge service by using JavaScript code running on the browser to call a bridge service, which in turn calls a public-facing data service from the web server using C#

The key takeaway for this chapter is that you must consider the design of your web site in the context of the data services (or any other services) you plan to consume. If you are developing the data service, consider who the audience is, whether your web site is the only known consumer, and design the web site around these decisions. Think carefully how to best apply the strengths of both the client and server models to deliver an excellent user experience.

CHAPTER 6

■■■

Mashing Up Data Services

In Chapter 5, you created a solution using AJAX and ADO.NET Data Services. We outlined how we can use ADO.NET Data Services in ASP.NET solutions and introduced the AJAX add in for ADO.NET Data Services and provided a number of practical demonstrations of how to use this technology. In this chapter, we will focus on how we can a consume data services on the Web using a new concept called mashups. We will demonstrate, with a number of exercises, how to combine your data services using a new mashup editor from Microsoft called Popfly.

Let's Do the Mash

According to Wikipedia the term "mashup" originally referred to the practice of mixing two or more songs together for use in genres such as hip hop and rap. In modern computing, the word has been applied to describe the process of creating new applications by combining or mashing together two or more preexisting application sources. These new mashup applications are used to create new and interesting services and products for consumers.

You can already find lots of different examples of mashups on the web, and new ones are appearing all the time. ProgrammableWeb is a web site dedicated to mashups, with over 3,450 listed at the time of this writing. An example of one of these mashups is BidNearBy, a neat mashup that combines eBay, Craiglist, and Amazon plus brand-name stores on a Google map so users can locate items near them (see Figure 6-1). Although this mashup is more complex behind the scenes than the example we'll build in this chapter, it demonstrates multiple mashups on one web site.

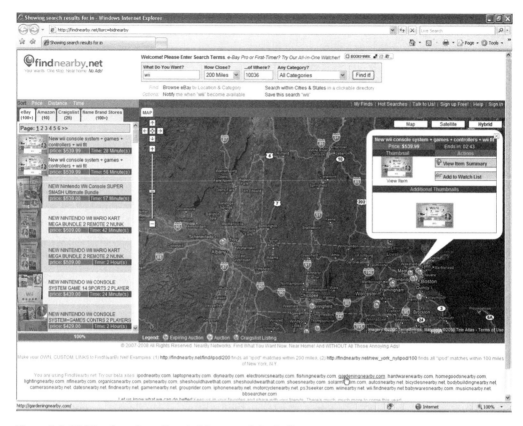

Figure 6-1. *BidNearby: eBay, Google Maps, and Craigslist*

Mashups have been around since the early years of the Internet but were difficult to create because of the business model used by players such as Yahoo and Microsoft: they required customers to sign up for services with a vendor-specific ID and providing those services in a vendor-specific portal. In this way, Yahoo and Microsoft would control customers' data and lock them into using only their products and services. If users wanted to have the news from Microsoft and sports coverage from Yahoo, they would have to sign up with both vendors and log into each portal to view the information. This data-access model left no easy way for users to view all of their data in one place, let alone combine proprietary data from multiple sources. Along with this restriction, vendors also published proprietary API interfaces for their services that were not web friendly and were built using C interfaces and dynamically linked libraries.

The old proprietary model fell by the wayside when Web 2.0 came along. Look at portals of today, such as Microsoft Live or iGoogle: they allow users data to be shared across multiple competing vendors, so you can now get news from Microsoft and sports from Yahoo in a single portal. With the Web 2.0 mind shift, companies started to recognize that the social networking aspects of the Internet could mean big money, and for them to excel in this new market, they must provide easy access to consumer data. Simply put, Web 2.0 web sites put consumers in charge of their data and enable them to easily share that data with friends and family. "Consumer data" doesn't necessary need to be sensitive information, such as social security numbers; the term refers to anything important to a customer, including family photos, local weather forecasts, or a query on a search engine for a product to buy. To enable easy access, vendors have started to change their proprietary interfaces to use open standards such as SOAP, XML-Remote Procedure Call (XML-RPC), and REST. In addition, data is also exposed by data feeds using RSS formats. ADO.NET Data Services fit perfectly into the mashup space, because they allow data to be easily shared by providing a RESTful uniform interface.

So how do we create a mashup? Mashup development follows a linear design process that can be summarized as follows:

1. Pick a subject.

2. Locate your data sources.

3. Sign up for the data vendors' APIs.

4. Determine the intersections of the data.

5. Combine the data in a visual display.

Sources of Mashups

To determine the sources of a mashup, you must understand its purpose. The idea of a mashup may come from a business problem or your personal life experiences. For example, recently John was stranded overnight at a connecting airport, which meant he needed a hotel room. A good mashup to solve this problem would be a web page that shows hotels close to the airport. The site could be enhanced by adding entertainment options in the area, because everyone gets bored looking at hotel walls.

The main sources of mashups can be categorized as mapping, photo, video, news, weather, search, and e-commerce. These sources can be provided by big and small vendors and are often listed on popular mashup web sites, such as ProgrammableWeb. These services usually require you to sign up for a developer's API to prevent you from overusing the service and completely replicating the original web site. Some of the popular mashup sources are listed in Table 6-1.

Table 6-1. *Mashup Sources*

Source	Category	Available at	APIs Used
Microsoft Virtual Earth	Mapping	`dev.live.com/virtualearth`	JavaScript interaction
Google Maps	Mapping	`www.google.com/apis`	JavaScript interaction
Yahoo Flickr	Photos	`www.flickr.com/services`	REST, SOAP, and XML-RPC
Microsoft Live Photos	Photos	`dev.live.com/spacescontrol`	SOAP and REST
Google Picasa	Photos	`www.google.com/apis`	REST
Google Search	Search	`code.google.com`	SOAP and REST
Microsoft Live Search	Search	`dev.live.com/livesearch`	SOAP
Yahoo Search	Search	`developer.yahoo.com/search`	REST
YouTube	Video	`www.youtube.com/dev`	JavaScript interaction
eBay	E-commerce	`developer.ebay.com`	SOAP and REST
Microsoft Live Expo	E-commerce	`dev.live.com/expo`	SOAP and REST
Yahoo Shopping	E-commerce	`developer.yahoo.com/shopping`	SOAP and REST

Intersecting Data

Once you have identified your subject area and sources and signed up for all the vendors' APIs, the next step is to determine the intersections of the data. Much like when you join or intersect two tables in a SQL JOIN statement, you are essentially trying to identify something in the output of one data source that can be used as input for the other. You can follow three simple steps to find these intersecting points:

1. List the input and output values from each source within your mashup.

2. Join them together by using one or more intersecting fields.

3. If the sources don't quite fit together, another API or source must be used between the two original data sources (this step is optional).

Listing Input and Output Values

Suppose we wanted to create a mashup that showed nearby coffee shops on a map. To achieve this, we would probably use two sources, one that enabled us to search for coffee shops by location and another rendered these locations as pins on a map.

Table 6-2. *Source, Input, and Output Values for Our Coffee Shop Example*

	Business Directory API Source	**Mapping Display Source**
API method	`SearchForAddressByZipCodeAndBusinessType()`	`AddPin()`
Input(s)	ZipCode, 'Coffee Shop'	Latitude, Longitude, PinDescription
Output(s)	Description, BusinessName, AddressLine1, AddressLine2, City, ZipCode	'Visual Display Only'

Joining Sources

If we consider the intersections of the data in Table 6-2, we basically want to take the Business-Name (coffee shop name) field and show this in conjunction with the pins on the map. Here, we have a problem because we only have the address details of the coffee shop, not the latitude and longitude points that the mapping display requires. We'll need to follow the last step.

Adding Additional Sources Until the Mashup Details Fit Together

The final step is to add another source to the mashup that can be used to convert the addressing details that are output from the `SearchForAddressByZipCodeAndBusinessType()` method into latitude and longitude points by a process called geocoding. To do this, we need a new source that calls a worldwide geocode service, which accepts an address and converts it to latitude and longitude points. This new source would fit between the two other sources to provide these points to the `AddPin()` method.

Mashup Environments

Most mashup environments are What You See Is What You Get (WYSIWYG) visual interfaces that are used to graphically build mashups. Often, they allow you to drag and drop the different sources of a mashup onto a design surface where you can connect them together using either code or basic input fields. Some environments have built-in social networking aspects, which allow users to share their creations with others using popular social networking applications such as Facebook. The vendors of these environments vary from start-ups to big players such as Google, Microsoft, and Yahoo. We'll briefly describe four popular mashup environments, and later in the chapter, we'll dive deeper into Microsoft Popfly and explain how to use it with ADO.NET Data Services.

Google Mashup Editor

Google Mashup Editor (see Figure 6-2) is an online tool that uses tags that compile into AJAX UI components. Users can combine data from RSS feeds with Google services such as Google Base and Google Maps. As at time of this writing, there is limited access to the beta release of the Google Mashup Editor. A screen shot of the Google Mashup Editor is shown in Figure 6-2.

- *Features*
    - IntelliSense online text editor
    - Google HTML tags, such as `gm:data`, `gm:list`, and `gm:item`, are used to provide access to Google services and outside data feeds
    - Ability to publish mashups as Google applications
    - Ability to create Google gadgets that can be shared with other users
- *Data services support*: REST JSON support via JavaScript

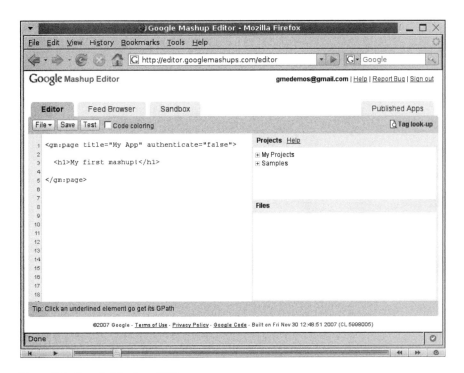

Figure 6-2. *Google Mashup Editor*

Microsoft Popfly

Popfly, Microsoft's contribution to the mashup space, is built around social networking concepts, so mashups can be created and shared by users (see Figure 6-3). Popfly blocks contain a JavaScript code library that is used to retrieve data from an endpoint, and the online tool allows you to connect similar blocks together. Popfly also includes a basic web page editor that can be used to embed mashups.

- *Features*
    - Online community
    - Sliverlight online mashup editor
    - Ability to create and rate other users' blocks
    - Ability to create and share web pages
    - Search for other users blocks and mashups
    - JavaScript-based scripting language
- *Data services support*: REST JSON support in blocks via JavaScript

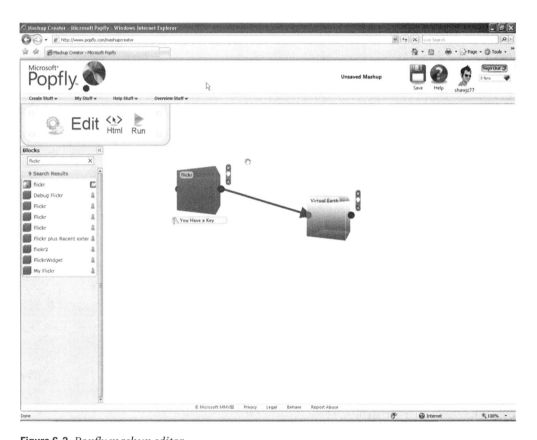

Figure 6-3. *Popfly mashup editor*

■**Tip** Apress has published a book by Microsoft employee Eric Griffin called *Foundations of Popfly* (2008) that describes Microsoft Popfly in detail.

Yahoo Pipes

Yahoo Pipes (see Figure 6-4) is a powerful visual composition tool that allows aggregation and manipulation of Web content. The basic concepts are similar to Popfly: you can connect pipes (like Popfly blocks) that link to underlying data sources to create mashup output. Pipe's doesn't allow you to view the source code of the prebuilt pipes like Popfly does. However, the environment has an advantage of providing relevant programming type methods that allow counting, sorting, and filtering of data (these methods are available in Popfly, but the feature is nicer in Pipes). The Pipes visual tool gives a really clear view of the processing is taking place without requiring you to drill down into the pipe.

- *Features*
    - Visual online tool used to connect pipes together
    - Prebuilt modules for importing data, user input, and operators
    - Ability to publish mashups as Yahoo widgets
- *Data services support*: REST JSON support

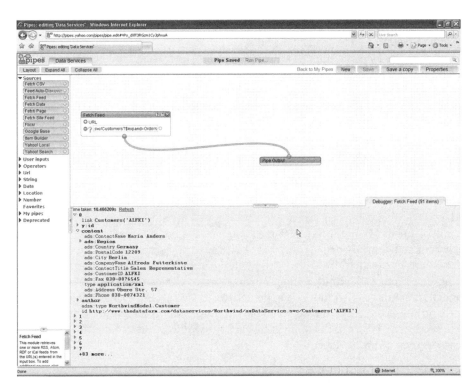

Figure 6-4. *Yahoo Pipes*

Using Microsoft Popfly

Microsoft Popfly was introduced in May 2007 as a mashup editor aimed at nonprogrammers. Popfly, which uses Web 2.0 social networking concepts, encourages users to share mashups with their friends via Microsoft's online community where users can view blocks, code, and web pages that have been created by others. Community members can also rate one another's efforts.

Popfly services center around Windows Live, so to access Popfly, you need a Windows Live ID. So before you start you must register your e-mail address with Windows Live. After creating an ID or using an existing ID, you can simply log in by clicking the Sign In button on the Popfly home page (http://www.popfly.com). The online Popfly environment is created in Silverlight, a free tool from Microsoft, so you'll need to install a version of this before you can use Popfly. We recommend the most recent version, Sliverlight 2.0 at the time of this writing. To install Sliverlight, navigate to http://silverlight.net/, and click the Getting Started link to install Sliverlight 2 for Windows.

The key features of the Popfly environment are as follows:

- Blocks
- Mashup design surface
- Web page creation
- Mashup sharing
- Block development capabilities

Blocks

Creating mashups in Popfly is simple. You are not required to understand the underlying APIs associated with the sources of the mashups, because Popfly encapsulates these sources into visual blocks; in other words, Popfly wraps up vendors' APIs or services so that they can be used in your mashup. Some blocks are generic such as the RSS feed block, which can be used to get RSS data from any web site, shown in Figure 6-5. Also, specific blocks can be created for services, such as an RSS feed from Yahoo news.

To create a mashup, you simply select the blocks that are associated with the mashup and drag these onto the visual design surface. Once the blocks are on the design surface, you can then configure them and link them together to achieve the desired output. The Popfly environment contains a ready-made collection of blocks from well-known sources such as Virtual Earth, Flickr, and Facebook. For easy access, blocks are stored in categories such as mapping, images and video, and local community. Although you'll find many different categories blocks, they basically fall into two types: display and data. A mashup can contain as many data blocks as required, but only one display block can be used on the design surface at any one time.

Each block has input and output points, shown to you as circles, and these are used as simple connection points to other blocks. On the left-hand side of the block is the input, and on the right-hand side is the output. A block can have multiple inputs but only one output. To remove a block, click the "X" icon. To configure it, click the wrench, and for help, click the light bulb. You can see these icons in Figure 6-5.

Figure 6-5. *RSS Feed block*

After you click the wrench icon to configure a block, after a brief zoom animation a screen appears that shows a list of operations on the surface of the block. Blocks have two modes of configuration: simple, shown in Figure 6-6, or advanced, shown in Figure 6-7. By default, the simple mode is used, so you can simply choose an operation from a drop-down menu and specify the inputs.

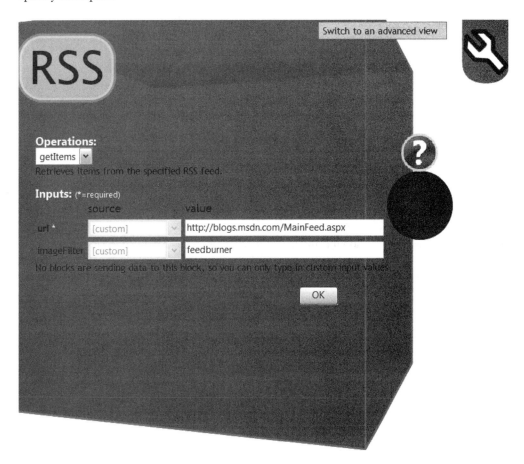

Figure 6-6. *Popfly's simple block configuration mode*

```
Go back to the simple view
```
```
RSS
```
Feel free to tweak the JavaScript below, if you know how.   OK

```
rss.__reserved.pendingCalls = 1;
rss.getItems("http://blogs.msdn.com/MainFeed.aspx", "feedburner", fu
    {
        try
        {
            data["RSS"] = result;

            environment.output(result); // Output the result beca

        }
        catch (ex)
        {
            environment.reportError(ex);
        }
    }
);
```

Figure 6-7. *Popfly's advanced block configuration mode*

Similar to other Microsoft development concepts, a block's architecture contains two components: an XML description file and a code-behind file. The XML file describes the block's properties and operations, which will appear on the mashup creator surface in configuration mode. The code-behind file contains JavaScript that executes the defined operations. The description and code files together create a functional block.

Mashup Design Surface

The mashup design surface (shown in Figure 6-3) is an interactive online tool where blocks can be linked together. It allows developers to design mashups without having to write a single line of code. Connecting data services to blocks is just a case of drawing a line between them. On the interface's left side, the blocks are categorized (Display, Images & Video, Maps, News & RSS, Shops, and so on). The design surface allows you to search for by name using the search textbox.

Web Page Creation

Popfly comes with a WYSIWYG web page editor that you can use to create web pages containing shared mashups. You can access the web page creator by clicking Main Menu ➤ Create Stuff ➤ Web Page. The editor, which works similar to SharePoint Designer, allows you to configure the look of your mashup on a web page and includes HTML editor features that give you the ability to create hyperlinks, embed images, and change page styles.

After creating these web pages, you can share them with the Popfly community or externally on the Internet using the Popfly community's built-in hosting features.

Sharing Mashups

Popfly is all about being nice and sharing with your friends. Once you have created your blocks or web pages, you can share them with others. In turn, you can see how other users have developed their code. Additionally, if you like the functionality of the code but want it to be extended slightly, you can simply create a new version by copying, or *ripping*, the original code. The option to share the mashup is specified in the My Stuff ➤ Projects section of Popfly and is achieved clicking the MashOut option. The options for sharing your mashup are as follows:

- *Embed the mashup*: The mashup can be used in any HTML page, including the web page creation tool provided with the Popfly Environment. The HTML that is automatically generated is similar to the code generated on a YouTube link; here's an example.

```
<iframe style='width:500px; height:375px;
'src='http://www.Popfly.com/users/joeblogs➥
/RestaurantRatingMashup.small'
frameborder='no' allowtransparency='true'>
</iframe>
```

- *Download as a Windows Vista Gadget:* Popfly creates an installation package that can be used to install the mashup as a gadget. However, on the default visual desktop size of the gadget, this means that the mashup potentially won't fit into the gadget, and you will need to scroll up and down.

- *Windows Live spaces*: You can add the mashup to your pages within your Windows Live spaces.

- *Share on Facebook, Diggit, Reddit*: This option allows the mashup to appear as an application on multiple social networking web sites.

- *E-mail the mashup*: E-mail a link to the new mashup using your registered Windows Live e-mail account. This link can then be used to navigate to the shared mashup with a browser.

In addition to these sharing options, the Popfly team is currently working on support for hosting Window Forms and Windows Presentation Foundation applications.

Tip Sharing other users' code can cause issues when the underlying block is changed. Currently, the only way to keep in control of your mashup is to create all the blocks yourself. If you like the functionality of other users' blocks, its best to create your own version of ripped blocks.

Block Development

If there isn't a block available that matches your mashup requirement, you can create your own block using the online block creation tool or Visual Studio. Recall that a block consists of two components: an XML file and a JavaScript file. The XML file is the definition of the operations, input, and output, while the JavaScript file contains the implementation. The online block creation tool is hosted on the Popfly web site and displays these files in two large text boxes with no IntelliSense feature. This tool doesn't provide a good development experience, so we recommended only using online block creation for simple tweaking to blocks. Use Visual Studio for any significant block development. Let's compare the two ways of creating a block. We'll start by creating a block that simply outputs "Hello World" in Exercise 6-1.

EXERCISE 6-1: CREATING A HELLO WORLD BLOCK

This exercise will walk you through how to create a Hello World block using the online block creation tool and Visual Studio 2008.

Sign Up for Popfly

The first step is to create a Popfly account by signing in with your Windows Live account.

1. Navigate to `http://www.Popfly.com`.

2. Click Sign In.

3. Accept the terms and conditions, and click OK.

Create the Hello World Block Using the Online Tool

1. On the Popfly web site, navigate to Create ➤ Block. The screen shown in Figure 6-8 will appear.

2. By default, a sample Hello World block is shown. To run this block, click the Save & Run icon in the top right-hand corner of the screen. This will show a dialog block that asks for the project's name, description, and tags. Name the project Hello World Basic, and leave all the other fields blank. Click OK.

3. Allow the web site to display pop-ups, and click the Save & Run icon to launch another browser displaying the block as part of an example mashup. Click Run, which has the play-button image. This will display "Hello, world!"

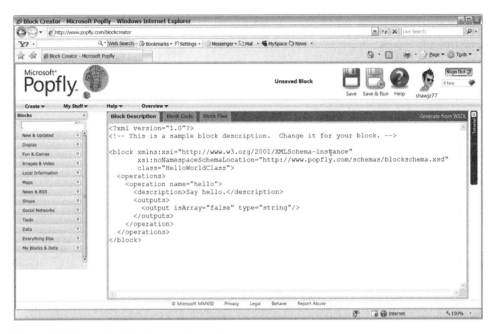

Figure 6-8. *The online block creation tool*

Create the Hello World Block Using Visual Studio 2008

1. Download the Visual Studio Popfly Explorer by navigating to `http://www.Popfly.com`, clicking Create Stuff ➤ Popfly Explorer, and clicking Download Popfly Explorer.

2. Install the Popfly Explorer by double-clicking the Popfly MSI installer. Leave the default options.

3. To confirm that Popfly has been successfully installed, open Visual Studio 2008, and make sure a new Popfly menu appears.

4. Create a new Popfly block by selecting File ➤ New ➤ Web Site. Select Popfly Block, and specify the project location, type **DataServicesHelloWorld** for the name, and click OK. Choose Basic Block from the options presented, and click Finish again.

   The files that are created are `default.js` and `default.xml`. These files contain a default implementation of a Hello World block.

5. Now that we have created the block, let's test it by uploading it to our Popfly space. First sign in to Popfly using the Popfly Explorer in the Visual Studio Solution Explorer, as shown in Figure 6-9. If the Popfly Explorer doesn't appear, click the Popfly menu, and select Show Popfly Explorer.

Figure 6-9. *Signing in from Popfly Explorer*

6. To publish the block to the Popfly environment using Visual Studio, click the Popfly menu, and choose Save Project to Popfly. When the Popfly project dialog appears, type **DataServicesHelloWorld** as the name of the data block. Next, click Accept and Publish and then Ok. If prompted, choose Open Local Copy.

7. Run the block in Visual Studio by pressing F5, and the Popfly environment will appear in a browser. Click the green Run icon to start the mashup, and click the Debug Console icon to see information messages.

■**Tip** You can create only a single block within a Visual Studio project. If multiple blocks are required, create each block in its own web site project.

Because the block XML and the JavaScript files are the key components of Popfly blocks, understanding them well is essential, so we will now describe these in greater detail.

XML Definition Files

Blocks' XML definition files store metadata associated with the JavaScript and are used by the online tool. Their purposes are to describe the block, in terms of the inputs and outputs, and provide description tags that can be used to locate the block. The metadata definition stored in the BlockDefinition.xsd file determines how the XML is structured and validates the

XML. If you would like to view this definition, navigate to `http://www.popfly.com/schemas/` `blockschema.xsd`. To explain the key parts of the XSD file, let's first walk through the structure of the XML file for the Hello World block. We will change the block to accept two input parameters and output a custom object.

The top element contains a `<block>` node, which has a class attribute pointing to the JavaScript class definition associated with the block. We will change the class name from `HelloWorldClass` to `ApressHelloWorldClass` as follows:

```
<block class="ApressHelloWorldClass">
```

The next important part is the collection of operations that define the service. These are contained within a parent `<operations>` node, and at least one operation is required by the designer. Each operation defined should map to the methods within the JavaScript class. Each operation's `<operation>` node contains the name of the JavaScript function and a human-friendly description used by the Popfly online designer. We will leave the operation as `hello`. The `callMode` attribute is by the Popfly API to understand how the method is called, and it can take one of three values: `auto`, `async`, or `sync`.

```
<operations>
<operation name="hello" callMode="auto" >
            <description>Say Hello.</description>
```

The input and output of the operation need to be defined next. The input parameters are contained within an `<inputs>` parent node. Each input needs to match the parameter of the JavaScript function contained in the `name` attribute of the operation. We will modify the `hello` operator to accept two input parameters: a first name and a last name. When specifying an input node, additional attributes can be set to establish whether the parameter is required and its type. In addition, the input node can contain three values: a description, a default value, and constraints. The description is used by the designer, and the default value should be specified when the `required` attribute is set to `true`. The constraints node is used to validate user input, such as setting a range of values or allowing only certain values (e.g., from an option group). We will constrain the block to only allow names of the Beatles. The inputs for the block follow:

```
<input name="FirstName" required="true" type="string">
<description>First Name</description>
    <defaultValue>John</defaultValue>
    <constraints>
            <constraint mandatory="true" type="oneOf">
                <value>John</value>
                <value>Paul</value>
                <value>Ringo</value>
                <value>George</value>
            </constraint>
    </constraints>
</input>
<input name="LastName" required="true" type="string">
<description>Last Name</description>
    <defaultValue>Lennon</defaultValue>
```

```
        <constraints>
              <constraint mandatory="true" type="oneOf">
                    <value>Lennon</value>
                    <value>McCartny</value>
                    <value>Starr</value>
                    <value>Harrison</value>
              </constraint>
        </constraints>
</input>
```

You can output data from blocks in two ways: as an object definition or an array of objects or as HTML. The hello world block presently outputs "Hello world!" as HTML. Instead of using HTML, we will change this output to use an object definition, which is helpful because objects have properties that can be set by other connected blocks in mashups. Output parameters are contained within an <outputs> parent node. The output parameter that we will specify is a HelloWorldObject:

```
<outputs>
<output isArray="false" type="HelloWorldObject"/>
</outputs>
```

■**Tip** You should always try to return objects from blocks.

The final part of the definition is to specify one or more objects that can be used in the block. Each object requires a JavaScript class definition created in the code file:

```
<objects>
    <object name="HelloWorldObject">
        <field name="FirstName" type="string" isArray="false" />
        <field name="LastName" type="string" isArray="false" />
    </object>
</objects>
```

The block's XML file is ultimately linked to the functions that are exposed by the service. The block's final XML code is shown in Listing 6-1.

Listing 6-1. *The Hello World Block's Updated XML*

```
<?xml version="1.0"?>
<!-- This is a sample block description.  Change it for your block. -->

<block xmlns:xsi="http://www.w3.org/2001/XMLSchema-instance"
       xsi:noNamespaceSchemaLocation="http://www.popfly.com/schemas/blockschema.xsd"
       class="ApressHelloWorldClass">
  <operations>
    <operation name="hello">
```

```xml
                <description>Say hello.</description>
                <inputs>
                    <input name="FirstName" required="true" type="string">
                        <description>First Name</description>
                        <defaultValue>John</defaultValue>
                        <constraints>
                            <constraint mandatory="true" type="oneOf">
                                    <value>John</value>
                                    <value>Paul</value>
                                    <value>Ringo</value>
                                    <value>George</value>
                            </constraint>
                        </constraints>
                    </input>
                    <input name="LastName" required="true" type="string">
                        <description>Last Name</description>
                        <defaultValue>Lennon</defaultValue>
                        <constraints>
                            <constraint mandatory="true" type="oneOf">
                                    <value>Lennon</value>
                                    <value>Mccarty</value>
                                    <value>Starr</value>
                                    <value>Harrison</value>
                            </constraint>
                        </constraints>
                    </input>
                </inputs>
                <outputs>
                  <output isArray="false" type="HelloWorldObject"/>
                </outputs>
            </operation>
            <objects>
                <object name="HelloWorldObject">
                    <field name="FirstName" type="string" isArray="false" />
                    <field name="LastName" type="string" isArray="false" />
                </object>
            </objects>
        </operations>

</block>
```

JavaScript Class Definition

JavaScript is a dynamic, weakly typed, prototype-based language. Each object that is defined can have properties and methods dynamically assigned to it. The language has no concept of classes; instead, prototype functions are used to define properties, methods, and inheritance. In class-based programming, such as in .NET C#, the structure of the class is defined statically. When the class is instantiated, the language uses the structure of the class to hold the instance data. However, in prototype programming, objects are cloned from prototype functions, instead of the class definitions being static properties, and methods can be dynamically assigned to the object at runtime. Prototype functions are used extensively in the AJAX toolkit to help with the development experience with JavaScript and its ability to simulate object-orientated capabilities.

■**Tip** We recommend further background reading on JavaScript and Prototype functions using books such as *Pro JavaScript Techniques* by John Resig (Apress, 2006).

In Popfly, JavaScript prototype functions are used to define objects that are used by the interface. Let's now define the functions that will implement our block's XML interface. The first part of the block's JavaScript file contains references to two JavaScript assemblies. These assemblies are not required for the online tool but are needed in Visual Studio to provide IntelliSense. Here are those references:

```
/// <reference name="MicrosoftAjax.js" assembly="System.Web.Extensions,
Version=3.5.0.0, Culture=neutral, PublicKeyToken=31BF3856AD364E35" />

/// <reference name="Microsoft.Popfly.Explorer.Wizard.BlockAPI.js"
assembly="Microsoft.Popfly.Explorer.Wizard, Version=1.0.0.0, Culture=neutral,➥
 PublicKeyToken=c1ceb53b217f2480" />
```

The next part of the JavaScript code is a default constructor for the class definition:

```
function ApressHelloWorldClass()
{
}
```

If the class requires initialization of variables, these can be specified as a prototype function in the `initialize` function of the `ApressHelloWorldClass`. Popfly will call this function if the `hasInitialize` attribute is set to `true` on the Block node (`<Block class="ApressHelloWorldClass" hasInitialize="true">`). The class function follows:

```
ApressHelloWorldClass.prototype.initialize = function() {
}
```

Each operation that needs to be exposed by the JavaScript class is defined as a prototype function. In the Hello World block definition, we modify the `hello` operations to pass two parameters and return a custom `HelloWorldObject`:

```
ApressHelloWorldClass.prototype.hello = function(firstName, lastName) {

    var helloWorldResult = new HelloWorldObject(firstName, lastName);
    return helloWorldResult;
};
```

We must now define the objects as another function definition. Note that this doesn't need to be a prototype function, because shared instances aren't required.

```
function HelloWorldObject(firstName, lastName)
{
    this.FirstName=firstName;
    this.LastName=lastName;
}
```

Finally, we would like the HelloWorldObject to implement a toString() method so that it will display a formatted string when it is output into the environment. The string can be output as HTML.

```
HelloWorldObject.prototype.toString = function() {
    var html = "<div>";
    html += "<strong> My favorite Beatle is " + this.FirstName + " " + this.LastName
    + "</strong>"
    html += "</div>";
    return html;
};
```

The final JavaScript code is shown in Listing 6-2.

Listing 6-2. *Hello World Updated Block JavaScript file*

```
<?xml version
// This is some sample JavaScript code.  Change it for your block.
function ApressHelloWorldClass()
{
}


ApressHelloWorldClass.prototype.hello = function(firstName, lastName) {
    var helloWorldResult = new HelloWorldObject(firstName, lastName);
    return helloWorldResult;
};


HelloWorldObject.prototype.toString = function() {
    var html = "<div>";
    html += "<strong> My favorite Beatle is " + this.FirstName + " " + this.LastName
    + "</strong>"
    html += "</div>";
    return html;
};


function HelloWorldObject(firstName, lastName)
{
    this.FirstName=firstName;
    this.LastName=lastName;
}
```

If you would like to try the new updated block XML and JavaScript, open the Hello World block from Popfly by selecting Create ➤ Block. Locate the DataServicesHelloWorld block. Open the Block Description, and overwrite it with the XML file shown in Listing 6-1. Overwrite the block's code using Listing 6-2. After that, click the Save & Run icon to run the new block. A new browser window will load; click the Run icon to see the output, which should be "My favorite Beatle is John Lennon". Click the wrench icon on the block to change the first name and last name properties.

Handling Errors

Exception handling in Popfly blocks should generally be avoided, because if an exception is thrown, all mashup processing will stop. For example, if we are processing a collection of objects and stop on the first one, no other objects would be displayed. If errors need to be shown to end users, these should be returned as strings in the display using the `environment.output("<text>")` function. Pop-up alerting using the JavaScript `alert()` function should be avoided, because using this takes the current focus from the browser.

Developing Popfly Blocks with Data Services

There are two categories of Popfly blocks: display and API. The display block is used to visually display something to users. The API Popfly block is used encapsulate calls to web services and APIs, which are then exposed externally as Popfly operations. In this respect, any data services that are called are treated like any other API. Only one consideration must be made for data services. Because they are often hosted on a different domain, you must use cross-domain call for these services. Cross-domain calls, logically at least, are those that interact with a service outside the current server domain, for example, to retrieve Yahoo data from a server inside the Amazon domain.

Here's why this is important when developing Popfly blocks: by default, the browser security will either prompt the user for permission to make the cross-domain call or throw an error with no prompting. To prevent this situation, the Popfly environment contains a number of helpers to retrieve data from data services and other HTTP sources. These methods are `getText()`, `getXml()`, and `getHttpResponse()` and are explained in detail in the following sections.

Data Retrieval Methods

The key parameters of the data retrieval methods are the URL and headers. The URL defines which data service to call, and the headers specify one or more HTTP headers to pass into the call. This provides the ability to return the data in a JSON format by specifying the application or JSON MIME type in the HTTP `Accept` header.

getText() Methods

These methods perform an HTTP GET that retrieves an HTML or XML HTTP response from the URL given. The `async` method uses a callback function that is invoked once the data has been fetched, and is similar to an AJAX callback function. Here are the methods:

- `text = environment.getText(<url>)`
- `text = environment.getText(<url>, <callback>)`

getXml() Methods

These methods retrieve the HTTP response and parse it into an XML document. HTTP headers can be passed into the request by creating these to a JavaScript variable first:

- `var headers = [ new Header("key", "value"), new Header("content-type", "text/xml")];`
- `httpResponse = environment.GetXml("http://someurl", null, headers);`

The `<key>` parameter is used for blocks that have developer keys. The `<data>` parameter is used when performing a HTTP POST operation.

Here are the methods:

- `<xmlobject> = environment.getXml(<url>, <key>, <headers>, <data>)`
- `<xmlobject> = environment.getXmlAsync(<url>, <key>, <headers>, <data>, <callback>)`

getHttpResponse() Methods

These methods are similar to `getXml` except that you can specify a return type to load the response into:

- `<xmlobject> = environment.getHttpResponse(<url>, <key>, <headers>, <data>, <returnType>)`
- `<xmlobject> = environment.getHttpResponseAsync(<url>, <key>, <headers>, <data>, <callback>, <returnType>)`

Creating a Data Services Block

To help you understand how to create Popfly blocks, let's walk through an Exercise 6-2, which shows how we would expose the Northwind data service we created in Chapter 2. To do this, we must host the Northwind service on a public-facing server. For the purpose of this demonstration, we have hosted the Northwind service on `http://dataservices.spheregen.com/Northwind/Northwind.svc`.

EXERCISE 6-2: CREATING A DATA SERVICES BLOCK

This exercise will walk you through how to create a Hello World block using the online block creation tool and Visual Studio 2008.

1. First, we must create a Visual Studio solution to host the data block. Let's create a Visual Studio 2008 Popfly block project: In Visual Studio, select File ➤ New ➤ Web Site, and select Popfly Block. Specify the project location, and type **DataServicesNorthwind** for the name. Click OK, and choose Basic Block from the options presented. Click Finish.

2. Now, we must create the XML metadata associated with the service. This data block will expose a single method, getNorthwindCustomers(). This method will accept a City argument and output a collection of Customer objects. The input parameter that is specified will contain a default value of London. The default.xml file in the new DataServicesNorthwind project should be overwritten with Listing 6-3.

Listing 6-3. *Northwind XML Definition*

```
<?xml version="1.0"?>
<block xmlns:xsi="http://www.w3.org/2001/XMLSchema-instance"
    xsi:noNamespaceSchemaLocation="http://www.popfly.com/schemas/
blockschema.xsd"
    class="NorthwindClass">
    <operations>
        <operation name="getNorthwindCustomersByCity" callMode="auto">
            <description>Retrieves Northwind Customers By City</description>
                <inputs>
                    <input name="CityName" required="true" type="string">
                        <description>City Name</description>
                            <defaultValue>London</defaultValue>
                    </input>
                </inputs>
                <outputs>
                    <output isArray="true" type="custom" object="Customer"/>
                </outputs>
        </operation>
    </operations>
    <objects>
        <object name="Customer">
            <field name="CustomerID" type="string" isArray="false" />
            <field name="CompanyName" type="string" isArray="false" />
        </object>
    </objects>
</block>
```

3. The next step in the process is to add the JavaScript definition that acts against the XML definition. The methods must be written as JavaScript object functions that are defined as prototypes. The JavaScript class name must match the <block class="NorthwindClass"> attribute that was specified in the XML definition file, and the public prototype methods must match the XML definition's operations. Thus, we need to have a single prototype function called getNorthwindCustomers() that contains a City string argument. Using the code in Listing 6-4, overwrite everything in the default.js file in the project except the references to the Microsoft AJAX and Popfly Explorer assemblies—you must not remove those.

Listing 6-4. *Northwind JavaScript Definition*

```
/// <reference name="MicrosoftAjax.js" assembly="System.Web.Extensions,➥
xsi Version=3.5.0.0, Culture=neutral, PublicKeyToken=31BF3856AD364E35" />
/// <reference name="Microsoft.Popfly.Explorer.Wizard.BlockAPI.js"➥
xsiassembly="Microsoft.Popfly.Explorer.Wizard, Version=1.0.0.0,➥
```

```
Culture=neutral, PublicKeyToken=c1ceb53b217f2480" />
/// -----------------------------------------------------------------
//declare/define the class
function NorthwindClass() {
}

//define the getCustomers function in the class
NorthwindClass.prototype.getNorthwindCustomersByCity= function(CityName)
{
    var jsonText = environment.getHttpResponse("➥
http://dataservices.spheregen.com/Northwind/Northwind.svc/➥
 Customers?$filter=(City eq '" + CityName + "')➥
        ", null, [{ "Key": "Accept", "Value": "application/json"}], null);
    var response = (eval("(" + jsonText.responseText + ")")).d;
    var results = []
    var currentResult = {}
    for (var i in response)
    {
        currentResult = new Customer(response[i]["CustomerID"],
                            response[i]["CompanyName"]);
        results.push(currentResult);
     }
     return results;
}

Customer.prototype.toString = function() {
    var html = "<div>";
    html += "<strong>" + this.CompanyName + "</strong>"
    html += "</div>";
    return html;
};
//define the customer object that will be returned
function Customer(customerId, companyName) {
    this.CustomerID= customerId;
    this.CompanyName= companyName;
}
```

4. Now that we have created the block, we can test it by uploading it to our Popfly space. Simply run the project in Visual Studio by pressing Ctrl-F5. Then, sign in to Popfly, and follow the prompts to upload the project.

Creating a Restaurant Rating Mashup

Let's create a Popfly mashup that display top-rated restaurants on a map. The mashup consists of four blocks: user selection, geocoding, restaurant rating, and Virtual Earth. Essentially, the mashup starts by displaying two input boxes to ask the user for a city and type of cuisine.

The Restaurant Rating block is then searched using these parameters. Restaurants that are received by the restaurant rating block are fed into the geocoding block, which converts these details into geographic latitude and longitude coordinates. These points, along with the restaurants' details, are sent to the Virtual Earth mapping display block, which displays the restaurants at the specified coordinates as pushpins. This mashup's concepts are shown in Figure 6-10.

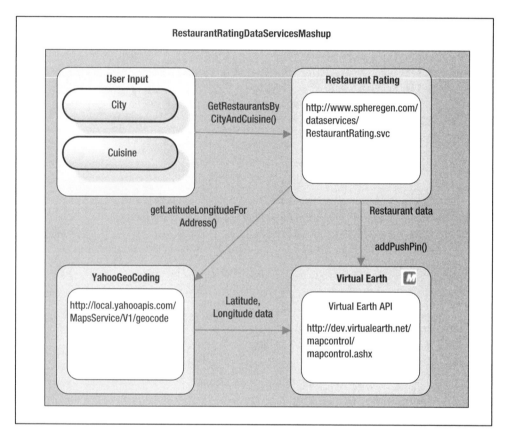

Figure 6-10. *Restaurant Rating mashup conceptual overview*

Exercise 6-3 explains the steps to create the restaurant rating data service. The resultant code for these exercises can be found on the CD ROM provided within the folder named *RestaurantRating*. The restaurant rating data service block, as at the time of this writing, will appear on the Popfly web site in the Data category. If you can't find the blocks online for any reason, the exercise can be reproduced by recreating all the blocks in Popfly. Again, remember that the data services block requires that you have a public-facing server to host the service.

EXERCISE 6-3: CREATING THE RESTAURANT RATING DATA SERVICES BLOCK

This aim of the restaurant rating block is to retrieve a collection of entities from the restaurant rating data service using two $filter operations for the city and cuisine. To display something meaningful to the user along with the pushpin, the block will also use the $expand operator to retrieve the main photo and cuisine description for the restaurant. By default, Popfly works with lists of data as untyped lists. To enhance the usability of the block, typed entity definitions will be placed into the XML file associated with the block. To avoid cross-domain issues, the data service will be called using Popfly's getHTTPResponse method.

A restaurant rating database is used as the source of the block, and it is created using the scripts located in the RestaurantRating\Database folder in this book's downloadable code. If you haven't got the code at hand, you can manually create the database structure using the entity model shown in Figure 6-11.

Creating the Restaurant Rating Data Service

1. Create the ApressRestaurantRating database, tables, and relationship. First, go to SQL Server 2005 or 2008 and open the Query Analyzer. Click File ➤ Open File, and navigate to the CD ROM database's scripts\ SQLDDL.sql script. Press F5, and check for any errors in the script execution.

2. With Query Analyzer still open, insert example records into the database. Click File ➤ Open File, and navigate to the database's scripts\SQLCreateScript.sql script. Press F5, and check for any errors in the script execution.

3. Create a web application by clicking File ➤ New Web Site. Type **RestaurantRating.WebApp** as the name of this project, and click OK.

4. Add an Entity Framework model item by right-clicking the project and choosing ADO.NET Entity Data Model. Name this RestaurantRatingModel.edmx, and click OK.

5. From the Entity Data Model wizard dialog, choose Generate from Database. Click Next, and click New Connection. Choose the ApressRestaurantRating database, and click Next. Select all of the tables, and click Finish.

6. Add an ADO.NET data service item by right-clicking the project and choosing ADO.NET Data Service. Name this RestaurantRating.svc, and click OK.

7. Open the RestaurantRating.svc.cs file, and grant full read access to the both the service and entity sets as shown in Listing 6-5.

Listing 6-5. *The Resource Permissions Access Script*

```
using System;
using System.Collections.Generic;
using System.Data.Services;
using System.Linq;
using System.ServiceModel.Web;
using System.Web;
```

```
namespace Apress.Data.Services.RestaurantRating.WebApp
{
    public class RestaurantRating : DataService<ApressRestaurantRatingEntities>
    {
        // This method is called only once to initialize service-wide policies.
        public static void InitializeService(IDataServiceConfiguration config)
        {
            config.SetEntitySetAccessRule("*", EntitySetRights.AllRead);
            config.SetServiceOperationAccessRule("*",
                        ServiceOperationRights.AllRead);
        }
    }
}
```

8. Verify that the service works correctly by right-clicking the `RestaurantRating.svc` file and selecting Set As Start Page. Then, press F5 to debug.

9. To familiarize yourself with the entities provided by the Entity Framework, open the EDM by double-clicking `RestaurantRatingModel.edmx`; the EDM is shown in Figure 6-11. Note that the restaurant entity is the main entity that will be retrieved from the block.

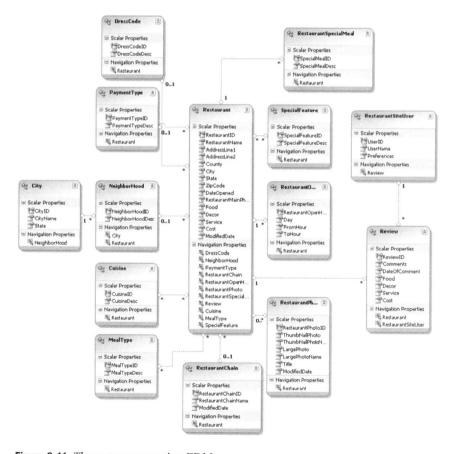

Figure 6-11. *The restaurant rating EDM*

10. The restaurant rating data service should now be hosted using a public-facing server. For the purpose of this exercise we have hosted the service on `http://dataservices.spheregen.com/RestaurantRating/RestaurantService.svc`.

Creating the Restaurant Rating Popfly Block

1. Create a new Popfly block in Visual Studio by selecting File ➤ New ➤ Web Site. Select Popfly Block, and specify the project location. Type **RestaurantRatingDataServices** for the name, and click OK. Choose Basic Block from the options presented, and click Finish.

2. Open the `default.xml` file, and overwrite this using the XML in Listing 6-6.

Listing 6-6. *Restaurant Rating XML File*

```xml
<?xml version="1.0" encoding="utf-8"?>
<block xmlns:xsi="http://www.w3.org/2001/XMLSchema-instance"
  xsi:noNamespaceSchemaLocation="http://www.popfly.com/schemas/blockschema.xsd"
  class="RestaurantRatingDataServices">
    <providerName>Apress</providerName>
        <providerUrl> http://dataservices.spheregen.com/RestaurantRating/
  RestaurantService.svc</providerUrl>
        <suggest output="geodisplay" input="userinput"/>
        <operations>
            <operation name="getRestaurantsByCityAndCuisine" callMode="auto">
                <description>Get a list of Restaurants By City and Cuisine
                </description>
                    <inputs>
                        <input name="City" required="true" type="string">
                            <description>City where the Restaurant is located
                            </description>
                                <defaultValue>New York</defaultValue>
                        </input>
                        <input name="Cuisine" required="true" type="string">
                            <description>The type of Cuisine that is served at
                             the Restaurant</description>
                            <defaultValue>Thai</defaultValue>
                        </input>
                    </inputs>
                    <outputs>
                        <output isArray="true" type="custom"
                            object="Restaurant" />
                    </outputs>
            </operation>
        </operations>
        <objects>
            <object name="Restaurant">
                <field name="RestaurantID" type="string" isArray="false" />
                <field name="RestaurantName" type="string" isArray="false"/>
                <field name="AddressLine1" type="string" isArray="false"/>
```

```
                <field name="AddressLine2" type="string" isArray="false"/>
                <field name="County" type="string" isArray="false"/>
                <field name="City" type="string" isArray="false"/>
                <field name="State" type="string" isArray="false"/>
                <field name="ZipCode" type="string" isArray="false"/>
                <field name="FullAddress" type="string" isArray="false"/>
                <field name="DateOpened" type="dateTime" isArray="false"/>
                <field name="Food" type="integer" isArray="false"/>
                <field name="Decor" type="integer" isArray="false"/>
                <field name="Service" type="integer" isArray="false"/>
                <field name="Cost" type="decimal" isArray="false"/>
                <field name="Rating" type="decimal" isArray="false"/>
            </object>
        </objects>
    </block>
```

3. Open the default.js file, and overwrite the JavaScript definitions using the code in Listing 6-7. The dataUrl variable is used to point to the data service that we have hosted.

Listing 6-7. *Restaurant Rating JavaScript Definition*

```
function RestaurantRatingDataServices()
{
    this.dataUrl = "http://dataservices.spheregen.com/RestaurantRating/➥
    RestaurantService.svc/Restaurant";
}
RestaurantRatingDataServices.prototype.getRestaurantsByCityAndCuisine➥
= function
 RestaurantRatingDataServices$getRestaurantRating(city, cuisine)
{
    var jsonText = environment.getHttpResponse(this.dataUrl +➥
     "?$expand=Cuisine&$filter=(City eq '" + city + "') and➥
(Cuisine/CuisineDesc eq '" + cuisine + "')", null, [{ "Key": "Accept",➥
    "Value": "application/json"}], null);
    var response = (eval("(" + jsonText.responseText + ")")).d;

    return this.parseResponse(response);
};


RestaurantRatingDataServices.prototype.query = function
RestaurantRatingDataServices$query(query) {
    var jsonText = environment.getHttpResponse(this.dataUrl + "?" + query,➥
    null,    [{ "Key": "Accept", "Value": "application/json"}], null);
    var response = (eval("(" + jsonText.responseText + ")")).d;

    return this.parseResponse(response);
};
```

```
RestaurantRatingDataServices.prototype.parseResponse =
function ResturantRatingDataServices$parseResponse(response)
{
    var results = []
    var currentResult = {}
    for (var i in response) {
        currentResult = new Restaurant(response[i]["RestaurantID"],
                                       response[i]["RestaurantName"],
                                       response[i]["AddressLine1"],
                                       response[i]["AddressLine2"],
                                       response[i]["County"],
                                       response[i]["City"],
                                       response[i]["State"],
                                       response[i]["ZipCode"],
                                       response[i]["DateOpened"],
                                       response[i]["Food"],
                                       response[i]["Decor"],
                                       response[i]["Service"],
                                       response[i]["Cost"]);
    results.push(currentResult);
    }

    for (var i = 0; i < results.length; i++) {

        results[i].toString = function() {
    var output = "<p>";
    for (var field in this) {
        if (field == "toString") {
            continue; //Don't show output for this function!
    }
        output += field + " : " + this[field] + " <br/>";
            }
            output += "</p>";
            return output;
        };

    }

    return results;
};

Restaurant.prototype.toString = function() {
var html = "<div>";
    html += "<strong>" + this.RestaurantName + "</strong>"
    html += "</div>";
    return html;
};
```

```
function Restaurant(restaurantID, restaurantName, addressline1,
                    addressline2, county,
                    city, state, zipCode, dateOpened, food,
                    decor, service, cost, rating ) {
    this.RestaurantID = restaurantID;
    this.RestaurantName = restaurantName;
    this.AddressLine1 = addressline1;
    this.AddressLine2 = addressline2;
    this.County = county;
    this.City = city;
    this.State = state;
    this.ZipCode = zipCode;
    this.FullAddress = addressline1 + ", " + addressline2 + ", " + county +
        ", " + city + ", " + state + ", " + zipCode;
    this.DateOpened = dateOpened;
    this.Food = food;
    this.Decor = decor;
    this.Service = service;
    this.Cost = cost;
    this.Rating = (food + decor + service)/3;
};
```

4. Now that we have created the block, let's test it by uploading it to our Popfly space. First sign in to Popfly using the Popfly Explorer in Visual Studio.

5. To publish the block to the Popfly environment from within Visual Studio, click the Popfly menu, and choose Save to Popfly. When the Popfly project dialog appears, type **RestaurantRatingDataServices** as the name of the data block, and click "Accept and Publish" and then OK. If prompted, Choose Open Local Copy.

6. Run the block in Visual Studio by pressing F5. The Popfly environment will appear in a browser, and you can click the green Run icon to start the mashup. Click Debug Console icon to see information messages.

■**Note** Full debugging capabilities are built into Popfly, so you can step into and over the blocks' code within Visual Studio.

In Exercise 6-4, we'll create the other custom block, User Input.

EXERCISE 6-4: CREATING THE USER INPUT BLOCK

Here are the instructions to create the User Input block:

1. Create a new Popfly block in Visual Studio by selecting File ➤ New ➤ Web Site. Select Popfly Block. Specify the project location, and type **RestaurantRatingUserInput** for the name. Click OK.

2. Open the `default.xml` file, and overwrite the block XML using the code listed in Listing 6-8. Then, overwrite the JavaScript definitions in `default.js` using the code in Listing 6-9. This specifies two user HTML input boxes and a search button event that is executed asynchronously.

Listing 6-8. *User Input Block XML Definition File*

```
Xml Definition

<?xml version="1.0" encoding="utf-8"?>
<block xmlns:xsi="http://www.w3.org/2001/XMLSchema-instance"➥
xsi:noNamespaceSchemaLocation=http://www.popfly.com/schemas/blockschema.xsd➥
 class="UserInputClass" hasInitialize="true">
    <providerLogoUrl>/content/components/icons/userInputLogo.png➥
    </providerLogoUrl>
    <blockLogoUrl>/content/components/icons/userInputSquareLogo.png➥
    </blockLogoUrl>
    <blockIconUrl>/content/components/icons/userInput.png</blockIconUrl>
    <suggest output="flickr"/>
    <operations>
        <operation name="getCityAndCuisine" callMode="async">
                <description>Retrieves the City And Cusine</description>
            <inputs/>
            <outputs>
                <output isArray="false" type="custom" object="CityAndCuisine"/>
            </outputs>
        </operation>
    </operations>
    <objects>
        <object name="CityAndCuisine">
            <field name="City" type="string" isArray="false" />
            <field name="Cuisine" type="string"  isArray="false" />
        </object>
    </objects>
</block>


JavaScript Definition

function UserInputClass() {
};

UserInputClass.prototype.initialize = function() {
    this.dataUrl = "http://dataservices.spheregen.com/RestaurantRating/
    RestaurantService.svc/";

    // Emit this first so it can be on top of blocks used later
    environment.output("<div id=userInputBlockDiv style=background:#333;
                                  color:#fff;padding:1em;></div>");
```

```
    //Get List of Cities from DataService
    var jsonText = environment.getHttpResponse(this.dataUrl +
    "City?$orderby=CityName", null, [{ "Key": "Accept",➥
"Value": "application/json"}], null);
    var response = (eval("(" + jsonText.responseText + ")")).d;

    var currentResult = {}
    for (var i in response) {
        currentResult = new CityObject(response[i]["CityID"],
                                      response[i]["CityName"],
                                      response[i]["State"]);

        Array.add(UserInputClass.cityCollection, currentResult);
    }

    //Get List of Cuisines from DataService
    var jsonText = environment.getHttpResponse(=➥
this.dataUrl + "Cuisine?$orderby=➥
CuisineDesc", null, [{ "Key": "Accept",➥
"Value": "application/json"}],➥
                        null);
    var response = (eval("(" + jsonText.responseText + ")")).d;

    var currentResult = {}
  for (var i in response) {
        currentResult = new CuisineObject(response[i]["CuisineID"],
                                      response[i]["CuisineDesc"]);

        Array.add(UserInputClass.cuisineCollection, currentResult);
    }
};

    UserInputClass.prototype.getCityAndCuisine = function(callback) {

    var cityOptions = "<option>[Enter City]</option>";
    var cuisineOptions = "<option>[Enter Cuisine]</option>";

    //Build the option list for cities
    for (var i = 0; i < UserInputClass.cityCollection.length;  i++) {
        cityOptions += "<option value='" + environment.
                                escapeQuotes(UserInputCla➥
                                    ss.cityCollection[i].CityName) + "'>" +
                                UserInputClass.cityCollection[i].CityName➥
        +   "</option>";
    }
```

```
    //Build the option list for cuisines
    for (var i = 0; i < UserInputClass.cuisineCollection.length; i++) {
        cuisineOptions += "<option value='" +➥
        environment.escapeQuotes(UserInput➥
        Class.cuisineCollection[i].CuisineName) + "'>" + ➥
        UserInputClass.cuisineCollection[i].CuisineName + "</option>";
    }

    var num = UserInputClass.getCityAndCuisine_Counter;

    //Add HTML
    document.getElementById("userInputBlockDiv").innerHTML +=
    " City : <SELECT id='userInput_getCityFromDropdown'>" + cityOptions +
      "</SELECT><BR/>" + " Cuisine :
        <SELECT id='userInput_getCuisineFromDropdown'>"
                + cuisineOptions
  + "</SELECT><BR/>" +
    "<BUTTON id='userInput_getCityAndCuisineButton'>Go</BUTTON><BR/>";

    Array.add(UserInputClass.getCityAndCuisine_Callbacks, function() {
        callback(new UserInputTwoValues(document.getElementById
                    ("userInput_getCityFromDropdown").value,
                      document.getElementById("userInput_getCuisineFrom➥
                      Dropdown").value));
    });

    UserInputClass.getCityAndCuisine_Counter++;

    document.getElementById("userInput_getCityAndCuisineButton").onclick = ➥
        UserInputClass.getCityAndCuisine_Callbacks[0];

};

function UserInputTwoValues(value1, value2) {
    this.City = value1;
    this.Cuisine = value2;

    this.toString = function() {
        return this.City + ", " + this.Cuisine + " ";
    }
};

function CityObject(cityID, cityName, state) {
    this.CityID = cityID;
    this.CityName = cityName;
    this.State = state;
};
```

```
function CuisineObject(cuisineID, cuisineName) {
    this.CuisineID = cuisineID;
    this.CuisineName = cuisineName;
};

// Allow multiple instances, each with their own callback:
UserInputClass.getCityAndCuisine_Counter = 0;
UserInputClass.cityCollection = new Array();
UserInputClass.cuisineCollection = new Array();
UserInputClass.getCityAndCuisine_Callbacks = new Array();
```

3. To publish the block to the Popfly from within Visual Studio, click the Popfly menu, and choose Save to Popfly. When the Popfly project dialog appears, type **RestaurantRatingUserInput** as the name of the block, and click "Accept and Publish" followed by OK. If prompted, choose Open Local Copy.

In Exercise 6-5, we'll create the mashup and link the blocks together. We have taken the Yahoo Geocoding and Virtual Earth blocks from the Popfly site. In these blocks are missing from this site or are not functioning correctly at a later date, we took the liberty of ripping these blocks and placing them in this chapter's code's RestaurantRating folder at the time of this writing, so you can use the versions of the blocks we used if you need them.

EXERCISE 6-5: CREATING THE RESTAURANT RATING MASHUP

We will now create the mashup using the blocks that have been published:

1. Open Popfly by navigating to http://www.popfly.com.

2. Create a mashup by clicking Create Mashup ➤ Mashup.

3. Click the RestaurantRatingDataServices block in the My Blocks & Data section, and drag it onto the design surface.

4. Click the RestaurantRatingUserInput block in the My Blocks & Data section, and drag it the design surface.

5. Search the Popfly web site for the Yahoo Geocoding block and Virtual Earth blocks. Click and drag them onto the design surface as you did for the previous blocks.

Connecting the Blocks

1. Click the right circle of the RestaurantRatingUserInput block and then click the left circle of the RestaurantRatingDataServices block to connect these two.

2. Click the right circle on RestaurantRatingDataServices followed by the left circle on the Yahoo Geocoding block to connect these two blocks.

3. Clicking on the right circle of RestaurantRatingDataServices followed by the left circle of the Virtual Earth block to connect these. Please note that you will receive a warning on connecting the blocks together, but it will go away once the Yahoo Geocoding block is connected.

4. Connect the Yahoo Geocoding and Virtual Earth blocks by clicking on the right circle on the Yahoo Geocoding followed by the left circle of the Virtual Earth block.

The mashup should now look like Figure 6-12.

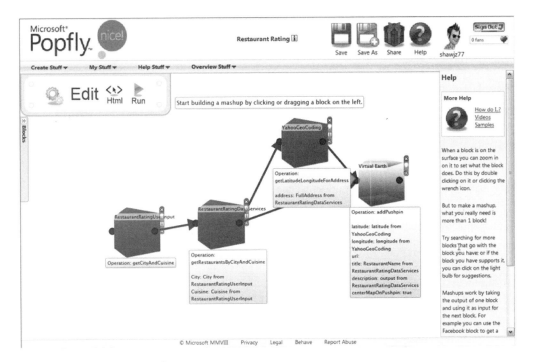

Figure 6-12. *Restaurant mashup*

Setting the RestaurantRatingDataServices Properties

Configure the RestaurantRatingDataServices block by clicking the wrench icon and specifying the information in Table 6-4.

Table 6-4. *The getRestaurantsByCityAndCuisine Opeartion Values*

Input	Source	Value
City	RestaurantRatingUserInput	City
Cuisine	RestaurantRatingUserInput	Cuisine

Setting the Yahoo Geocoding Properties

Configure the Yahoo Geocoding block by clicking the wrench icon and specifying the information in Table 6-5.

Table 6-5. *The getLatitudeLongitudeForAddress Value*

Inputs	Source	Value
Address	RestaurantRatingDataServices	FullAddress

Setting the Virtual Earth Properties

Configure the Virtual Earth block by clicking the wrench icon and specifying the information in Table 6-6.

Table6-6. *The addPushpin Values*

Inputs	Source	Value
Latitude	YahooGeoCoding	latitude
Longitude	YahooGeoCoding	longitude
URL	[custom]	
Title	RestaurantRatingDataServices	RestaurantName
Description	RestaurantRatingDataServices	[entire Restaurant object]
CenterMapOnPushpin	[custom]	true
Properties		
DefaultZoomLevel		12
UsePhotoUrlAsIcon		true

Saving and Running the Mashup

1. To save the mashup, click the Save icon and type **Restaurant** as the project name and **Restaurant DataServices** as the tag. Click "Accept and Save".

2. To test the mashup, click the green Run icon. The browser navigates to the mashup and should show a Virtual Earth map with two drop-down menus. Specify New York in the City field and Thai in the Cuisine field, and click OK. This focuses the Virtual Earth map on New York and place a new pushpin in the Thai restaurant's location.

3. Share the mashup by clicking the Share icon, so that we can include the mashup in a web page.

In Exercise 6-6, the final one in this chapter, we'll create the web page that hosts the mashup.

EXERCISE 6-6: CREATING A POPFLY WEB PAGE TO HOST THE MASHUP

This exercise provides steps to create a simple web page to host our restaurant rating mashup within the Popfly environment.

1. Create a web page in the Popfly online environment by clicking Create Stuff ➤ Web Page.

2. In the web creator interface, click the page style ribbon, and click the header. In the Customize Header dialog, type **Top Restaurants in your area** as the Site Title and **Restaurant Rating Website** in the Site Slogan.

3. Change the theme of the web site by clicking Theme, selecting "Food and Beverage", and choosing one the theme's pictures.

4. Change the default zones by clicking on Zone 1. Click the Layout icon, and specify Single Area.

5. Add the mashup by clicking Zone 1, selecting Mashup icon, and choosing Restaurant Rating.

6. Save the web page by clicking the Save icon. Type **Restaurant Rating Website** for the title and **Restaurant Data Services Website** for the tag, and click Accept and Save.

7. Test the web page by clicking the preview icon. The final mashup web page should look like the one shown in Figure 6-13.

Figure 6-13. *Our mashup on a web page*

Enterprise Mashups

Although mashups started as a consumer phenomenon, some credible examples bring the advantages of mashup while addressing corporate concerns over security, governance, and enterprise-ready architecture. Mashups can help corporations embrace Web 2.0 ideals by leveraging existing SOA investments and improving time to market for online services that would typically take years to complete.

Web 2.0 technologies such as wikis, tags, and mashups are increasingly being used to breathe new life into corporations, and this trend has been dubbed "Enterprise 2.0." An enterprise mashup can contain anything important to a corporation and can contribute directly or indirectly to its bottom line. Enterprise mashups can affect all parts of the business from information workers to sales and management.

Mashups help maintain data integrity and facilitate the use of one view of a system: Historically, employees have often used multiple spreadsheets to store data from numerous line of business (LOB) systems. If the LOB is updated, this data change must be manually added to the spreadsheet. If, for example, sales data spreadsheets were slow in being updated, incorrect financial decisions might be made.

A mashup in the enterprise environment could be a solution born from a specific problem isolated to a single user or a specific issue. In time, other users may also wish to use or build on the mashup, and the mashup might evolve considerably. For example, assume a manager must approve an expense report. In normal circumstances, managers just click OK to approve the report, and that's the end of story. However, what if a manager is needs a business intelligence view of the current budget and data from an LOB system to make an intelligent decision about a questionable expense report? The business intelligence, LOB data, and expense report could be mashed together on a single page so that the manager has all the facts before clicking the OK button.

Here are a few more ideas for enterprise mashups to solve common problems that might be faced by department and industry vertical:

- *Sales*

  - You're going to a conference, and you want to know whether anyone from your LinkedIn or Facebook network is also going to attend.

  - You're using a popular online sales management tool, such as Salesforce.com or Microsoft CRM 4.0, and you want to know if any of your leads have direct or indirect associations are also LinkedIn or Facebook friends.

  - You want to map your leads onto a map to see how to best distribute your sales team.

- *Human resources*

  - Your human resource system has direct access to job applicant LinkedIn profiles to search for people who are known experts in their field as voted by the LinkedIn community.

  - Direct access to view job listings and candidates from a number of job sites.

- *Real estate*: You want to view current properties that are available in a certain area.

- *Supply chain distributer*: See your supply chain inventory levels on a map and the logistics data stored in a system such as Microsoft Dynamics NAV.

Security

The key issue with enterprise mashups is security. If companies are creating dynamic services that use data from multiple resources, the data will require a federated security model to access these services (clean separation between the service and the client and the associated authentication and authorization procedures). Microsoft is currently working on its cloud-computing platform that will provide some of these services such as the federated security model; we'll cover cloud computing the Chapter 9.

Data Services

Data Services will be used as a key enabler in an enterprise mashup environment. If you wanted to expose data from your legacy CRM application based on Oracle or DB2, you could simply use the entity framework and expose a Data Services layer as a RESTFul service. If SOA best practices are followed, data services, along with traditional services, can be placed within a repository store such as Universal Description Discovery Integration (UDDI). This UDDI will, in turn, provide a set of reusable components that software developers and managers can use to locate services that can be mashed together.

SharePoint

The next version of SharePoint will reportedly contain built-in AJAX libraries support and will most likely contain Popfly-like capabilities for creating enterprise mashups. Mashups can also be created using SharePoint 2007. IDV Solutions (`http://www.idvsolutions.com`) has created a tool called Visual Fusion Server that can be used to connect to multiple enterprise sources, data files, spreadsheets, and so on to leverage these within a SharePoint dashboard; you can see a demonstration at `http://wondersoftheworld.idvsolutions.com/default.aspx`.

Summary

Mashups have been listed as one of the top strategic technologies that will change how users interact with the web over the next five years. "Strategic technologies," as defined by leading market research company Gartner (who every year lists the top five strategic technologies), are those that could disrupt IT or business, often require a significant investment, and could cripple organizations if adopted too late.

Mashups come in two flavors: user-based mashups and enterprise mashups. User-based mashups are often created by nonprogrammers who typically use one of the mashup environments described in this chapter, like Popfly, to create mashups that will be shared with friends and family in social networking web sites. Enterprise mashups are used in the corporate space and must have tighter security, because companies need to control how employees and other consumers access their data. Enterprise mashups empower users to make decisions on using the most up-to-date data and remove the reliance on IT to create numerous, customized data interfaces. However, before implementing enterprise mashups, companies first need to invest in SOA and centralized dashboards.

And here are a couple of potential sources of profit in mashups:

- Companies might specialize in creating mashup widgets for consumers.

- Companies specializing in Data as a Service (DaaS) solutions, such as backing up common data source databases, Excel, Word, etc.; see Chapter 9 for more information.

- Advertisement space might be sold on interesting mashups.

- Companies could specialize in providing enterprise mashup infrastructure services such as delivering technology that stores and runs mashups. A decent example of one company that is doing this is JackBe (http://www.jackbe.com).

However, for mashups to reach their full potential requires a shift in the mindset of typical nonprogrammers: they need to begin to think of mashup editors as a way to manage their data. Most everyday users have data on different media, web sites, databases, and so, and mashups provide a way of having a single view of this data. Marketing dollars will need to be spent by big companies, so that users could see how easily mashups can be created and how mashups help in everyday situations such as going to the movies, eating out, or planning a vacation.

CHAPTER 7

■■■

Silverlight 2.0 Solutions

The most common way to create a web site is to present HTML web pages back to the user for rendering in a browser. Chapter 5 describes how developing applications that render HTML content has evolved over the last decade; it details how ASP.NET can be employed to render HTML server side using data returned from ADO.NET data services, and how client-side AJAX techniques can be used to consume data services within the browser to manipulate the HTML DOM. In this chapter we are going to look at an alternative technology for creating web sites called Silverlight, and how to consume data services within Silverlight solutions.

In order to work through the examples in this chapter, you will need to ensure the following software is installed on your computer:

- Visual Studio 2008 and .NET Framework 3.5 Service Pack 1

- Microsoft Silverlight Tools for Visual Studio 2008 SP1

- Microsoft Expression Blend 2 SP1

■Note You'll find links to download all the software listed here at `http://silverlight.net/GetStarted/`. The Silverlight Tools for Visual Studio 2008 SP1 download includes the Visual Studio tooling for Silverlight, the Silverlight 2 SDK, and the development runtime of the Silverlight 2 plug-in that enables debugging support in Visual Studio.

The Web Application Spectrum

The fact that HTML is as old as the Internet itself makes it a ubiquitous markup language understood by all browsers (albeit with varying results in different browsers). The ubiquitous nature of HTML is its strength, but as a markup language it does have limitations; HTML web pages are normally based around a flow layout, where content will best fit the size of the browser window and the text size of the browser. Beyond this there is little control over content layout, and typography is limited to flow from left to right. Image content does not scale smoothly when a user zooms in because images are served from raster-based file formats (such as GIF or JPG images), which means they are made up of fixed pixels. There are graphic design limitations to HTML, because it expects content to be rendered only in rectangular boxes, and beyond static images, there is little support for rich interactive content such as animation, audio, or video.

As web applications have evolved and matured, demand has grown for richer user experiences. AJAX techniques that manipulate the HTML DOM client side provide a richer experience than traditional server-side applications, but content is still limited by HTML itself. Requirements that demand richer content have driven the adoption of new technologies that augment HTML content with richer media. Technologies that meet these requirements include Flex and Silverlight, which are used to deliver a new breed of web applications commonly known as Rich Internet Applications (RIAs).

What is the cost of a richer user experience? Primarily, it is limiting your target audience to specific browsers and devices; unless a user has the Silverlight plug-in installed, he will not be able to view Silverlight content. However, the Silverlight plug-in is a lightweight download, and much like Flash it is becoming increasingly commonplace on an end user's computer. The Silverlight plug-in currently works only on Internet Explorer, Firefox, and Safari browsers (on both Windows and Mac operating systems). This accounts for the vast majority of computers out there, but if you need to target all browsers, operating systems, and devices (including mobile devices), you will need to stick to HTML content until Silverlight is supported on other browsers and operating systems.

The second cost of a richer user experience is bandwidth; a site with only rich content will undoubtedly cause longer download times when an application is first accessed. As broadband becomes increasingly common, this is less of an issue, but even then it still needs to be considered. For this reason, it can be useful to mix Silverlight content with HTML where it suffices, because this reduces the payload of the application's pages.

With so many choices for web application development now at developers' fingertips, it can be somewhat daunting to decide which technologies to apply to your application. One way to view this is as a spectrum of presentation technologies as shown in Figure 7-1.

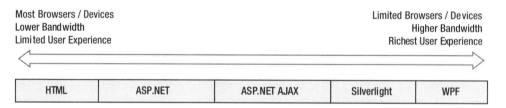

Figure 7-1. *The web application spectrum*

For the majority of developments, the options at either end of this spectrum will be too limiting to justify the cost of development. Therefore, this book concentrates on the middle three options. ASP.NET and AJAX solutions were described in Chapter 5. The rest of this chapter describes Silverlight and how to consume data services from Silverlight applications.

Light Up the Web

Silverlight is a relatively new technology that installs a cross-browser-compatible plug-in to a browser to run Silverlight content from within an HTML page. Silverlight uses its own XML-based markup language called XAML to render content within the plug-in. Silverlight XAML markup is a subset of that offered by Windows Presentation Foundation (WPF) used to develop rich user experiences on the Windows platform. XAML offers many benefits over traditional HTML; content is rendered using vector graphics, which means that the content scales correctly to the size of the window it is being rendered in. XAML provides much more control over content layout than HTML, which means that your application can respond more effectively to sizing a browser window across different screen resolutions. XAML also provides much more support for rich media, such as streaming video and animation to provide richer user experiences.

Silverlight was first released in 2007 as version 1.0. Silverlight 1.0 uses XAML markup to present content that is controlled using code written in JavaScript. Silverlight 2.0 builds upon the capabilities of XAML markup and replaces the interpreted JavaScript code model with compiled code that runs on the browser within the Silverlight common language runtime (CLR), much like native .NET applications run with the .NET CLR. This compiled code can be written using any native .NET language, such as C# or VB .NET. Using compiled code provides many benefits over the JavaScript model; compiled code provides much improved performance over JavaScript, and the object-oriented constructs of a language such as C# make for much more maintainable solutions than can be achieved using JavaScript. An additional benefit for web developers used to developing ASP.NET applications is that the development paradigm and design-time experience now feel very familiar, with a markup language similar to ASP.NET markup and a code-behind file written in C# or VB .NET.

Compiled code running in the Silverlight CLR runs against a lightweight version of the .NET Framework. This framework follows an identical namespace structure to its bigger parent, but only appropriate classes remain available within Silverlight. So for example, the System.ServiceModel namespace used by WCF still exists within Silverlight, but only for the purpose of consuming services; thus classes under this namespace that are used in .NET to develop WCF services are not available within Silverlight. Likewise, the System.Windows.Controls namespace used by WPF exists, but WPF XAML features not supported in Silverlight XAML have been removed.

Silverlight Controls

Much like ASP.NET web sites, Silverlight 2.0 applications have a clean separation of concerns between content contained in markup and code to handle logic for the content. A Silverlight 2.0 application is constructed of user controls, each of which consists of XAML markup and a code-behind file (written in C# in our examples).

XAML is a specific format of XML used by both Silverlight and WPF applications as a markup language. The significance of using a markup language is that it creates a familiar paradigm for web designers and developers to collaborate in a similar fashion to working on traditional HTML web pages. Using markup languages makes it easy to create design-time WYSIWYG tooling. The Silverlight tools for Visual Studio 2008 provide such an experience for developers, while Expression Blend 2 SP1 provides a design-time experience tailored for designers. Both products are able to work against the same Visual Studio solution, which means that designers and developers can work side by side during the project cycle to deliver solutions in the most productive manner possible.

Silverlight user controls are composed of other controls in XAML markup. Silverlight provides a rich set of prebuilt controls out of the box, and like ASP.NET you can use these controls to compose your own user controls to reuse elements of your application's design. At the root of a Silverlight application is a startup object, which is the root user control to execute when a Silverlight application is executed by the plug-in from an object element in an HTML web page. This is normally the Page.xaml file that is created when a new Silverlight application is created, but it can be changed from within the project properties if necessary.

Silverlight control properties are set in XAML markup as element attributes much like ASP. NET markup. However, unlike ASP.NET markup, the declarative syntax uses XML namespaces. All Silverlight controls ultimately inherit from the System.Windows.Controls.Control class, which provides control properties that are common to all controls. Most importantly, the Control class includes the Name property, used to identify an instance of a control in XAML. Identifying a control in XAML means that you are able to reference the control in the code-behind. The Control class's properties are defined under the XML namespace http://schemas.microsoft. com/winfx/2006/xaml, which by default is declared in XAML using the name x. Thus, by default, the Name property is declared in XAML using the syntax x:Name="ControlName".

Some Silverlight controls are contained in additional assemblies from core Silverlight Framework. These can be found in the Silverlight 2.0 SDK. Silverlight assemblies can be referenced in much the same way as referencing any other .NET assembly. Controls used from additional referenced assemblies are referenced in XAML using additional XSD namespace references.

XAML provides an additional markup concept to those familiar with markup languages like HTML; nested XAML controls can use a feature called **Attached Properties**, which means that the markup for a child control can set the properties of a parent container control. This feature can provide clearer markup for nested controls; for example, a Grid control can define the layout rows and columns in markup, and then child controls of the Grid control do not have to be declared underneath each row and column, as each child control can refer to the attached property within its own markup.

Listing 7-1 shows some example XAML markup that includes a Grid control and DataGrid control. The DataGrid control is referenced in markup using an additional XML namespace defined at the top of the XAML as data, and the DataGrid uses attached properties to place the control within the second row of the Grid layout control.

Listing 7-1. *Example XAML Markup*

```
<UserControl xmlns:data="clr-namespace:System.Windows.Controls;
assembly=System.Windows.Controls.Data"
x:Class="Apress.Data.Services.CustomerService.SilverlightClient.Page"
    xmlns="http://schemas.microsoft.com/winfx/2006/xaml/presentation"
    xmlns:x="http://schemas.microsoft.com/winfx/2006/xaml"
    Width="750" Height="500">
    <Grid x:Name="LayoutRoot" Background="White">
        <Grid.RowDefinitions>
                <RowDefinition Height="40"/>
                <RowDefinition Height="*"/>
        </Grid.RowDefinitions>
...
        <data:DataGrid x:Name="CustomersDataGrid"
Grid.Row="1" AutoGenerateColumns="False"
ItemsSource="{Binding Mode=OneWay}" Margin="10"
Width="650" HorizontalAlignment="Left" >
...
```

```
        </data:DataGrid>
    </Grid>
</UserControl>
```

Layout Controls

One core feature that XAML improves upon over HTML is more control over layout, and how the interface will render and resize when the parent window size is changed by a user. This is achieved in XAML by the use of layout controls that inherit the `System.Windows.Controls.Panel` base class. Layout controls can be nested and used together to provide complete control over how your user control will render when it is resized. Table 7-1 lists the layout controls provided by Silverlight and describes how they are used.

Table 7-1. *Core Silverlight Layout Controls*

Silverlight Control	Description
Grid	Provides a grid layout based on rows and columns to place child controls
Canvas	Provides a canvas layout based on specific coordinates of the canvas
StackPanel	Provides a stack layout for child controls based on the size of container

The `Grid` and `Canvas` controls will be familiar concepts to developers used to writing HTML, because the `Grid` is akin to writing table-based markup and the `Canvas` is similar to absolute positioning. However, the `StackPanel` layout is a concept not available in HTML at all. It enables you to render child controls using either a horizontal or vertical stack (based on the setting of the `Orientation` property). Each stacked child control can be set to fill the space that the stack control is set to occupy. For example, if you had two `Rectangle` controls set horizontally within the `StackPanel` control, they would each fill up half the width of the `StackPanel` control's space.

Input Controls

Silverlight provides many controls akin to those you find in an HTML or ASP.NET form. Table 7-2 lists the most commonly used data input controls in Silverlight and details what the equivalent HTML element would be where appropriate.

Table 7-2. *Core Silverlight Input Controls*

Silverlight Control	Description
Button	Provides a simple button control similar to an input button element.
ListBox	Provides a list box of items for selection, similar to a select element.
TextBox	Provides a text input box similar to an input text element.
CheckBox	Provides a check box similar to an input check box element.
RadioButton	Provides a radio button similar to an input radio button element.
ScrollBar	Provides a scrollbar to a region of layout. There is no HTML equivalent.
Slider	Provides a slider control. There is no HTML equivalent.

Shape Controls

Shape controls in Silverlight allow you to create shapes to present content in. These shapes are rendered as vector graphics, meaning that they scale appropriately depending on their size. Shape controls inherit from the `System.Windows.Controls.Shape` base class. Table 7-3 lists the shape controls available in Silverlight.

Table 7-3. *Core Silverlight Shape Controls*

Silverlight Control	Description
Rectangle	Renders a rectangle shape
Elipse	Renders an elipse shape
Line	Renders a straight line
Path	Defines a path of vector coordinates to make up a shape

The final shape listed here is a special shape called a `Path` control. The `Path` control is special because it defines a series of coordinates that make up an exact shape of any variety, including shapes containing curves. This enables a new level of design freedom from that capable in HTML. You can consider the `Rectangle`, `Elipse`, and `Line` controls as predetermined paths; in fact it is possible in Expression Blend to convert any one of these shapes into a path, which you can then change into an irregular shape.

Data Binding

Data binding is as important in Silverlight as it is in ASP.NET; it enables developers to glue together the application's presentation with the underlying data without writing lines of error-prone code to achieve it. In all data binding scenarios, an application will have data represented in an object or collection of objects. A property of a source object can be bound to property of any Silverlight XAML element, by writing an expression in XAML markup. Additionally, some controls support the ability to bind to collections of objects, using binding expressions on the properties of template child elements.

Binding Single Object Properties

A property of a source object can be bound to any dependency property of a control that inherits from `System.Windows.FrameworkElement`. You can express the binding using XAML markup such as the following:

```
<TextBox x:Name="myTextBox" Text="{Binding MyProperty, Mode=OneWay}" />
```

This example binds the `TextBox` control's `Text` property to a source object property called `MyProperty`. A control's property binding can use any one of three modes:

- `OneTime` binding
- `OneWay` binding
- `TwoWay` binding

`OneTime` binding means that after being initially bound, updates to the underlying source object are not reflected in the control's property. `OneWay` binding means that updates from the source object's property are reflected in the control's property, but changes made to the control's property are not reflected in the source object. `TwoWay` binding means that updates to properties in either the control's property or the source object's property are refreshed on both sides. In order to use `TwoWay` binding, the source object must implement the `INotifyPropertyChanged` interface.

In addition to declaratively binding a source object's property to a control's property in XAML as described previously, you must also write some code in the code-behind to relate the control to the instance of the source object you want to bind to. To achieve this you need to set either the control's `Source` property or the `DataContext` property in the code-behind. These two mechanisms work in the same way, except that all child properties of a parent control inherit the same `DataContext` property. If the control's binding source is an object exposed by another control, the source will most likely be set in XAML markup; otherwise the binding source is most likely to be set in code. For example, the `TextBox` control XAML listed previously may have its `Source` property set using the following code:

```
TextBox.Source = MyObject;
```

In this code, `MyObject` would contain a property called `MyProperty` used in the controls `Text` property binding.

Binding to Collections

In addition to binding single objects to individual properties, Silverlight enables you to bind to any collection that implements the `IEnumerable` interface. Silverlight provides a set of controls that support binding to collections. Table 7-4 lists the core Silverlight controls that can bind to collections of data.

Table 7-4. *Silverlight Data Bound Controls*

Silverlight Control	Description
`ItemsControl`	Binds items to a repeater with no specified design
`ListBox`	Binds items into a list control
`TabControl`	Binds items into a tab strip control
`DataGrid`	Binds items to a table style list containing columns of data

Both the `ListBox` and `TabControl` controls inherit from the `System.Windows.Controls.ItemsControl` class. To implement data binding, the `DataContext` property of the control needs to be set to a collection implementing the `IEnumerable` interface. Unlike ASP.NET, there is no need to explicitly execute a `DataBind` method; items are automatically bound to the collection.

Silverlight controls that bind to collections are also able to implement two-way data binding. This means that not only can a control such as the `DataGrid` bind to data read from a collection, but the grid can also push updates to the data made in the grid directly back to the collection. To enable two-way data binding, the collection being bound to must implement the `INotifyCollectionChanged` interface (with each item in the collection implementing the `INotifyPropertyChanged` interface) and the `ItemsSource` property of a control must be set to two-way binding. A good collection type to use for two-way binding is the

`System.Collections.ObjectModel.ObservableCollection<T>` class, because it implements the `INotifyCollectionChanged` interface. The `ObservableCollection<T>` class inherits the `Collection<T>` type and therefore behaves similarly to a `List<T>` collection.

The controls listed previously are able to implement templating, much like data bound controls in ASP.NET. Templating gives you the freedom to render whatever child controls you see fit to render for each item in a collection. Silverlight provides many specific types for templating, which all inherit from the `System.Windows.FrameworkTemplate` class.

Consuming Services

Silverlight 2.0 is a great technology for providing a rich user experience in web applications, but it would not be very useful if you were unable to consume services easily to work with the data you are using to present back to a user. Fortunately, Silverlight provides comprehensive support for consuming services over HTTP, whether they are SOAP, RESTful, or plain old XML (POX) services.

No matter what kind of service you are consuming, all service requests made by Silverlight must occur asynchronously. The reason for this is to ensure that threads on the browser are not locked for any longer than necessary; this is the same reason that service requests made on AJAX pages are always made asynchronously. An asynchronous pattern involves having a callback method to handle the response from the service request once it is returned to the browser.

Depending on the type of service you are consuming, you need to handle service calls using a different part of the Silverlight framework, which closely follows the .NET Framework API for consuming services. The three categories of service you may call are

- SOAP services
- ADO.NET data services
- All other REST and POX services

Consuming SOAP Services

Silverlight supports the consumption of basic profile SOAP services (in WCF these are endpoints configured to use the `BasicHttpBinding`). SOAP services are consumed by generating a WCF client proxy (service reference) in your Silverlight application using Visual Studio in exactly the same way as you would to consume a SOAP service for using a .NET client.

When a WCF client proxy is created in a Silverlight application, the client configuration is stored in a configuration file called `ServiceReferences.ClientConfig`. This XML file contains the WCF client endpoint configuration, which is identical to the configuration you would see in any .NET WCF client configuration file for the same service endpoint.

Consuming the SOAP service using the generated proxy is the same as making the service call from any .NET WCF client, except that service operations can only be called asynchronously. Therefore, you need to wire up an asynchronous event handler for when the service responds to the asynchronous request.

One final word of caution; SOAP faults are not supported in Silverlight. This is due to security restrictions in the browser that stop the Silverlight plug-in from seeing any SOAP faults.

Consuming ADO.NET Data Services

The Silverlight 2 SDK (downloaded as part of the Silverlight Tools for Visual Studio 2008 SP1) contains several additional Silverlight assemblies that you can add to your Silverlight application when required. Once of these additional assemblies is the `System.Data.Services.Client` assembly, which is a version of the ADO.NET Data Services client library, compiled against the Silverlight CLR.

The Silverlight version of the ADO.NET Data Services client library works in an identical manner to the .NET version, with the exception that synchronous calls to ADO.NET Data Services are not supported. This means that client proxy classes generated using `DataSvcUtil.exe` can be added directly into a Silverlight application. Because Silverlight provides support for LINQ, the complete LINQ to URI syntax for calling data services remains the same.

If you attempt to call the data service using the generated proxy synchronously, you will receive a `NotImplementedException` from the client assembly. This is because synchronous calls are not supported in Silverlight. In order to execute the call to the data service asynchronously, you must

- Make a call to the data service as normal using a LINQ query.

- Cast the result variable from this query to a new variable of type `DataServiceQuery<T>`, where `T` is the entity type of each item in the LINQ result set.

- Call the `BeginExecute` method against the `DataServiceQuery<T>` variable, passing in a new `AsyncCallback` delegate into the method.

- Implement the callback method taking a type `IAsyncResult` as an argument, which you can then use to examine the response.

- Within the callback method, cast the result argument to the type `DataServiceQuery<T>`, and call the `EndExecute` method to return the result from the service call.

The result from the asynchronous callback is of type `IEnumerable<T>`, so it can be easily bound to a Silverlight control that supports data binding, such as the `DataGrid` control. Listing 7-2 shows example code to call a data service and then bind the response to the query in an asynchronous callback.

Listing 7-2. *Consuming a Data Service Asychronously from Silverlight Code*

```
private void ExecuteSearch(string searchText)
{
    // create client proxy
    CustomerEntities dataService = new CustomerEntities(
        new Uri("CustomerDataService.svc", UriKind.Relative));

    // query data service using LINQ
    var customers = from c in dataService.Customers.Expand("Salutation")
                    .Expand("Gender")
                    where c.LastName.Contains(searchText)
                    select c;
```

```
            DataServiceQuery<Customer> customerQuery =
                (DataServiceQuery<Customer>)customers;

            // execute the query asynchronously
            customerQuery.BeginExecute(new AsyncCallback(OnSearchComplete),
                customerQuery);
        }

        void OnSearchComplete(IAsyncResult result)
        {
            // Get a reference to the Query
            DataServiceQuery<Customer> customerQuery =
              (DataServiceQuery<Customer>)result.AsyncState;

            // assign results to customers collection.
            Customers = customerQuery.EndExecute(result).ToList();
        }

        public List<Customer> Customers
        {
            get
            {
                return (List<Customer>)CustomersDataGrid.DataContext;
            }
            set
            {
                CustomersDataGrid.DataContext = value;
            }
        }
```

Consuming Other REST and POX Services

Because there is no standard way that other REST and POX services are described (like a WSDL or an ADO.NET data service $meta URI), consuming other REST and POX services is a little harder to achieve because you cannot generate a service proxy to consume.

To communicate with other REST and POX services, you need to use the WebClient and HttpWebRequest classes under the System.Net namespace. The WebClient class is used to make HTTP GET requests, while the HttpWebRequest class is used to make HTTP requests against all other HTTP verbs.

As with all other Silverlight service requests, the response must be dealt with in an asynchronous callback. The response must be parsed as there is no client proxy to handle deserializing the response.

For services that return data in XML format, there are two options for handling the response. You can use the System.Xml.Serialization.XmlSerializer class to deserialize the response into a type you define in your solution (you can use XSD.exe to generate the type for you based on the response XML). Alternatively, you can use LINQ to XML to parse the response XML.

For services that return data in JSON format, you can use the WCF `DataContractJsonSerializer` class to deserialize the response into a type you define in your solution.

Handling Cross-Domain Requests

As with AJAX solutions, service requests made from Silverlight solutions require the service endpoint to exist on the same domain name as the client web page for security reasons.

Silverlight does provide a mechanism enabling cross-domain requests to services. This mechanism is based on the **service** declaring that it can be called publicly across domains. This feature is nothing new; Flash has used such a mechanism for a long time.

To enable Silverlight clients to access a service across a different domain, the service must expose either a `crossdomain.xml` file or a `clientaccesspolicy.xml` file. Both of these files must exist in the root of a service's host web site. The `crossdomain.xml` file is familiar to Flash developers, because it is the same file used to declare a service for public consumption by Flash. Therefore, adding this file to your service will enable not only Silverlight clients, but also Flash clients to call your service across domains. An example `crossdomain.xml` file is shown in Listing 7-3.

Listing 7-3. *An Example crossdomain.xml File*

```
<?xml version="1.0"?>
<!DOCTYPE cross-domain-policy
  SYSTEM "http://www.macromedia.com/xml/dtds/cross-domain-policy.dtd">
<cross-domain-policy>
  <allow-access-from domain="www.yoursite.com" />
  <allow-access-from domain="yoursite.com" />
  <allow-access-from domain="*.anothersite.org" />
</cross-domain-policy>
```

The second supported file format to enable cross-domain requests to your service is a file called `clientaccesspolicy.xml`. This is a Silverlight-only file, but it provides more functionality than the more broadly supported `crossdomain.xml` file, because it enables you to limit cross-domain access to specific URI paths in your service's web site. An example `clientaccesspolicy.xml` file is shown in Listing 7-4.

Listing 7-4. *An Example clientaccesspolicy.xml File*

```
<?xml version="1.0" encoding="utf-8"?>
<access-policy>
  <cross-domain-access>
    <policy>
      <allow-from>
        <domain uri="http://clientdomain.com"/>
      </allow-from>
      <grant-to>
        <resource path="/public-services/" include-subpaths="true"/>
      </grant-to>
    </policy>
  </cross-domain-access>
</access-policy>
```

Web Page Interoperability

In 1623 John Donne wrote the famous phrase "No man is an island, entire of itself." The same is true for a Silverlight application; it is a good citizen of a web page that may well contain HTML and JavaScript in addition to Silverlight content. In fact, if bandwidth is a consideration in the architecture of your application, you will certainly want to think about using HTML content augmented with Silverlight content instead of presenting all your content in Silverlight. This solution gives the best of what both mediums have to offer.

You can interoperate between an HTML page and Silverlight content in both directions: from Silverlight managed code to the HTML DOM and from JavaScript into methods in your managed code. These two interoperability options enable certain architectural scenarios for designing your web application:

- **Manipulating the HTML DOM using C# in managed code**: For example, you could render the results from a data service call into HTML.

- **Calling into a C# method from JavaScript**: For example, you could call into a method that executed business logic in managed code or executed some presentation logic against a Silverlight control.

There is a performance boost you will gain from running logic in compiled managed code in C# as opposed to interpreted JavaScript. There are also maintainability benefits from using an object-oriented language like C# over a procedural language. However, the extensible and flexible nature of JavaScript as a functional language has made it hugely popular, and for simple logic it is a productive language to work with. You may also have skill-set reasons for having a bias of one of these languages over the other. Whatever your situation, the interoperability that Silverlight provides enables you to choose the option that best fits your circumstances.

Accessing the HTML DOM from Managed Code

Silverlight provides access to the HTML from managed code via the `System.Windows.Browser` namespace. The `HtmlDocument` object exposes the web page's HTML DOM that the Silverlight content is hosted in. A reference to the `HtmlDocument` object can be obtained by accessing the `HtmlPage.Document` static property. The `HtmlDocument` object provides the `GetElementById` method for obtaining references to elements (typed as `HtmlElement`) in the HTML DOM.

The `HtmlElement` object contains two methods called `GetProperty` and `SetProperty` for getting and setting element properties in the HTML DOM. Additionally, the methods `GetStyleAttribute` and `SetStyleAttribute` get and set CSS style properties. HTML DOM events can also be handled in managed code by calling the `AttachEvent` method of the `HtmlElement` object, where you instantiate a new `EventHandler<HtmlEventArgs>` delegate to handle the event. Listing 7-5 shows a Silverlight control code-behind that accesses the HTML DOM.

Listing 7-5. *Accessing the HTML DOM from the Silverlight Code-Behind*

```
using System;
using System.Windows.Controls;
using System.Windows.Browser;
namespace Apress.Data.Services.SilverlightHtmlSample {
```

```
public partial class Page : UserControl {
    private HtmlDocument document;

    public Page() {
        InitializeComponent();
        document = HtmlPage.Document;

        document.GetElementById("InputTextBox").SetProperty("disabled", false);
        document.GetElementById("InputTextBox").SetAttribute("value",
            "This text is set from managed code.");

        // Add event handler for button.
        HtmlElement searchButton = document.GetElementById("SearchButton");
        searchButton.AttachEvent("onclick",
            new EventHandler<HtmlEventArgs>(OnSearchButtonClicked));
    }


    void OnSearchButtonClicked (object sender, HtmlEventArgs e) {
        HtmlElement inputTextBox = document.GetElementById("InputTextBox");
        inputTextBox.SetAttribute("value", inputTextBox.GetAttribute("value")
        .ToUpper());
    }
}
```

Silverlight also enables you to call JavaScript methods from managed code by calling the `HtmlPage.Window.Invoke` method, passing in the name of your JavaScript method as a string, followed by the method's argument list. For example:

```
HtmlPage.Window.Invoke("myJavaScriptFunction", variableOne, variableTwo);
```

This code would call a JavaScript function called `myJavaScriptFunction`, passing in two objects into the functions arguments named `variableOne` and `variableTwo`.

Accessing Silverlight Managed Code from JavaScript

You can expose method of your Silverlight control to the web page so that you can call into your managed code from JavaScript.

The method of achieving this is largely attribute driven; you first add the `[ScriptableType]` attribute to the Silverlight controls class to mark the control as being accessible by JavaScript.

Next you need to expose a name to identify the Silverlight content through the HTML DOM. To do this you need to call the `HtmlPage.RegisterScriptableObject` method, passing in a string to identify the Silverlight control and a reference to it. For example, the code might read `HtmlPage.RegisterScriptableObject("MyControl", this);`.

Any method you wish to expose from your Silverlight control needs to have the `[ScriptableMember]` attribute attached to it. Once this is done, you are now ready to call these methods from JavaScript.

To call a Silverlight method from JavaScript, you must obtain a reference to the object element using the `getElementById` method. So for example, if you want to execute a managed code method from JavaScript called `MyMethod` from the object element called `silverlightControl`, and you register your scriptable Silverlight control with the name `MyControl`, you would call `silverlightControl.content.MyControl.MyMethod();` in JavaScript.

Debugging Silverlight Code

Visual Studio 2008 provides support for debugging Silverlight applications, providing a similar experience to debugging any other .NET code. In order to debug Silverlight applications, you need to ensure that you have the developer version of the Silverlight plug-in installed, which is installed as part of the Silverlight Tools for Visual Studio 2008. Make sure that you do not install the release version of the Silverlight plug-in over the top of this installation, or you lose debugging support in Visual Studio.

Silverlight debugging works in exactly the same way as debugging any other .NET application. Code is debugged from the compiled code file (XAP file), which is contained in the `ClientBin` folder of the web site hosting the Silverlight application (the Silverlight project will place the XAP file in the folder for you when the Silverlight project is built).

EXERCISE 7-1: BUILDING AN ADO.NET DATA SERVICES CLIENT IN SILVERLIGHT

In this exercise, you will create a Silverlight application hosted in a web site that will consume a data service that is hosted within the same web site. Because the client and the service are contained within the same domain, there is no need to add cross-domain configuration to the service. You can download the files you need for this exercise from the Apress web site (`http://www.apress.com/book/sourcecode`); the files comprise a web site containing the same customer data service used in Chapter 5, without any ASP.NET client code. You will add a new Silverlight application, host it in the same web site, and develop a Silverlight client that consumes the service and binds the result data to a `DataGrid` control. This exercise is deliberately similar to the exercises in Chapter 5 so that you can compare the markup and code for a similar use case. Ensure that you have the developer version of the Silverlight plug-in installed so that you can debug the application.

1. Open the starting solution in Visual Studio and view the `CustomerDataService.svc` file in the browser to make sure that the service is working correctly. Try out a couple of queries in the browser to test that database connectivity is functioning correctly.

2. Right-click the `Client` folder and select Add ➤ New Project from the context menu. Select the Silverlight Application template from the dialog box, name the application `Apress.Data.Services.CustomerService.SilverlightClient`, and click OK. The Add Silverlight Application dialog box will appear, as shown in Figure 7-2.

Figure 7-2. *The Add Silverlight Application dialog box*

3. This dialog box enables you to create a new web site to host the application or link the application to an existing web site. You are going to host the Silverlight application in the existing web site, which is selected by default as shown in Figure 7-2. Notice that check boxes also exist to add a test page to the existing web site. This will generate a web page with the appropriate HTML markup to host your Silverlight application. Leave all the default options selected and click OK. Visual Studio will work for a few seconds while it creates a new Silverlight application and makes the appropriate changes to the web site.

4. Once finished, Visual Studio will open the Page.xaml file from the new created Silverlight application (which can be seen in Solution Explorer in the Client folder). The designer shows a split view, with the canvas displayed in the top part of the page and the underlying XAML markup shown below it. Right-clicking anywhere in the designer and selecting View Code will bring up the C# code-behind for the Page.xaml file.

5. Check the solution builds without error. Navigate to the web site within Solution Explorer. Examine the two page files that have been created for you (Apress.Data.Services.CustomerService. SilverlightClientTestPage.aspx and Apress.Data.Services.CustomerService. SilverlightClientTestPage.htm). These test pages contain the plumbing needed to host a Silverlight application in a web page using either ASP.NET markup or HTML markup. Also notice that the web site now contains a ClientBin folder, containing the file Apress.Data.Services.CustomerService. SilverlightClient.xap. This file is the compiled Silverlight assembly that will run in the host web site.

6. You are now going to add some XAML markup to the Page.xaml file to lay out the control. While you could do this in Visual Studio, Expression Blend provides better design-led tooling. You can work on the same solution in both Visual Studio and Expression Blend simultaneously to take advantage of the best of both environments. Open Expression Blend and in the Project tab click Open Project. Navigate to the solution file (Apress.Data.Services.CustomerService.sln) and click Open.

7. The Expression Blend screen is divided into three areas: the toolbox is on the left, the design surface is in the middle, and the option tabs are on the right. Click the Project tab. All the solutions files will be visible in this tab. Navigate to the Page.xaml file and open it so it appears in the design surface. If you click the Split tab, you will be able to view the XAML markup created as you change the design surface.

8. By default the XAML contains one single Grid control to lay out content. You are going to create two rows on content within this grid, the first of which will contain two columns. Click the Selection tool in the toolbox (the first icon in the toolbox) and double-click in the middle of the canvas. In the Objects and Timeline pane, you can see the Grid control named LayoutRoot is selected.

9. Notice the rulers to the top and left of the canvas on the design surface. As you move your mouse down the left side and along the top, an orange line will appear and move with your mouse. This line represents where a Grid row or column will be created when you click the mouse. Move the mouse down the left edge to create two rows as shown in Figure 7-3.

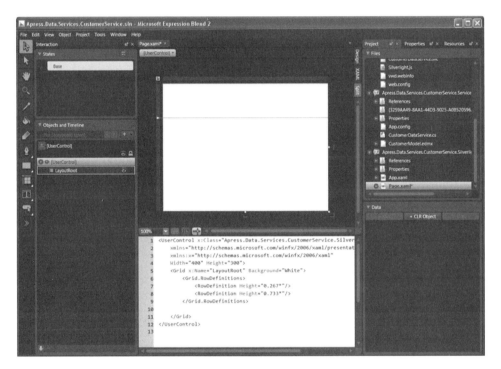

Figure 7-3. *The Page.xaml file in Expression Blend after creating two rows in the Grid control*

10. Notice the RowDefinition markup that has been created in the XAML window. You want the second of these two rows to size to the remaining space, by setting the Height property to *. This can be achieved by either editing the XAML or clicking the small arrow icon to the side of the left margin on the first row.

11. Add a new Grid control from the toolbox to the design surface by double-clicking the Grid control (the Grid control is three icons up from the bottom of the toolbox). Delete the HorizontalAlignment, Margin, and Width properties from the generated XAML. In the XAML window, add the markup Grid.Row="0" to the Grid element to explicitly state that this grid will appear within the first row of the outer grid. Double-click the new created Grid control in the Object and Timeline pane so that the grid is selected (it will be highlighted yellow).

12. On the design surface, move the mouse over the top rule area and create a column near the right margin of the canvas. Make the first column star sized so that when the canvas is made wider, the first column stretches to fit the space.

13. Add a `TextBox` control from the toolbox to the first column of the first row by drawing it within the column to fill the space. In the Properties tab, set the name of the control to be `SearchTextBox`. Delete the text from the Common Properties pane. Add the property `Grid.Column="0"` to the `TextBox` XAML to specify that the control will appear in the first column of the parent `Grid`.

14. Repeat the preceding step for a `Button` control, but placing it in the second column, naming the button `SearchButton`, and setting the `Text` property to `Go` (the `Text` property can be found under common properties in the Properties pane). The overall XAML should now look like the following listing. Save the page and close Expression Blend.

```
<UserControl
    x:Class="Apress.Data.Services.CustomerService.SilverlightClient.Page"
    xmlns="http://schemas.microsoft.com/winfx/2006/xaml/presentation"
    xmlns:x="http://schemas.microsoft.com/winfx/2006/xaml"
    Width="750" Height="500">
    <Grid x:Name="LayoutRoot" Background="White">
        <Grid.RowDefinitions>
            <RowDefinition Height="40" />
            <RowDefinition Height="*" />
        </Grid.RowDefinitions>
        <Grid Grid.Row="0" Margin="7">
            <Grid.ColumnDefinitions>
                <ColumnDefinition Width="*" />
                <ColumnDefinition Width="50" />
            </Grid.ColumnDefinitions>
            <TextBox Grid.Column="0" x:Name="SearchTextBox" />
            <Button Grid.Column="1" x:Name="SearchButton" Content="Go"  />
        </Grid>
    </Grid>
</UserControl>
```

15. Switch back to Visual Studio and reopen the edited `Page.xaml` file. You are going to add a `DataGrid` control to the bottom row. Open the XAML page (showing the XAML markup) and place the cursor just before the end of the closing `Grid` tag of the `Grid` control named `LayoutRoot`. In the toolbox, double-click the `DataGrid` control to add the control to the `LayoutRoot` control. Visual Studio will automatically add an XML namespace to the top of the XAML markup that refers to the `System.Windows.Controls.Data` assembly. By default this will be referenced using the XML namespace `xmlns:data`. Notice that markup for the `DataGrid` control has been added near the bottom of the XAML as `<data:DataGrid>` `</data:DataGrid>`.

16. Add a `Grid.Row` property to the `DataGrid` so that it is positioned in the second row of the grid. Name the `DataGrid` control `CustomersDataGrid` and set the `AutoGenerateColumns` property to true. The `DataGrid` markup should now read `<data:DataGrid x:Name="CustomersDataGrid" Grid.Row="1" AutoGenerateColumns="True"></data:DataGrid>`.

17. In order for the `DataGrid` to bind to data you will return from the data service call, you need to set the binding mode on the `ItemsSource` property. Add the `ItemsSource` property to the XAML markup and set it to `OneWay` binding. The property should read `ItemsSource="{Binding Mode=OneWay}"`.

18. You are going to add a click event handler to the `Button` control. Move the cursor into the `Button` control markup and add a `Click` event to the markup, following the IntelliSense to generate the event handler in code. Select View Code to see the event handler `SearchButton_Click` created in C#.

19. You need to reference the ADO.NET Data Services Silverlight client library within your application in order to be able to call a data service. In Solution Explorer, navigate to the Silverlight application project `references` folder. Right-click the folder and select Add Reference. From the .NET tab in the dialog that appears, select the `System.Data.Services.Client` assembly and click OK.

20. The `Apress.Data.Services.CustomerService.DataClient` console application project already contains a generated data service proxy file called `CustomerDataService.cs`. Copy this file into the Silverlight application so that the application can reference a client proxy for your data service.

21. In the `Page.xaml.cs` code-behind file, add a using declaration to use the `CustomerModel` namespace. This is the namespace of the client proxy. Also, add a namespace to use the `System.Data.Services.Client` namespace.

22. Add a new method to the code called `ExecuteSearch` and change the button's click event handler so that it looks like the following code:

```
private void SearchButton_Click(object sender, RoutedEventArgs e)
{
    // get the text from the search text box
    string searchText = SearchTextBox.Text;

    ExecuteSearch(searchText);
}

private void ExecuteSearch(string searchText)
{
    //TODO: Execute Search here
}
```

23. Now you need to add code to call the data service via the client proxy. To do this you will add code to the `ExecuteSearch` method, which must call the data service asynchronously using a callback method you will call `OnSearchComplete`. The code for the implemented `ExecuteSearch` method is shown here:

```
private void ExecuteSearch(string searchText)
{
    // create client proxy
    CustomerEntities dataService = new CustomerEntities(
        new Uri("CustomerDataService.svc", UriKind.Relative));

    // query data service using LINQ
    var customers = from c in dataService.Customers.Expand("Salutation")
                    .Expand("Gender")
                    where c.LastName.Contains(searchText)
                    select c;
```

```
        DataServiceQuery<Customer> customerQuery =
            (DataServiceQuery<Customer>)customers;

        // execute the query asynchronously
        customerQuery.BeginExecute(new AsyncCallback(OnSearchComplete),
            customerQuery);
    }

    void OnSearchComplete(IAsyncResult result)
    {
        //TODO: Handle data service callback here
    }
```

24. Within the OnSearchComplete method you will assign the search result to a Customers collection prop-
    erty you will define in your code. This property will handle data binding to the DataGrid control to present
    the data, by setting the collection to the DataGrid control's DataContext property. The code for the
    implemented OnSearchComplete method and the Customers property is shown in the following listing:

```
    void OnSearchComplete(IAsyncResult result)
    {
        // Get a reference to the Query
        DataServiceQuery<Customer> customerQuery =
          (DataServiceQuery<Customer>)result.AsyncState;

        // assign results to customers collection.
        Customers = customerQuery.EndExecute(result).ToList();
    }

    public List<Customer> Customers
    {
        get
        {
            return (List<Customer>)CustomersDataGrid.DataContext;
        }
        set
        {
            CustomersDataGrid.DataContext = value;
        }
    }
```

25. Build the solution and view the test page in the browser. Enter the text **smi** into the text box and click the Go
    button. The search results from the data service query should appear bound to the DataGrid, as shown in
    Figure 7-4.

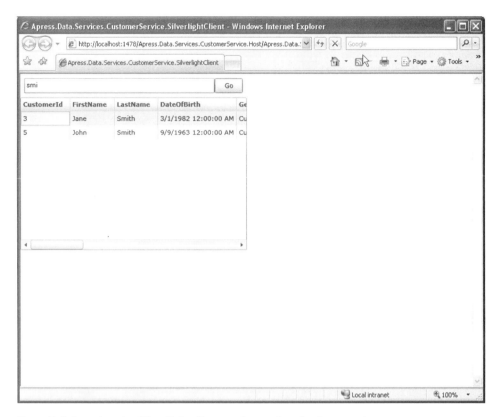

Figure 7-4. *Running the Silverlight client and querying the data service*

26. When you run the application, you will notice that the DataGrid does not correctly show the value of properties such as Gender and Salutation, because these are not POCO properties, and by default the DataGrid control will cast their value to a string. To fix this issue, you need to turn off autogenerated columns and define your column data bindings explicitly. Open the Page.xaml file markup. Set the AutoGenerateColumns property to false and add explicit data columns with member bindings to each property you want to return in the grid. Change the DataGrid control markup to look like the following listing:

```
<data:DataGrid x:Name="CustomersDataGrid" Grid.Row="1"
    AutoGenerateColumns="False"
    ItemsSource="{Binding Mode=OneWay}"
    Margin="10" Width="650" HorizontalAlignment="Left" >
    <data:DataGrid.Columns>
        <data:DataGridTextColumn Header="Customer Id"
            Binding="{Binding CustomerId}" />
        <data:DataGridTextColumn Header="First Name"
            Binding="{Binding FirstName}" />
        <data:DataGridTextColumn Header="Last Name"
            Binding="{Binding LastName}" />
```

```
        <data:DataGridTextColumn Header="Date Of Birth"
            Binding="{Binding DateOfBirth}" />
        <data:DataGridTextColumn Header="Gender"
            Binding="{Binding Gender.GenderName}" />
        <data:DataGridTextColumn Header="Salutation"
            Binding="{Binding Salutation.SalutationDescription}" />
    </data:DataGrid.Columns>
</data:DataGrid>
```

27. Change the `UserControl` `Width` and `Height` properties to be 750 and 500 pixels, respectively, to allow the larger `DataGrid` results to display correctly. Build the solution and view the test page in the browser, again searching for a last name containing the text "smi." Note how the `Gender` and `Salutation` columns show the correct information, and that column headers are no longer named after the property names. Figure 7-5 shows the running application.

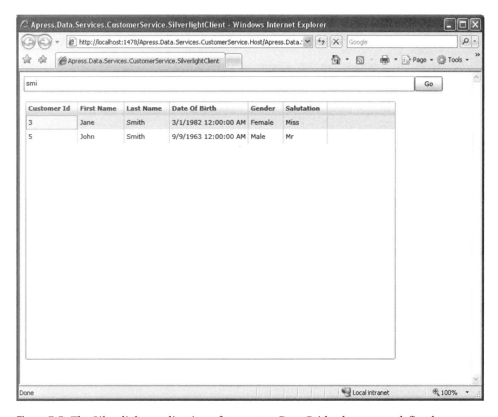

Figure 7-5. *The Silverlight application after custom DataGrid columns are defined*

In this exercise you have built a simple Silverlight application that consumes a data service to search for customers.

Summary

The aim of this chapter is not only to describe how to consume ADO.NET data services from Silverlight client applications, but also to make you think about when you should apply Silverlight as a technology to build richer user experiences for web applications, and just as importantly, when you should apply other technologies, such as the server-side ASP.NET or AJAX techniques described in Chapter 5.

A key takeaway from this chapter is that there is no one-size-fits-all approach to developing web applications, where a single technology is "better" than another. A more considered approach to web development is to view these technologies as a confluence, where each technology has strengths and weaknesses; the task (as always) that we face as developers is to understand when to best apply a technology to exploit the features that it has to offer. As with REST and SOAP services, these technologies are not in competition; they are complementary to each other, each suited to a different purpose. Any thinking to the contrary is gross simplification, which leads to misuse.

Silverlight can be applied to your web application developments in one of the following three ways:

- Building an entire web site front end using Silverlight, providing the richest, but also heaviest, user experience

- Augmenting an HTML page (delivered using ASP.NET and/or AJAX) with rich Silverlight content and driving business logic and service calls from AJAX

- Augmenting a Silverlight page with HTML content and driving business logic and service calls from within Silverlight

Each of these scenarios has strengths and weaknesses, but one thing to consider is that the vast majority of applications developed using any one of these paradigms will require communication with services if the software needs to do anything beyond just delivering a rich user experience. For each scenario listed here, ADO.NET Data Services provides the ideal target technology for developing RESTful services that surface data from a data source.

■■■

CHAPTER 8

Using ADO.NET Data Services with BizTalk

In Chapter 4 we explored how we could implement ADO.NET data services on top of existing assets such as a WCF (Windows Communication Foundation) SOAP service or a .NET API. We explained how an ADO.NET Data Services layer that used a LINQ to SQL provider could negate a lot of "legacy" .NET code and would create a cleaner business tier. This works well when the assets are .NET based, but what if these assets are on a legacy system that can only be accessed using a complex API or, worse still, the system isn't Windows based? Time for us to introduce Microsoft BizTalk Server. This is Microsoft's Enterprise Application Integration (EAI) tool that comes with a collection of adapters you can use to access these assets. In addition to adapters, it contains a comprehensive suite of tools to assist with workflow, business rules, and transformation services. It also supports various messaging standards such as EDI, SWIFT, and HIPAA, discussed briefly later in the chapter. If we are able to consume data services within BizTalk, we can use the data exposed by the data service to interact with BizTalk's extensive set of messaging features.

Why BizTalk?

So why are we writing about BizTalk exactly and why is BizTalk relevant to ADO.NET Data Services? Let's look at the problem. When data is spread across multiple Line of Business (LOB) systems, such as accounting data in a JD Edwards system and invoicing data in a SAP system, it becomes difficult to create a process, which has to span these systems. This is where BizTalk comes in. BizTalk has a set of tools that can be used to orchestrate processes to create one reusable business process. In the future, one or more of these systems could have an endpoint that is a data service. This could occur when a data service is put on top of a legacy database or when an external vendor has decided to do this. Therefore, we should be able to consume a data service within BizTalk so that it can be used within a wider business process.

BIZTALK FOR THE MASSES

We are throwing a Windows Server Enterprise product into the mix that many readers may not have experience with. So before we provide a step-by-step exercise of how to go about consuming a data service with BizTalk, we'll give a brief 101 introduction of this nearly ten-year-old product and what it's used for.

Microsoft BizTalk Server isn't as rare as you think; currently, it is used by 7,000 customers across the globe, including 90 percent of the Fortune 100 companies. Since its introduction in 2000, it has sparked a revolution in the integration industry. This is partly because of the ease of use of the product. In its first release, the focus of the product was to provide something that was able to transform data from one form to another using a simple mapping tool. This version of BizTalk was COM based and came with a few adapters that supported basic protocols such as FILE, FTP, and SMTP. The second major release of BizTalk was in 2004. This was one of the first products to be written fully in a .NET language, and it came with enterprise class features.

The product has a rich feature set that includes the following areas:

- **Orchestrations**: Orchestrations are used to compose system endpoints that fit into a business workflow. A Visual Studio design tool is used to create an orchestration from many different shapes: send, receive, delay, parallel actions, and so forth. The definition of an orchestration is then deployed as an XML file into a SQL Server database (BizTalk management database). The orchestration process is controlled by the BizTalk runtime engine, which dehydrates/rehydrates (deserializes/serializes) the orchestration from a SQL Server database using message subscription rules.

- **Schema designer**: BizTalk works best with XSD XML files. The schema designer is a Visual Studio design tool that is used to create XSD-compliant schemas. These schemas are then used by BizTalk to validate XML messages. The schema designer also contains a flat file extension that can be used to define other types of formats such as flat files. The flat file format is mapped to the XSD schema, which BizTalk then uses to transform a flat file into an XML representation.

- **BizTalk Mapper**: The BizTalk Mapper is another Visual Studio design tool used to provide the transformation rules between two message schemas. The BizTalk "map" can then be used as part of an orchestration to transform an incoming message to another specific endpoint format.

- **Business Activity Monitoring**: Business Activity Monitoring (BAM) consists of a set of tools that allows certain parts of messages to be tracked by a SQL Server database. These parts can then be used as part of a cube to provide business intelligence reporting for management. An example could be to track an order and date received. A report could then be produced to see how many orders have been received during a certain month.

- **Business rules**: The business rules engine allows you to create business rule policies that are executed when a message is being processed by the BizTalk engine. A business rule could be to check that an order number exists in a Line of Business system using complex validation rules involving one or more XML elements. The business rules composer design-time tool is employed to develop these rules in a visual format using various sources such as XML files, databases, and .NET objects.

- **WCF/Web Services Wizard**: The Web Services and WCF Wizards allow you to expose an orchestration or a set of schemas as a service endpoint.

- **Support for various messaging protocols and standards**: BizTalk supports a wide range of messaging protocols such as HTTP, TCP, FILE, and FTP. The messaging standards supported include EDI, SWIFT, RosettaNet, HIPPA (EDI subset), and HL7 (EDI subset).

Two of the product's primarily selling points are its ability to scale out to meet business needs and its extensive support of connecting systems. Scaling of BizTalk is achieved by its publish-and-subscribe architecture pattern, where the core engine would decide on which processes to activate on each server within the server farm. BizTalk Server 2006 R2 is the current version of the product, and it includes an additional set of features such as support for WCF, WS-*, an array of Line of Business adapters, and even support for the Radio Frequency Identification (RFID) protocol. BizTalk 2009 will be latest version of the product, to be released in 2009. It will align the product with Visual Studio 2008 and .NET Framework 3.5. In addition, there will be increased support for EDI and SWIFT message types.

■**Note** You might be interested in other books that cover BizTalk in greater detail, such as *BizTalk 2006 Recipes* by Mark Beckner et al. (Apress, 2006); Some titles provide in-depth analysis of specific features in BizTalk such as *Pro EDI in BizTalk Server 2006 R2*, also by Mark Beckner (Apress, 2007).

Publish-and-Subscribe Architecture

The most important aspect to understand about BizTalk is that it uses publish-and-subscribe architecture. This is an EAI pattern that allows systems to be loosely coupled.

WHAT ARE ENTERPRISE INTEGRATION PATTERNS?

Similar to a software design pattern an Enterprise Application Integration pattern is an architecture technique that aims to provide best practices to solve well-known obstacles associated with message processing issues. Various EAI patterns tackle areas such as message ordering, message routing, splitting a message into many parts, message transformation, enriching message content, and so forth. Some of the well-known patterns include the Aggregator and the Scatter-Gather pattern. The Aggregator pattern is used to combine the results of individual but related messages so that they can be processed as a whole. The Scatter-Gather pattern is used to coordinate the flow when receiving messages from multiple recipients.

Essentially, the publisher sends a message with one or more properties that describe content to a central point. The messaging system then sends the message on to one or more subscribers. This is an asynchronous messaging pattern that is more scalable than a point-to-point architecture because the message publishers only need to send a message; it's up to the messaging system to deliver this message correctly. In BizTalk the published messages are stored in a MessageBox database in SQL Server. A message in BizTalk consists of a message context and one or more message body parts. The message context contains one or more "promoted" properties that are also stored along with the message in the MessageBox. These properties are stored in the context and used by the messaging system to publish the message to one or more subscribers.

Figure 8-1 gives an overview of the BizTalk publish-and-subscribe mechanism: a message is received and then transformed into an end-system format, which is then sent to this system for processing. The orchestration contains three shapes: logical receive, transformation, and send. Following is a more detailed walkthrough of the processing of a message in BizTalk:

1. Message A is received by a receive port from one of the many adapters that come with BizTalk such as FILE, FTP, and so forth.

2. Message A runs through a pipeline process that decodes, disassembles, and validates the message. While it runs through the pipeline, the message context is populated with a number of promoted properties from the adapter, port, and the message itself.

3. Message A is saved into the BizTalk MessageBox database.

4. A publish/subscribe polling event takes place and sends Message A to an orchestration that has a subscription based upon its message type.

5. The orchestration receives Message A through a logical receive port and transforms it into Message B.

6. The newly transformed Message B is sent to a logical send port within the orchestration.

7. The Message B is saved back into the BizTalk MessageBox database.

8. A publish/subscribe polling event takes place and sends Message B to a send port pipeline process.

9. Message B runs through a send pipeline process before it is sent it to the physical adapter endpoint such as FILE, FTP, and so forth.

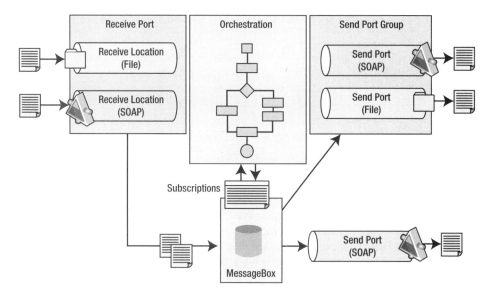

Figure 8-1. *Overview of BizTalk process*

Message Standards

A **messaging standard** is something that has been created by a worldwide body. The aim of most messaging standards is to solve an issue or increase productivity, or for regulatory purposes. There are many standards bodies around the world that discuss and agree on new standards for a particular sector. An example of one of these standards is the Electronic Data Interchange (EDI) format, which is used by retail and healthcare industries.

An extensive array of messaging standards are supported by BizTalk across multiple industrial sectors. This is achieved with BizTalk support for both flat file parsing and XML processing. Even in the world of web standards, many large companies are still using 20-year-old messaging standards:

- **RosettaNet**: Standard for high-end technical manufacturing
- **CIDX**: Standard for the chemical industry
- **EDI**: Standard for supply chains, manufacturing, and so forth
- **HIPAA**: Standard for the U.S. healthcare industry (a subset of EDI)
- **SWIFT**: Standard for financial messaging

Transformations (Mapping)

The extensive support for messaging standards usually means that there are going to be mapping requirements between these standards and other systems. For example, a supply could send a message that states that your product type is Apples but your end system calls this product Pears. Another transformation could be to summarize the input message before it is sent to the end system, for example, "Add all the order amounts together and send this as one amount to the end system."

The BizTalk Mapper is a visual tool that runs inside Visual Studio and is used to create and edit maps to transform messages from one format to another. This is achieved with a collection of functoids that can be dragged onto the design surface and connected together with the source and destination schemas. Functoids exist for string manipulation, looking up values from a database, math functions, and so on. Behind the scenes BizTalk stores maps as Extensible Stylesheet Language Transformations (XSLT) style sheets. In the context of ADO.NET Data Services, we may want to create a map between an input message that will provide values to an Atom message that is then sent to a data service. Figure 8-2 illustrates a simple map that uses a string manipulation functoid to combine the first and last name into a Name field in an output message.

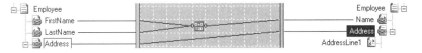

Figure 8-2. *BizTalk Mapper example*

Pipelines

BizTalk works mainly with the XML document format. To take advantage of the BizTalk XML processing features, pipelines are used to convert messages from their native format into XML. Pipelines do this through a number of logical stages that decode, disassemble, and validate a message. Essentially pipelines clean up and retrieve key parts of the message before it is processed by an orchestration.

Orchestrations

The orchestration design surface is a visual tool that is used to bind business processes together. An orchestration looks like a flowchart and has similar features to Windows Workflow. Following is an overview of the steps to create an orchestration, with a detailed discussion to follow:

1. Define schemas to describe the format of the messages.

2. Add shapes to represent the business process.

3. Create transformations between the formats of the messages.

4. Define the ports through which the messages are sent and received.

5. Bind the send and receive shapes to the ports.

6. Add the physical endpoints in BizTalk Administration Console.

The first step to create an orchestration is for the developer to identify the messages or schemas that are used in the business process. Messages are defined in BizTalk as XSD schemas. The BizTalk Editor tool is provided to create these schemas. If the process is interacting with an LOB or a web service, a number of BizTalk tools can automatically generate these schemas. Schemas often map to business entities such as Employee, Customer, Supplier, Company, and Sales.

The next step is for the developer to use the BizTalk Editor to mark properties in the schema that are useful in the business process (e.g., an order amount or a company number). These properties can then be used to make decisions on the path that the message must take in the business process, that is, if an order is for a certain supplier, update SAP. Additionally, properties can be used by the messaging engine to decide the orchestration that must be activated. For example, there could be a specific process for a company such as Wal-Mart that is completely different from processes for other suppliers. Instead of creating a number of decision shapes in one orchestration, a promoted property can be set in the orchestration, which is then used by the message engine to route the message to that process. Once the schemas and promoted properties have been defined, the developer then essentially drags shapes from the toolbox onto a design surface, which creates the business flow. There are shapes for decision, parallel action, custom code-behind expression, message construction, transaction scope, delay, termination, suspend, and send and receive ports. An example of a business process could be a message that is received from an endpoint such as the file system and then transformed to another message format, which is then sent on to a system to update. This would require three shapes, receive, send, and transformation, and also two logical ports that would need to be bound to the receive and send shapes.

Finally, an orchestration also has the ability to span over time for a long running transaction. An example of this could be an order process that contains a manual process. If the manual process takes a day before completing, the orchestration would dehydrate (serialize to the `MessageBox` database) and then rehydrate (deserialize from the `MessageBox` database) and carry on with the process once the manual process is complete. This is achieved with correlation tokens that are created when a message is sent to the manual process. When the process is complete and a message is sent back, the BizTalk engine that will check the message for the correlation token, which then rehydrates the orchestration business process. For example, a correlation token could be simply an order number from the message. Figure 8-3 illustrates a typical orchestration that has a decision shape that determines whether an order needs approval before updating an end system.

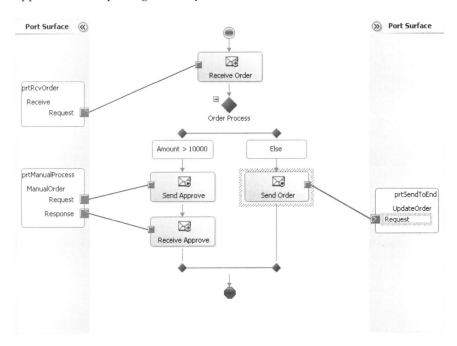

Figure 8-3. *Order orchestration overview*

Adapters

BizTalk Server 2006 R2 comes with a number of adapters that come in two flavors, messaging protocol or system interface. Each adapter is either installed out of the box with BizTalk Server or has a separate MSI install. If there isn't an adapter available for a particular system or protocol, developers can create their own adapters by using the SDK. Table 8-1 lists a subset of some of the most useful adapters. A complete list of adapters can be found at `http://www.microsoft.com/biztalk/en/us/adapters-included.aspx`.

Table 8-1. *Subset of BizTalk Adapters*

Source	Description
BizTalk Adapter Pack 1.0	Includes adapters for SAP, Siebel eBusiness applications, and Oracle databases, and the WCF LOB Adapter SDK. This adapter pack is included with BizTalk Server 2006 R2 licenses as of March 1, 2008.
SAP, PeopleSoft, JD Edwards, Siebel	Enables exchange of business function messages between BizTalk Server and LOB systems.
IBM DB2	Enables reading and writing information from and to IBM mainframe DB2.
FILE	Enables reading from and writing to files in the Microsoft Windows file system.
FTP	Enables exchange of files between BizTalk Server and FTP servers.
HTTP	Enables sending and receiving information by using HTTP.
SOAP	Enables sending and receiving messages by using SOAP over HTTP.
SQL	Enables reading and writing information from and to a Microsoft SQL Server database.
WCF	Includes seven adapters and wizards that enable easy communication to and from BizTalk Server and web services-based applications via WCF.
Windows SharePoint Services	Enables the exchange of XML and binary messages between BizTalk Server and SharePoint document libraries.

Configuring Your Environment

Two versions of BizTalk are available at the time of writing: BizTalk 2006 R2 and BizTalk 2009. Both versions share the same messaging engine and features that have been discussed. BizTalk 2006 supports Visual Studio 2005 and BizTalk 2009 supports Visual Studio 2008. Therefore, we have included two sections that discuss configuring your BizTalk environment. All exercises that are provided will work in both Visual Studio 2005 and Visual Studio 2008.

BizTalk 2006 R2

There are a few guides on MSDN (such as the one at `http://msdn.microsoft.com/en-us/library/aa577356.aspx`) on how to set up BizTalk 2006 R2. The main issue that you will have installing the development environment is that BizTalk Server 2006 R2 is only supported in Visual Studio 2005. This causes an issue because ADO.NET Data Services requires Visual Studio 2008. In a production environment this won't matter, because the development tools aren't required, but this doesn't help if you're developing on a single machine. Unfortunately, unless Microsoft creates a service pack that allows the support of Visual Studio 2008, you will need to install Visual Studio 2005. Additionally, BizTalk is a huge product, and we don't require all the features here. If you want to install all the features of BizTalk, please go to the MSDN article via the link provided and use those setup instructions; otherwise, now follows a simple exercise to set up only the required features of BizTalk on your Windows 2003 R2 environment. Here's a short list of the additional software required to complete the exercises:

- Visual Studio 2005 SP1

- SQL Server 2005 SP2 Developer Edition

- BizTalk Server 2006

- WCF LOB Adapter SDK SP2

EXERCISE 8-1: CONFIGURING YOUR BIZTALK 2006 R2 ENVIRONMENT

This aim of this exercise is to install BizTalk Server 2006 R2 in your local development environment.

Installing Visual Studio 2005

1. Install Visual Studio 2005–required features by running the installation program. Once the Visual Studio Wizard appears, choose the custom installation option and choose Visual C#, Visual Basic, and Visual Web Developer as shown in Figure 8-4. Finally, click Install to finish.

Select features to install:
- ☑ **Microsoft Visual Studio 2005 Professional Edition**
  - ☑ **Language Tools**
    - ☑ Visual C#
    - ☐ ✕ Visual J#
    - ☐ ✕ Visual C++
    - ☑ Visual Basic
      - ☑ Smart Device Programmability
      - ☑ Visual Web Developer
  - ☑ **.NET Framework SDK**
  - ☐ ✕ **Dotfuscator Community Edition**
  - ☐ ✕ **Tools for Redistributing Applications**
  - ☐ ✕ **Crystal Reports for Visual Studio**

Figure 8-4. *Visual Studio 2005 options*

2. Install Visual Studio SP1.

3. Install SQL Server 2005 using default settings.

4. Install SQL Server 2005 SP2 using default settings.

Installing BizTalk Server 2006 R2

1. Install the BizTalk Server 2006 R2 by running the installation program. When you do this, the Installation Wizard will appear. Select the Install Microsoft BizTalk Server 2006 R2 on this computer option and click Next. Choose to perform a custom install, and then select all available features except for Human Workflow Web Service. In the software prerequisites step, choose the Automatically install the redistributable prerequisites from the web option, click next, and finally click Install. This will install BizTalk 2006 and also the following software:

- Office Web Components

- Microsoft Data Access Components (MDAC) 2.8 SP1

- Microsoft XML Core Services (MSXML) 3.0 SP7

- MSXML 6.0

- SQLXML 3.0 SP3

- Microsoft .NET Framework 2.0

- Microsoft .NET Framework 3.0

- ADOMD.NET 8.0

- ADOMD.NET-KB893091-v8.00.0991-x86.EXE

- ADOMD.NET 9.0

2. Configure BizTalk 2006 in the Basic Configuration by clicking the Configure BizTalk 2006 link. When the BizTalk Configuration dialog appears, choose Basic Configuration and enter a username and password for an account. Make sure that the user is a member of the local administrators group. Once you have done this, click Next and ignore any security warnings.

BizTalk is now set up and configured.

BizTalk 2009

BizTalk 2009 can be run on the following operating systems: Windows 2003, Windows 2008, Windows XP with Service Pack 3, and Windows Vista with Service Pack 1. Once these have been installed, to configure BizTalk 2009 for a development environment you first need to install the following software prerequisites: Visual Studio 2008 SP1, SQL Server 2008, and BizTalk Server 2009.

BizTalk and ADO.NET Data Services

Now that you have installed BizTalk and gotten a brief overview of some of its features, the next topic to discuss is how to consume a data service within BizTalk. The logical starting point is that you first need to establish a way of communicating with the data service. Out-of-the-box adapters provided with BizTalk can be used to communicate with disparate systems such as data services. To get the most out of the enterprise functionality and flexibility of BizTalk, the key functional points that need to be met when consuming a data service are as follows:

- Specification of HTTP GET, PUT, POST, and DELETE operations against the data service needs to be allowed.

- The data service needs to appear as a flexible BizTalk endpoint that can be reconfigured by system administrators.

- Configuration of the data representation formats, Atom and JSON, needs to be allowed.

Review List of BizTalk Adapters

Let's start by reviewing the list of adapters that come with BizTalk to see whether any meet these requirements. To do this, you need to open up the BizTalk Administration Console and expand the list of adapters, using the following steps:

1. Open up the BizTalk Administration Console by selecting Start ➤ All Programs ➤ Microsoft BizTalk Server 2006 ➤ BizTalk Server Administration.

2. Expand the BizTalk Server 2006 Administration node.

3. Expand the Platform Setting node.

4. Expand the Adapters node to display the list of available BizTalk adapters as shown in Figure 8-5.

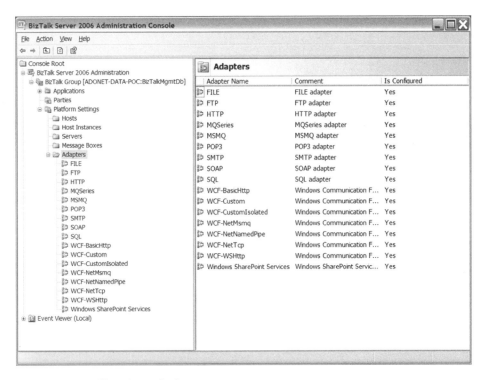

Figure 8-5. *BizTalk registered adapters*

From the list shown in Figure 8-5, the HTTP adapter appears to be the obvious choice, because you can simply point the HTTP adapter to the data service URL and then start communicating over HTTP. Let's review the HTTP adapter's options by creating a new BizTalk application called BizTalkWithDS with a send/receive port using the following steps:

1. Open up the BizTalk Administration MMC Console by selecting Start ➤ All Programs ➤ Microsoft BizTalk Server 2006 ➤ BizTalk Server Administration.

2. Create a dummy application in BizTalk by right-clicking the Applications node in the BizTalk Administration Console and selecting Create ➤ New Application. In the Application Properties dialog, name the application BizTalkWithDS.

3. Navigate to the new BizTalk BizTalkWithDS application by expanding the Applications node and navigating to BizTalkWithDS.

4. Create a new send/receive port in the BizTalkWithDS BizTalk application by right-clicking the Send Ports node and selecting New ➤ Static Solicit-Response.

5. In the Send Port Properties dialog, name this port DataServicesSendPort and select HTTP in the Type drop-down.

6. Click the Configure button next to the Type of Adapter drop-down to configure its properties as shown in Figure 8-6.

7. Enter `http://localhost/NorthwindDataService.svc/Customers('ALFKI')` in the Desti-nation URL text field, and then click OK to save these properties.

8. Click OK to save the new send/receive port.

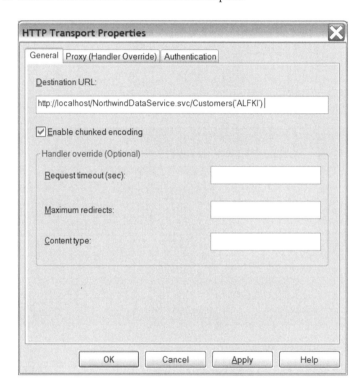

Figure 8-6. *HTTP adapter options*

Although the HTTP adapter allows communication over the HTTP protocol by default, this communication always uses the HTTP POST operation. If you review the HTTP adapter properties shown in Figure 8-6, there is nowhere to change this default behavior, which means that you cannot use this adapter.

The other BizTalk adapters in the list are used for different protocols such as FILE, FTP, and so forth and can't be used for HTTP communication. The only other adapters that could be used are the collection of BizTalk WCF adapters, the reasoning being that WCF allows multiple transports.

The WCF adapters are made up of adapters that represent WCF predefined bindings—customBinding, basicHttpBinding, WSHttpBinding, NetTCPBinding, NetNamePipeBinding, and NetMSMQBinding. You are not interested in communicating with your service in anything other than HTTP, so you can ignore the non-HTTP WCF adapters and just focus on the HTTP adapters that are based upon the basicHttpBinding, WSHttpBinding, and CustomBinding bindings.

First look at the BasicHttpBinding WCF-BasicHTTP adapter; this provides support for the ASMX-based web services and other services that conform to the WS-I Basic Profile 1.1 and are transported over HTTP or HTTPS. This sounds perfect; however, you need to make sure that you can specify a different HTTP operation. To see whether the basicHttpBinding WCF-BasicHTTP adapter fits the bill, switch the send/receive port to this adapter by selecting WCF-BasicHTTP adapter in the Type drop-down in the Send Port Properties dialog. This will present you with new set of adapter options as shown in Figure 8-7.

Figure 8-7. *WCF-BasicHTTP adapter options*

If you tab through the settings for the adapter, you will notice there are more configuration options than the traditional HTTP adapter, such as being able to set the text encoding and the identity of the call. However, you still have a similar problem to the basic HTTP adapter in that there is nowhere to set a different HTTP operation. If you switch your port to the WSHttpBinding WCF-WSHTTP adapter by changing the transport type property to WCF-WSHTTP in the Send Port Properties dialog, you will notice that this adapter also has the same problem in that it doesn't allow customizations. This leaves you with the `customBinding` WCF-Custom adapter, which allows you to extend the standard `basicHttpBinding` to provide the additional properties that you need. We will show you how to configure this in the next section.

WCF CUSTOM BINDING

The `customBinding` binding option can be used when none of the system-provided bindings meets the requirements of the service. It is essentially a container that you can use to fill with binding elements. Each of the binding elements that are added represents a processing step for sending and receiving messages, and at runtime these binding elements create the channels and listeners necessary. The binding elements can be built from a set of system-provided binding elements or can include user-defined custom binding elements. Three types of binding elements are available: protocol, encoding, and transport.

The execution of these binding elements occurs in a predefined order from protocol (optional), encoding, and finally transport.

Configuring the WCF-Custom Adapter

Review the options for the `customBinding` by again changing your send/receive port to use the WCF-Custom adapter and then clicking the Configure button, which will show the WCF-Custom Transport Properties dialog, as you can see in Figure 8-8.

If you now click the Binding tab, you are presented with a list of registered binding types from the Binding Type drop-down as highlighted in Figure 8-8. These bindings are held in the `machine.config` file, which is located in the .NET configuration folder. To view the list of the registered binding types, open the `machine.config` file in %windir% \Microsoft.NET\Framework\ v2.0.50727\CONFIG and locate `<bindingExtensions>` within the `<system.serviceModel>` tag.

You need to select the `customBinding` type from this list. To allow BizTalk to call data services, you require the `basicHttpBinding` elements that will provide you with the standard communication over HTTP. When you first select the `customBinding` option, you are given by default the `basicHttpBinding` elements, which are the `textMessageEncoding` (encoding) element with the `ReaderQuotas` subelement, and the `httpTransport` (transport) binding element.

To enable these elements to work over data services, you need to configure these to the following settings:

- `textMessageEncoding`
  - `messageVersion`: None
- `httpTransport`
  - `maxBufferSize`: 65536000
  - `maxBufferPoolSize`: 65536000
  - `maxReceivedMessage`: 65536000

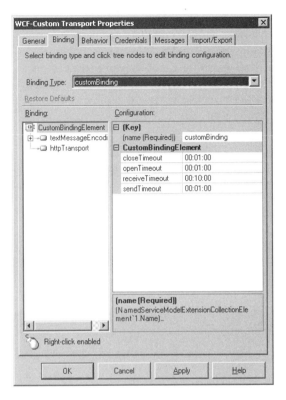

Figure 8-8. *Binding tab of the WCF-Custom Transport Properties dialog*

The reason for changing these elements is because the `textMessageEncoding` element will use SOAP to stamp message versions. This will cause an issue, as clients will then expect a SOAP-based message to be returned from your endpoint, though in this case you just want the raw HTTP response. In addition to changing the `textMessageEncoding`, you also modify the `httpTransport` element to increase maximum sizes that can be processed by the port; this is so it will allow larger Atom messages to flow through. Therefore, you increase the `maxBufferSize`, `maxBufferPoolSize`, and `maxReceivedMessage` properties by a factor of 10.

Now that you can communicate over HTTP, you need to be able to specify the HTTP operation based upon the type of request. To do this you need to intercept the message on the client (BizTalk Server) before it is sent and change the HTTP operation. This is achieved in WCF by implementing a client message inspector behavior that is executed in the WCF channel stack. To do this, you will need to implement a WCF endpoint behavior.

WCF BEHAVIORS

A **behavior** is a special type of class that extends runtime behavior during the service host/channel factor initialization process. Four types of behaviors are provided in WCF: service, endpoint, contract, and operation. Each of these types allows behaviors to be applied at different scopes: service, endpoint, contract, and operation.

The WCF endpoint behavior can be added to the WCF channel stack at runtime with code or added manually to the channel's XML configuration. If you add the behavior at runtime, there is no way for a user to configure different properties. To allow users the ability to change your behavior's properties at design time, you need to add the new behavior to the machine. config file in the <behaviors> section within the <system.serviceModel> tag. You also need to create the design-time properties, which is achieved by creating a class that inherits from the System.Model.Configuration.BehaviorExtensionElement.

To summarize, your behavior will consist of three classes.

- **BehaviorExtensionElement**: This class is inherited from the System.Model. Configuration.BehaviorExtensionElement.

- **HttpVerbBehavior**: This class will implement the IEndpointBehavior interface.

- **VerbMessageInspector**: This class will implement the IClientMessageInspector interface.

The following exercise provides instructions to create the WCF endpoint behavior and to supply the ability to surface it to the BizTalk custom adapter.

EXERCISE 8-2: CREATING CUSTOM WCF BINDING BEHAVIOR

This aim of this exercise is to create a WCF custom behavior that will execute before messages are sent from BizTalk. This exercise is broken down into sections for creating the C# project, implementing the classes, and registering the behavior in the global assembly cache (GAC) and the machine.config file.

The exercises in this chapter can be found with the code supplied with this book (which you can download from http://www.apress.com/book/sourcecode) located in the BizTalkSolutions folder.

Creating the HTTP Behavior C# Class Project

1. In Visual Studio 2008, create a new C# ASP.NET class project by selecting File ➤ New ➤ Project. Select the Class Library Visual Studio project template and enter **Apress.Data.Services.BizTalk.HttpVerbBehavior** as the project name.

2. Right-click the project and selecting Add Reference. Add the following assembly references:

   - System.configuration

   - System.Runtime.Serialization

   - System.ServiceModel

3. Delete Class1.cs.

Implementing the Behavior Extension Element

The key feature of our behavior will be the ability to specify an HTTP verb and content type that you require on the message; these properties are specified in the BehaviorExtensionElement and decorated with a [ConfigurationProperty] attribute as shown a little later in Listing 8-2. When the behavior is first executed by WCF, it will call the CreateBehavior() method that will send these configuration properties to the IEndPointBehavior implementation. The BehaviorType property is used by the WCF channel to initialize our implementation of the IEndPointBehavior.

1. Create a new class for the HttpVerbBehavior project by right-clicking the project and selecting Add ➤ New Item. From the Add New Item dialog choose the class project template and enter the name **Code.cs**.

2. To implement the functionality that you require, you need to reference six System.ServiceModel.* assemblies. Copy the structure shown in Listing 8-1.

Listing 8-1. *Class Structure*

```
using System;
using System.Collections.Generic;
using System.Linq;
using System.Text;
using System.ServiceModel.Description;
using System.ServiceModel.Channels;
using System.ServiceModel.Dispatcher;
using System.ServiceModel;
using System.ServiceModel.Configuration;
using System.Configuration;
using System.Net;

namespace Apress.Data.Services.BizTalk.HttpVerbBehavior
{
}
```

3. Add the implementation of the behavior extension element by entering the code in Listing 8-2 in between the namespace Apress.Data.Services.BizTalk.HttpVerbBehavior brackets.

Listing 8-2. *Behavior Extension Element*

```
public class HttpVerbElement : BehaviorExtensionElement
{
    public override Type BehaviorType
    {
      get { return typeof(HttpVerbBehavior); }
    }

    protected override object CreateBehavior()
    {
        return new HttpVerbBehavior(this.Verb, this.ContentType);
    }

    ConfigurationPropertyCollection _properties;

    [ConfigurationProperty("verb")]
    public string Verb
    {
      get { return (string)base["verb"]; }
      set { base["verb"] = value; }
    }
```

```
[ConfigurationProperty("contentType")]
public string ContentType
{
    get { return (string)base["contentType"]; }
    set { base["contentType"] = value; }
}


protected override ConfigurationPropertyCollection Properties
{
    get
    {
        if (this._properties == null)
        {
            ConfigurationPropertyCollection configProperties = new
                ConfigurationPropertyCollection();
            configProperties.Add(new ConfigurationProperty("verb",
                    typeof(string), null, null, null,
                    ConfigurationPropertyOptions.None));
            configProperties.Add(new ConfigurationProperty
                    ("contentType", typeof(string), null, null,
                     null, ConfigurationPropertyOptions.None));
                    this._properties = configProperties;
        }

        return this._properties;
    }
}
```

Implementing the IEndPointBehavior Interface

The IEndpointBehavior interface contains four standard methods: AddBindingParameters(), ApplyClientBehavior(), ApplyDispatchBehavior(), and Validate(). You are only concerned with the implementation of the ApplyClientBehavior() method, as the other three methods do not need to be implemented for WCF endpoint behaviors. The ApplyClientBehavior() method will add the implementation of the IClientMessageInspector (VerbMessageInspector) to the collection of behaviors that will be executed by the WCF channel

1. Add the implementation of the IEndPointBehavior interface by entering the code in Listing 8-3 in between the namespace Apress.Data.Services.BizTalk.HttpVerbBehavior brackets.

Listing 8-3. *Applying Client Behaviors in the IEndpointBehavior Interface*

```
public class HttpVerbBehavior : IEndpointBehavior
{
    public HttpVerbBehavior(string verb, string contentType)
    {
        this._verb = verb;
        this._contentType = contentType;
```

```
        }
        string _verb;
        string _contentType;

        #region IEndpointBehavior Members

        public void AddBindingParameters(ServiceEndpoint endpoint,
                System.ServiceModel.Channels.BindingParameterCollection
                bindingParameters)
        {
        }

        public void ApplyClientBehavior(ServiceEndpoint endpoint,
        System.ServiceModel.Dispatcher.ClientRuntime clientRuntime)
        {
                clientRuntime.MessageInspectors.Add(new
                VerbMessageInspector(this._verb, this._contentType));
        }

        public void ApplyDispatchBehavior(ServiceEndpoint endpoint,
                    System.ServiceModel.Dispatcher.EndpointDispatcher
                    endpointDispatcher)
        {
        }

        public void Validate(ServiceEndpoint endpoint)
        {
        }

        #endregion
}
```

Implementing the IClientMessageInspector Interface

The final, and most important, piece is the implementation of the client message inspector interface. The inspector interface contains two methods, AfterReceiveReply() and BeforeSendRequest(). You are only concerned with modifying the message before you send the request, so you don't need to provide an implementation of the AfterReceiveReply() method. You want to add two properties to the collection HttpRequestMessageProperty: these are the ContentType and the Method. You always need to set the ContentType for anything other than an HTTP GET because this is a requirement for data services. Also, if the original method is an HTTP GET, by default you want to suppress the HTTP request message body so that you pass only the HTTP URL to the data service.

1. Add the implementation of the IClientMessageInspector interface by entering the code in Listing 8-4 and in between the namespace Apress.Data.Services.BizTalk.HttpVerbBehavior brackets.

Listing 8-4. *Client Message Inspector*

```
public class VerbMessageInspector : IClientMessageInspector
{
```

```csharp
public VerbMessageInspector(string verb, string contentType)
{
    this._verb = verb;
    this._contentType = contentType;
}
string _verb;
string _contentType;

public void AfterReceiveReply(ref
        System.ServiceModel.Channels.Message reply,
        Object correlationState)
{
}

public object BeforeSendRequest(ref
        System.ServiceModel.Channels.Message request,
        IClientChannel channel)
{

    //Get the HTTP Request Message Property from the request
    HttpRequestMessageProperty mp = null;
    If (request.Properties.ContainsKey
                (HttpRequestMessageProperty.Name))
    {
        mp = (HttpRequestMessageProperty)request.
            Properties[HttpRequestMessageProperty.Name];
    }
    else
    {
        mp = new HttpRequestMessageProperty();
            request.Properties.Add(HttpRequestMessageProperty.Name
            , mp);
    }

    mp.Method = this._verb;

    //Set the contentType to default ATOM format
    if (String.IsNullOrEmpty(this._contentType))
    {
        this._contentType = "application/atom+xml";
    }

    //Set the Content Type
    mp = (HttpRequestMessageProperty)request.
            Properties[HttpRequestMessageProperty.Name];
    mp.Headers.Add(HttpResponseHeader.ContentType, _contentType);
```

```
        //If the method is GET then suppress the entity body
        if (mp.Method == "GET")
        {
            mp.SuppressEntityBody = true;
            Message msg =
            Message.CreateMessage(MessageVersion.None, "*");
            msg.Properties.Add(HttpRequestMessageProperty.Name, mp);
            request = msg;
        }

        return null;
    }
}
```

Registering the Assembly in the Global Assembly Cache

The final part is to register the behavior in the `machine.config` file and put the assembly in the GAC, the reason for the latter being that it allows BizTalk to access the assembly.

1. Sign the project assembly by right-clicking the HttpVerbBehavior project and selecting Properties. Now click the Signing tab. Check the Sign the Assembly option and choose <New> from the drop-down. In the Create Strong Name Key dialog, specify BizTalkSolutions as the name and uncheck the Protect my key with a User name and Password option.
2. Now click the Build Events tab in the Project Properties dialog. In the Post-build event command-line field, enter the following. This will register the assembly in the GAC after you build the project.

   ```
   echo Installing $(OutDir)$(TargetFileName) into the GAC...
   ```
3. Recompile the project by right-clicking the project and selecting Build.
4. Now open up the GAC by selecting Start ➤ Run and typing **assembly** in the text field. Locate the `Apress.Data.Services.BizTalk.HttpVerbBehavior` assembly, right-click it, and select Properties. You need to copy the public key token by highlighting the text, right-clicking, and selecting Copy.
5. Find the `machine.config` file by opening Windows Explorer and navigating to `%windir% \Microsoft.NET\Framework\v2.0.50727\CONFIG\machine.config`. Open this file and locate `<bindingExtensions>` within the `<system.serviceModel>` tag. The configuration is shown in Listing 8-5. The `PublicKeyToken` property needs to be overwritten with the public key token copied from the previous step.

Listing 8-5. *Machine.config Update*

```
<add name="httpVerbBehavior" type="Apress.Data.Service➥
s.BizTalk.HttpVerbBehavio➥
 r.HttpVerbElement, Apress.Data.Services.BizTalk.➥
 HttpVerbBehavior, Version=1.0.0.0, Culture=neutr➥
al, PublicKeyToken=2ede9548c38071a0" />
```

The behavior extension is now ready to be added to the BizTalk send/receive port created earlier. Reopen the send/receive port and navigate to the Behavior tab of the WCF-Custom Transport Properties dialog. To add the new extension, right-click IEndpointBehavior and select Add Extension. Highlight the new behavior you created earlier from the list as shown in Figure 8-9 and click OK.

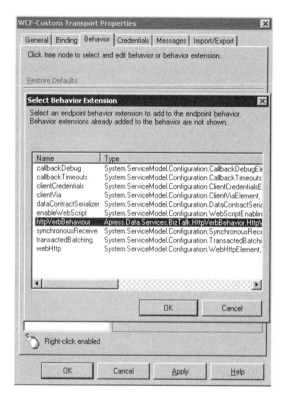

Figure 8-9. *Specifying the custom behavior*

The behavior element properties can now be entered; for the purpose of this demonstration, set the HTTP verb as GET and leave the content type blank (by default this will be the Atom format). To complete the configuration, you must enter the endpoint (address URI) in the General tab of the WCF-Custom Transport Properties dialog, http://localhost/NorthwindDataService.svc/Customers('ALFKI'), which will retrieve the ALFKI customer from the Northwind data service that you created in earlier chapters. Save the send port settings and close the Send Port Properties dialog.

You now need a way of testing the send/receive port. In older versions of BizTalk, you couldn't call a send/receive port directly without creating an orchestration. This is because the port uses the MessageBox to send requests and receive responses using port subscription tokens, which only orchestrations had the capability to subscribe to. In BizTalk 2006 R2 and onward, this architecture has changed so that you can create a WCF Net TCP send/receive port that will use a content-based routing filter (the subscription) on the send port to receive the response from the send/receive port. An illustration of how to execute the port is shown in Figure 8-10.

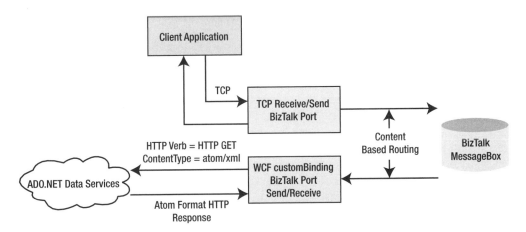

Figure 8-10. *Executing a data service endpoint using a console application*

In the following exercise, based on the illustration shown in Figure 8-10, you will test the port from a client test application. This client application will use the WCF Net TCP send/receive port to send a request into BizTalk that will activate the WCF customBinding communication with ADO.NET Data Services.

EXERCISE 8-3: TESTING THE DATA SERVICE ENDPOINT USING A CONSOLE APPLICATION

The aim of this exercise is to show how to test the new data service endpoint from a console application. To do this, you need to create a new receive location that uses the WCF Net TCP operation.

The exercises in this chapter can be found with the code supplied with this book (which you can download from http://www.apress.com/book/sourcecode) located in the BizTalkSolutions folder.

Creating a New WCF Net TCP Port

1. Navigate to the BizTalkWithDS application in the BizTalk Administration Console.

2. Create a new receive port by right-clicking the Receive Ports node and selecting New ➤ Request Response Receive Port. In the Receive Port Properties dialog, name the port **DataServicesActivation**.

3. Create a new receive location within the Receive Port Properties dialog by clicking Receive Locations in the left-hand tree and then clicking New in the right-hand pane. Name the receive location **DataServicesActivationLocation**.

4. Configure the receive location by specifying the WCF-NetTCP adapter type from the drop-down and then clicking the Configure button. In the WCF-TCP Transport Properties dialog, enter the endpoint address as **net.tcp://localhost/BizTalkToDataServices**, and then click OK to save the port.

5. Navigate to the receive locations listed in the BizTalkWithDS BizTalk application. Find the new DataServicesActivationLocation that has just been created. Enable the receive location by right-clicking it and selecting Enable. The receive location should now display a green check mark next to it.

Setting Up a Subscription

Now you'll link the new receive port to the data service's send/receive port. To do this you must add a subscription filter to the DataServicesSendPort send/receive port that you created earlier by following these steps:

1. Navigate to the BizTalkWithDS application in the BizTalk Administration Console.

2. Click Send ports and double-click the DataServicesSendPort to display the Send Port Properties dialog. Click the Filters tab on the left-hand side of the dialog.

3. To create the subscription filter, you have to click the arrow on the left-hand side of the grid, which will create a new subscription. Now choose BTS.ReceivePortName from the drop-down list of properties associated with BizTalk Server. Once you have done this, choose == in the Operator drop-down and finally enter the value **DataServicesActivation** into the Value field. The Group By drop-down should be set to And. Your settings should appear as shown in Figure 8-11.

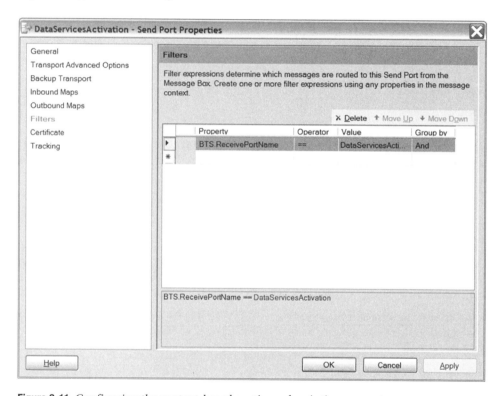

Figure 8-11. *Configuring the content-based routing subscription property*

4. Save the send port settings by clicking the OK Button.

5. Enlist and start the send port by right-clicking it and selecting Start.

Creating a Test Console C# Application

You now need a simple console application that will send a message to the WCF Net TCP channel, which will in turn use the content-based routing filter to route the message to the send/receive port to your WCF service. The WCF Net TCP binding will wait until its timeout for the response to be routed back to it. The console application will create the WCF Net TCP channel that will use a generic untyped service contract IBTSGeneric, which allows any response to be sent or received. Generic contracts are useful when you want an untyped interface to be exposed to clients, which will be none the wiser that the interface is actually forwarding the request to another endpoint.

1. In Visual Studio 2008, create a new C# ASP.NET class project by selecting File ➤ New ➤ Project. Select the Class Library Visual Studio project template and enter **Apress.Data.Services.BizTalk.BizTalkToDSClient** as the project name.

2. Right-click the project and select Add Reference. Add the following assembly references:

   - System.Runtime.Serialization
   - System.ServiceModel

3. Overwrite the code in Program.cs with the code in Listing 8-6.

Listing 8-6. *Test BizTalk Data Services Endpoint Console Application*

```
using System;
using System.Collections.Generic;
using System.Linq;
using System.Text;
using System.ServiceModel;
using System.ServiceModel.Channels;
using System.Xml;

namespace BizTalkClient
{
    class BizTalkClient
    {
        static void Main(string[] args)
        {
            NetTcpBinding b = new NetTcpBinding();
            EndpointAddress ea =
                new
            EndpointAddress("net.tcp://localhost/
            BizTalkToDataServices");
            ChannelFactory<IBTSGeneric> cf =
                new ChannelFactory<IBTSGeneric>(b, ea);
            cf.Open();
            IBTSGeneric c = cf.CreateChannel();
            Message msgToSend =
                Message.CreateMessage(MessageVersion.Default,
                "*",
                "Test Message  - will get stripped");
            Message responseMsg = c.Get(msgToSend);
            XmlReader xr = responseMsg.GetReaderAtBodyContents();
            xr.MoveToContent();
            Console.WriteLine(xr.ReadOuterXml());
            cf.Close();
```

```
        Console.Read();

    }
}
[ServiceContract]
public interface IBTSGeneric
{
    [OperationContract(Action = "*", ReplyAction = "*")]
    Message Get(Message msg);
}
}
```

An alternative to compiling this code is to import a predefined BizTalk application that contains all the assemblies and ports that are required. Now follows an exercise to import the BizTalk MSI.

EXERCISE 8-4: INSTALLING THE BIZTALK SERVICE APPLICATION

The aim of this exercise is to install a new application called BizTalkDS, which contains all the functionality that has been discussed in the previous exercises.

1. Import the BizTalk application MSI by opening the BizTalk Administration Console, right-clicking the Applications node, and selecting Import ➤ MSI File. In the Import MSI Wizard, browse to the MSI file location `BizTalkSolutions\Installations\CallableDataService\BizTalkWithDS.msi`, and click OK in the rest of the wizard's screens.

2. Notice that a new application called BizTalkDS will appear in the Applications node in the BizTalk Administration Console. Start the application by right-clicking it and selecting Start.

3. Add the behavior extension element binding to `machine.config` from by copying the configuration from `BizTalkSolutions\Installations\CallableDataService\ConfigForMachine.config` into `machine.config` as explained in the preceding walkthrough.

4. Execute the console application `BizTalkToDSClient.exe` to return the Atom feed for your ALFKI customer by navigating to `BizTalkSolutions\Installations\CallableDataService` and double-clicking `BizTalkToDSClient.exe`.

Summary

Microsoft Enterprise products are currently going through a revamp to align them with .NET 3.5 and beyond. The new version of BizTalk Server, BizTalk Server 2009, will provide additional features to work in an SOA environment, which include the SQL and Oracle WCF adapters shown earlier. It will provide support to use `webHttpBinding` as part of Visual Studio 2008 SP1 out of the box, which will enable easier consumption of data services without creating custom WCF behaviors. However, even the new version of BizTalk still has some way to go for queryable RESTful services, and there will be no support for data services. BizTalk

Server 2009 will be the last of its generation, paving the way for a new strategy in Microsoft code-named Olso. At the time of writing this new approach is under wraps in Microsoft. What is known is that this strategic approach will involve not only BizTalk, but also .NET 4.0, System Center, and the Visual Studio suite. The key component of this approach is the reintroduction of the Unified Modeling Language (UML). This will go some way toward bridging the gap between IT and business by providing business analysis with simple EDM-based modeling tools that can then be transformed into code. ADO.NET Data Services will play a key part of this approach because it will assist with how entities are surfaced from this modeling base and how they are activated from the cloud. To be able to query entities no matter where they are or what they are built upon is where Microsoft wants to be.

PART 4

The Future of ADO.NET Data Services

The ADO.NET Data Services journey has nearly come to an end. We have shown how this technology can be used to interface a wide ranging set of products that include Silverlight, AJAX, Popfly, and BizTalk.

So what is the future of ADO.NET Data Services? Its future lies within the slowly emerging technology called cloud computing. Cloud computing spans back through 20 years of desktop and server programming all the way to centralizing core processing. This shouldn't be confused with mainframe programming, because it is much more than having a powerful server for each company. Cloud computing is more aligned with the concept of distributed computing, where hardware and software is distributed over multiple storage spaces and vast amounts of processing power, which has the flexibility to handle increasing load. This will appeal to corporate IT directors because it will lower their staff costs by effectively outsourcing some of their companies' operational activities. The cloud computing dream will also enable smaller software companies to compete with larger firms by opening up the market. Microsoft has invested heavily in this approach by creating data centers in key locations, through which the company will supply both business process management software services and data as a service in the form of SQL Server Data Services.

Cloud computing also requires a new way of thinking about how users interact with their desktop. Rich Internet Applications (RIAs) such as Silverlight and AJAX solutions will provide the functionality of a desktop application but will run within the cloud. We will see ADO.NET Data Services and other WCF services providing a thin layer between the RIA and the cloud. The ADO.NET Data Services framework will also be added to technologies that require a queryable RESTful layer. An example of this is the Windows Live Hotmail Photo API; in the coming months it is due to appear on top of SQL Server Data Services.

At the time of writing, the next version of ADO.NET Data Services is currently being planned. It will provide alignment with the Entity Framework V2.0, WCF 4, and the .NET Framework. It will also feature offline capabilities that will enable developers to access data services offline. All in all, Microsoft will carry on invested in ADO.NET Data Services because of its importance in the cloud computing strategy.

CHAPTER 9

▪▪▪

Conclusion

This final chapter ends the book with a summary of the areas that we have covered and where ADO.NET Data Services is heading. The ADO.NET Data Services framework is a key enabling technology that fits as part of Microsoft's cloud computing strategy. It relates to a number of emerging technologies such as Microsoft's cloud computing platform, SQL Server Data Services, Oslo, and the Entity Framework V2.0. We then describe each of these new areas and how they relate to ADO.NET Data Services. Finally, we close out the book with the enhancements that are expected in the next version of ADO.NET Data Services, code-named Astoria vNext.

Where Are We?

ADO.NET Data Services is a new technology that is part of .NET Framework 3.5 Service Pack 1 and supports exposing data models as a set of queryable REST URI endpoints. ADO.NET Data Services exposes data that is represented by the Entity Data Model (EDM) via HTTP. This data can be interacted with through a thin layer of operations that map onto HTTP verbs (i.e., Create = POST, Read = GET, Update = PUT, Delete = DELETE). Following the core tenets of RESTful services, the entities exposed by the data service are addressable endpoints, which mean that it's possible to navigate entities and their relationships using just a URL. ADO.NET Data Services also provides a rich query framework that is used to control how data is retrieved through filtering, sorting, paging, and expanding entities. In addition, data has two serialization formats that allow it to be returned in either Atom or JSON formats. Rich client support is achieved with a Visual Studio plug-in or a command-line tool that is used to autogenerate a set of classes that represent the entities that have been exposed. The client assembly allows LINQ queries against the entities, which are then transformed into a URL query. This provides a further layer of abstraction that enables developers to use familiar syntax. The HTTP layer allows ADO.NET data services to be platform independent.

The key features of ADO.NET Data Services that we have covered are the following:

- Surface addressable entity sets that consumers can interact with using standard HTTP verbs such as GET, PUT, POST, and DELETE

- Well-known formats to represent data using Atom and JSON

- Extensive set of query string operations that can be used to filter, sort, page, and expand entities

- Querying services using standard LINQ syntax

- Surfacing multiple data sources using the Entity Framework, LINQ to SQL, or creating a custom CLR data source that supports `IQueryable<T>` and `IUpdateable<T>` interfaces

- Restricting entity access to read, write, update, or none

- Implementing business and security logic using query and update Interceptors

- Creating service operations for methods that don't exactly fit the exposed data model

- Batching support available to send multiple HTTP payloads to the server in a single atomic operation

- Optimistic concurrency checking that can be switched on the entity level

- Client library support for .NET applications, which include Window Forms applications, Windows Presentation Foundation (WPF) applications, and Web projects

- Asynchronous operations supported in the client library that provide support for Silverlight applications

- ASP.NET AJAX library available from CodePlex that is used to abstract the details of the HTTP requests so that developers can work directly with the JavaScript objects

- Consuming ADO.NET Data Services in enterprise server products such as BizTalk

- Consuming ADO.NET Data Services in mashups using Popfly

Cloud Computing

If you have been living under a rock for the past year, you wouldn't have heard about cloud computing. Cloud computing is a general term that describes anything that is based in the Internet. It is normally associated with developers who draw clouds in diagrams indicating where services or how systems communicate with each other. Cloud computing also incorporates such well-known trends as Web 2.0 and Software as a Service (SaaS), and more recently Data as a Service (DaaS). Its aim is to change the way we compute, moving from traditional desktop and on-premises servers to services and resources that are hosted in the cloud.

ADO.NET Data Services often seems to be mentioned in the same breath as cloud computing, which is the reason for covering this topic. However, before we dive into how ADO.NET Data Services fits into this arena, we'll first try to explain the benefits and drawbacks of cloud computing along with describing the service offerings from the key players.

Benefits of Cloud Computing

There are clearly benefits in building applications using cloud computing, some of which are listed here:

- **Zero up-front investment**: Delivering a large-scale system costs a fortune in both time and money. Often IT departments are split into hardware/network and software services. The hardware team provisions servers and so forth under the requirements of the software team. Often the hardware team has a different budget that requires approval. Although hardware and software management are two separate disciplines, sometimes what happens is developers are given the task to estimate CPU cycles, disk space, and so forth, which ends up in underutilized servers.

- **Usage-based costing**: You pay for what you use, no more, no less, because you never actually own the server. This is similar to car leasing, where in the long run you get a new car every three years and maintenance is never a worry.

- **Potential for shrinking the processing time**: If processes are split over multiple machines, parallel processing is performed, which decreases processing time.

- **More office space**: Walk into most offices, and guaranteed you will find a medium-sized room dedicated to servers.

- **Efficient resource utilization**: The resource utilization is handed by a centralized cloud administrator who is in charge of deciding exactly the right amount of resources for a system. This takes the task away from local administrators, who have to regularly monitor these servers.

- **Just-in-time infrastructure**: If your system is a success and needs to scale to meet demand, this can cause further time delays or a slow-performing service. Cloud computing solves this because you can add more resources at any time.

- **Lower environmental impact**: If servers are centralized, potentially an environment initiative is more likely to succeed. As an example, if servers are placed in sunny or windy parts of the world, then why not use these resources to power those servers?

- **Lower costs**: Unfortunately, this is one point that administrators will not like. If you have people administrating your e-mail server and network along with support staff doing other cloud-based tasks, this workforce can be reduced. This saves costs, though it also reduces jobs.

Drawbacks of Cloud Computing

There are some obvious drawbacks to cloud computing, which can be summarized into four key areas: security, reliability, speed, and contractual obligations. These challenges must be overcome by a chief technology officer before entering cloud computing. So when should you use cloud computing and when not?

When to use cloud computing:

- You have short-term requirements such as extra storage space or infrastructure that is needed for a business idea that can't wait for hardware procurement.

- You want to use simple applications that do not require extensive monitoring by support personal.

When not to use cloud computing:

- Your system involves storage or processing of personal, sensitive data that has associated consumer protection laws.

- You use applications that require regular monitoring by support staff.

In the following sections, we explore the questions that need to be asked for the four key areas.

Security

The security concerns of cloud computing are high on the agenda for most corporations. They want to make sure that their data is secure and won't be used against them in the future. In regards to security, some of these high-level questions need to be answered:

- Where is the data physically stored?
- How secure is the facility?
- Does the facility meet the PCI Data Security Standard (account protection standards)?

Reliability and Speed

The reliability of the cloud service and speed of access is important to many businesses. If data isn't physically located in data centers nearby, the law of physics come into play, because data has farther to travel (over various network links), which takes more time.

- How reliable is the service?
- How regularly is the data backed up?
- Do the data centers have high-speed links?
- Is there more than one high-speed link available in case one fails?

Contractual Obligations

The most important part of cloud computing that all large corporations need to look at is the contractual obligations of the vendor. This will involve a team of lawyers to hash out exactly what will be in the contract between you and the vendor. Top-level items that should be covered are the following:

- What Service Level Agreement (SLA) is needed for uptime? (Typically you want "four nine" uptime, that is, 99.9999% of the time.)
- What happens if the contract is terminated? Will I lose my data?
- What happens if I don't pay a bill? Will the service be switched off?
- How long is the minimum agreement in place for?
- What level of insurance liability cover does the vendor have?

Main Players

Over the last two or three years a lot of R&D money has been invested by some of the largest IT companies. The following section gives an objective view of the activities in cloud computing by companies listed in Table 9-1.

Table 9-1. *Ranked Cloud Computing Companies*

Company	Service Offerings
IBM	Blue Cloud, which is based upon the Hadoop Open Source project.
Google	Google Apps, a cloud computing offering in conjunction with IBM.
Yahoo	Cloud computing research. Yahoo is a major sponsor of the Hadoop open source project.
Amazon	Simple Storage System (S3), Elastic Compute Cloud (EC2), SimpleDB, Simple Queue Service (SQS), Amazon Web Services.
Salesforce.com	Force.com
Microsoft	Windows Azure, SQL Server Data Services (SSDS), Hosted Exchange, LiveMesh, FeedSync, CRM, and SharePoint.

IBM

IBM is to launch Blue Cloud to the corporate sector in 2008. The proposed offering will allow corporation data centers to operate like the Internet by enabling access across a distributed, globally accessible fabric of resources. IBM's aim is to break into the Web 2.0 market by helping clients take advantage of cloud computing architecture that integrates with their existing IT infrastructure via SOA-based web services. Essentially, this represents IBM's Enterprise 2.0 initiative, which aims to replicate Web 2.0 in the enterprise. This computing power will be based upon open standards, namely the Hadoop Open Source project—an implementation of the Google File System.

Google

Google is currently one of Microsoft biggest rivals. Their rise in the last 8 years has been momentous due to the massive amount of advertising revenue from their popular search engine. Trust us when we say there is no love lost between Microsoft and Google. Google has stated that it wants to eventually overtake Microsoft's grip on the desktop market and has started to work toward this aim by targeting Microsoft Office, which accounts for 50 percent of all of Microsoft's revenue.

Google has done this by providing a number of "cloud-based" services that were introduced in 2005 with Gmail, a free service that is similar to Windows Live Hotmail. The difference is that Gmail is based upon a flexible storage system that allocates any available space to users, giving users an average three times as much space as Microsoft's Hotmail system. This caused Microsoft to increase user's allocation to 5GB. Gmail is also different from Hotmail in that the Google search engine will provide ads based upon the content of the e-mail that users are reading. This provides a source of revenue for a free e-mail service. Gmail is now branded within a suite of tools called Google Apps. Google Apps is an online set of office tools that includes word processing, spreadsheets, and presentation software.

This suite of tools are similar to an early version of MS Office; if you just want to create a simple document or a spreadsheet, why do you need all the extra features that MS Office provides? Additionally, Google Docs allows the sharing of files between users to promote collaboration. Thus, if a file is being edited within Google Docs, there is no need to attach it to an e-mail. The business model is to provide Google Docs as a free service that allows files up to a certain size to be uploaded and shared. These online services are aimed at the consumer and have barely tapped the lucrative commercial market. Part of the issue is that Google's offerings are simply not yet trusted by large corporations because most of Google's products have a "beta" tag associated with them. The reason is not due to the offering itself, but that Google hasn't yet built a track record, which Microsoft has. In the case of Google's e-mail offering, corporations need to make sure that it's secure from hackers and spies.

Even Google concedes that its services don't have the bells and whistles that Microsoft products currently have, such as centralized e-mail backups that help them comply with regulatory rules. If an IT director goes with Google because of the cost difference compared to Microsoft, the director could be putting his neck on the line; most executives won't do this, which is the reason why Microsoft has a large foothold in its operating systems and the MS Office suite.

Finally, Google has also formed a partnership with IBM on its cloud computing strategy, which was mentioned previously. This joint IBM-Google cloud will run on Linux; IBM will supply the hardware and Google the software.

Yahoo

Yahoo, which has been in takeover negotiations with Microsoft recently, is looking to unleash a cloud computing strategy by providing research money for the fourth largest supercomputer in the world, based in Pune, India. Yahoo hopes that the result of this research will provide a cloud computing technology that will rival Amazon's S3 and Microsoft's SSDS. Similar to Google and IBM's projects, this will also be based upon the Hadoop open source project. The guiding principles are to provide a service that is reliable, robust, simple to use, and highly scalable; provide multiple rich access format; include rapid provisioning for new storage; and is operationally cheap. The four known products based on this approach are Yahoo oneConnect, Clippl, Live, and NewsGlobe. These products are consumer based, which allows easier sharing of videos and blogs along with mashup capabilities using Yahoo news and maps.

Amazon

When Amazon was established by Jeff Bezos in Seattle, it was one of the first major companies to sell goods over the Internet. The original idea was to be an online book store through which users could search for and buy the latest titles. This was coupled with an extensive supply chain and distribution model. Amazon was one of the few successful Internet companies to ride out the burst of the dot-com bubble. Building on its successful online book store, Amazon started to branch out into other retail areas such as supplying CDs, DVDs, software, and electronic items.

Due to the increase in its product line, the Amazon web site now attracts 615 million visitors according to a Compete survey, twice that of Wal-Mart. In fact, books are sold more than any other product on the Internet. Amazon delivers 40% of its sales through affiliates who list and sell products on the Amazon web site. Amazon required B2B services to accommodate its affiliates, now numbering in the thousands. This resulted in the launch of the Amazon Web Services project in 2002. What started as a project to assist Amazon buyers and sellers has now turned into a full-scale cloud computing platform. Amazon has four key products that it provides under the Amazon Web Services banner: the Simple Storage Service, Elastic Compute Cloud, SimpleDB, and Simple Queue Service. S3 is an online storage system that allows an unlimited number of data objects up to 5GB in size to be stored in it and then distributed via HTTP or BitTorrent.

There is a service charge for data stored and transferred. EC2 is a virtual site farm that allows users to run diverse applications from simulations to web hosting (even Microsoft-hosted products). SimpleDB allows users of the S3 and EC2 systems to utilize a high-performance database system. SimpleDB has no schema and stores data heterogeneously across disks. A simple API for storage and retrieval is provided to developers. SimpleDB shouldn't be confused with a traditional relational database model. SQS is a hosted queue that provides a location to store messages while they travel between two endpoints. SQS acts in a way similar to MSMQ and MQSeries.

ELASTIC COMPUTE CLOUD (EC2)

Amazon claims that up to 300,000 developers are working with EC2. The Elastic Compute Cloud is a collection of Amazon Virtual Machine Images (AWI) stored over thousands of servers. The best thing about the Amazon Virtual Machine is that it can be used with a wide range of operating systems including Linux and Windows. This means that databases such as SQL Server, Oracle, and MySql can be run in the cloud. We would relate the EC2 to EMC's VMWare Server virtualization where resources can be divided up into separate machine images.

Amazon has been in the cloud computing space a lot longer than Google and Microsoft and has created a solid set of infrastructure services. Unfortunately, many people still regard the company as a fancy bookshop, and time will tell as to whether Amazon will be able to compete with recognized software companies such as Microsoft and Google.

Salesforce.com

Salesforce.com was established in 1999 in San Francisco by former Oracle executive Marc Benioff. It has been one of the most successful providers of SaaS via its Customer Relationship Management (CRM) software. The reason for the success stems from its current platform, Force.com, which allows developers to create add-on applications. This is similar to the Microsoft model: provide the nuts and bolts, and developers do the rest. This has created a huge following, with even some of the largest corporations opting to use Salesforce.com's online services. What started as a CRM-based company has now developed into Salesforce.com supplying services for applications such as human resource management, resource planning, and supply chain management. All these run under the Force.com platform, which is the cloud infrastructure used to run Salesforce.com's SaaS applications. Force.com is the latest generation of the SalesForce.com platform, and it appeals to a wider audience than just salespeople. The company uses this platform to enable developers to create new visual interfaces, workflow services, integration with LOB systems, and database services from SOA-based components. Force.com is definitely the front runner in the cloud computing arena; whether the Oslo strategy (see the "Oslo" section later in this chapter) will create a platform similar to Force.com remains to be seen.

Microsoft

As an analogy of Microsoft's path to the cloud over the last 30 years, take the hit song "Vida La Vida," which translated means "Live the Life," off the latest Coldplay album. It's a song about a king who has everything, and the crowds would always cheer every time they saw him. Unfortunately, power went to the king's head, and soon he became a dictator; now the people all talk about a revolt and revolution.

Many know the Microsoft story, with a young Bill Gates selling MS-DOS to IBM in the early 1980s. That one sale helped Microsoft in the development of one the most popular desktop platforms ever: Microsoft Windows. The rise of Microsoft in the 1980s and 1990s seemed to be unstoppable. Many say that power went to Bill's head when the founder discounted the Internet as a passing fad and was quoted in 1993 as saying "The Internet? We are not interested in it." Oh how times have changed. Competitors such as Google, Apple, and Salesforce.com are aspiring to take Microsoft's throne, and now even Microsoft's most prized asset, MS Office, seems to be threatened. Microsoft's approach of providing software for a license fee is dying, and its business model must change to meet the new Web 2.0 generation.

The wakeup call arrived when Microsoft missed securing some serious revenue (around two billion dollars) by not providing an online CRM tool before Salesforce.com. Around this time was when Microsoft started to fundamentally change its business model from charging a license fee for individual SKUs to hosting software for a fee. To accommodate this new direction, Microsoft has invested millions of dollars in providing high-class data centers to support its cloud computing offerings.

The first of Microsoft's software to be cloud-aware was its MSN Messaging and free Hotmail services, which are now under the name Windows Live Hotmail. Next came the Enterprise Server products such as Microsoft Exchange, SharePoint, and more recently CRM 4.0. The next wave will be SQL Server (under the name SQL Server Data Services), BizTalk Server (under the code name Oslo, which also includes the next version of Visual Studio, System Center, and .NET Framework 4.0), and finally even its precious operating system (Cloud OS)! Steve Ballmer, the new CEO at Microsoft, explains that providing these types of services gives Microsoft further sales channels by providing value-added services such as support and "up time" guarantee bonuses. The timeline for Microsoft's migration to the cloud is illustrated in Figure 9-1.

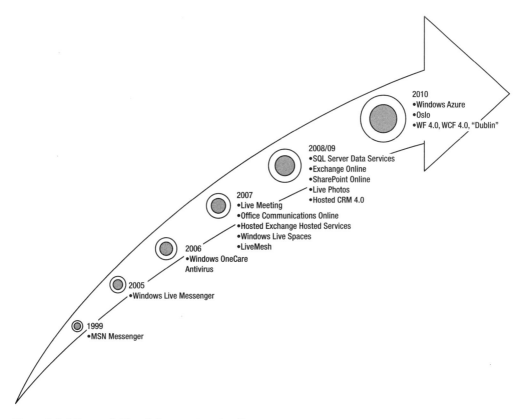

Figure 9-1. *Microsoft Cloud Computing timeline*

Where Does ADO.NET Data Services Fit In?

Now that you have read about the benefits and drawbacks of cloud computing and who the main players are, you are probably wondering where ADO.NET Data Services fits in. Presently, the answer is yes it fits into the cloud, because you can expose data sources and use a RESTful HTTP interface to access them. This can be considered in the cloud, can't it? Well, this all depends on your point of view. Presently, it is not possible to host a data service on anything other than the Windows Server that runs it, which is deemed "on-premises." This means that you can't just upload it to one of the cloud computing vendors described. The more likely position for ADO.NET Data Services in the cloud is as an enabling technology over the AtomPub protocol that will provide a standard way of querying resources over HTTP.

This has already started to happen with the announcement in February 2008 that the Windows Live Hotmail Photo API will provide AtomPub support, which will allow ADO.NET Data Services framework–style access to the service. SSDS will also provide similar support for AtomPub and eventually ADO.NET Data Services. These services can be split into three categories: consumer, infrastructure, and on-premises. The consumer and infrastructure services are hosted in the cloud by Microsoft or a cloud computing vendor, whereas the on-premises services that are currently supported by the ADO.NET Data Services framework are hosted by the client company. The ADO.NET Data Services framework provides a unified model to access these different types of services over the AtomPub protocol as shown in Figure 9-2.

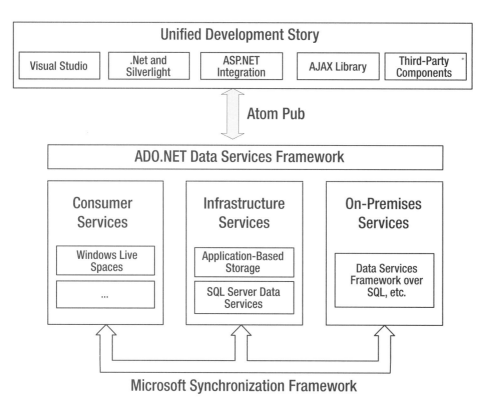

Figure 9-2. *ADO.NET Data Service framework: consumer, infrastructure, and on-premises*

Having data islands for each of these types of services could cause another issue because suddenly you lose your single view of the data. This is solved by the Microsoft Synchronization Framework (MSF), a general-purpose synchronization framework that allows you to synchronize between different data storage systems whether they exist on-premises or up in the cloud. This is achieved by setting up one or more endpoints that form a sync topology that determines how the data is synchronized into a single storage point, which is usually in SSDS. Also, MSF uses a provider pattern, which means that it can be used to synchronize multiple data stores such as Access databases, spreadsheets, vCards, XML documents, and so on. This "could" give you a single view of your entire data collection. MSF also has features that allow you to set up automated synchronization tasks based upon changes in the data sources . . . very neat.

One for the Road

Interested in what a likely cloud operating system could look like? A decent product available on the market, eDesk Online, is one of first examples of such a system. It allows document management, word processing, spreadsheet, CRM, and e-mail access in a web-based desktop-type environment. eDesk Online seems to be clearly ahead of the pack at the time of writing. To view demos of eDesk, navigate to `http://www.edeskonline.com` and click the link See the demo of eDesk Online; an interactive browser will appear as shown in Figure 9-3. The company promises in the future the same look and feel over multiple devices such as mobile phones, TVs, and so forth.

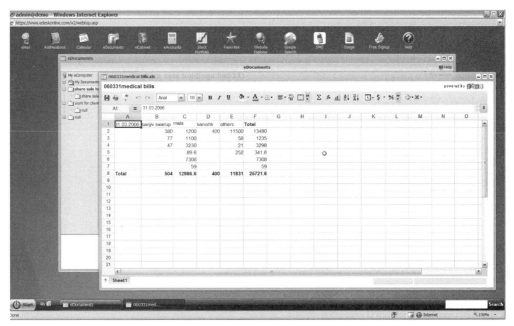

Figure 9-3. *eDesk web operating system*

SQL Server Data Services

SQL Server Data Services is Microsoft's hosted cloud solution for databases and shares very similar concepts to Amazon's S3 database. The underlying architecture consists of three layers. The first layer is the Global Data Services layer, which is used for existing services such as Windows Live Hotmail. The second layer is a set of Microsoft SQL Server instances that operate in a grid computing formulation in global data centers. The top layer is the interface to these SQL services, and it provides the core SSDS functionality that is visible to developers. Developers can access their data using either a REST or SOAP interface.

SSDS shares the basic concept of a database as you can store data, but it isn't a traditional Relational Database Management System (RDBMS). There aren't any features such as tables, keys, views, or stored procedures. There isn't a database schema, and even standard SQL isn't supported. This is similar to other major cloud database services, where a simple, discreet subset of standard RDBMS functionality is provided. The key reason for this is it's necessary to deprecate these features to achieve scalability and performance; having RDBMS features causes resource bottlenecks that could affect other users. Therefore, the aim of SSDS is to provide a lightweight database model that can be used to store collections of different data in nonrelational containers.

The core objectives of SSDS are as follows:

- **Location independent**: Data can be provided at any place at any time (works well when using the MSF).

- **Agility**: The solution provides a simple, flexible data model that supports REST and SOAP protocols.

- **Scalability**: Storage can scale without limits; businesses pay only for what they use.

- **Business SLA**: SSDA aims to be highly available, reliable, and secure. Most importantly, downtime is underwritten by Microsoft.

The basic concept of SSDS can be represented by the acronym ACE, which stands for Authority, Container, and Entity (ACE). Figure 9-4 illustrates this concept.

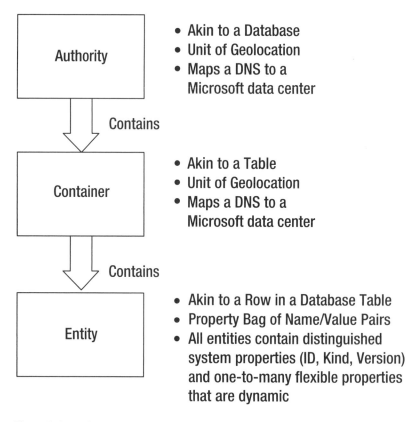

Figure 9-4. *Basic SSDS components*

At the top of the tree is the Authority, which relates to a database. When an Authority is provisioned, it is assigned a DNS name that maps to a specific geographic location. The Authority is used as the billing unit for any data that is employed. An Authority can hold zero or more Containers. A Container is similar to a table with the difference that it doesn't require a schema to describe it. This allows you to store a set of heterogeneous entities in a single Container. Containers contain entities that are property bag name/value pairs. There are two categories of entities that are supported: distinguished system properties and flexible properties.

Distinguished properties are common to all entities and include an ID, Kind, and Version. The ID is the unique identifier for the entity. The Kind is used to categorize similar entities together (e.g., City or Customer); due to having no schema, the same Kind doesn't guarantee the same structure. The Version is the current version of the entity and gets updated on every operation against it.

The second category of property is flexible properties, which the developer can use to specify the columns and format of how data is stored by the application. Flexible properties can be made up of `string`, `decimal`, `boolean`, `datetime`, and `binary` data types. The flexible properties by default are indexed automatically up to the first 256 bytes.

To access the SSDS, a scope needs to be created that points to the service's DNS. When accessing Containers and entities, the REST interface experience is similar to that of ADO.NET Data Services: you can access a Container in a way similar to how you would access an entity set. The difference is SSDS doesn't contain the extensive query support of ADO.NET Data Services.

The long list of Microsoft's target customers for SSDS will include small and medium-sized businesses looking to offload costs, developers looking to avoid infrastructure investments for data-intensive apps like mashups, and enterprises that might want easy archival and collaborative access to data sets.

ADO.NET Data Services will provide a standard RESTful query interface to the data stored in SSDS. However, it is currently not aligned with SSDS today (see the "Astoria vNext" section later in this chapter).

Oslo

Oslo is the code name for a project to update Microsoft technologies to service oriented architecture (SOA) and will affect multiple products and frameworks including BizTalk, .NET Framework 4.0, Visual Studio 10, and Microsoft System Center. The core foundation of this alignment is to provide a standard modeling platform that can be reused across a wide range of domains and which enables developers to write applications at a more abstract level. The goal is to reduce the gap between the model and the actual software that is eventually deployed by the developer. Microsoft wants to achieve this by providing a set of tools that will make developers program on the model itself, which effectively will keep it in sync with the original business model and in turn the documentation of the system. It will enable companies to easily create SaaS for their customers. The features of Oslo as outlined in the original unveiling are as follows:

- **Server**: BizTalk Server will provide the core foundation for distributed applications.

- **Services**: BizTalk Services Version 1.0 will provide a set of services that will allow developers to cross organizational boundaries using centralized security delegation and identity services.

- **Framework**: .NET Framework 4.0 will be enhanced to include model-driven development for Windows Communication Foundation and Windows Workflow Foundation.

- **Tools**: Visual Studio 10 will contain a set of new tools that help with the end-to-end application life cycle. This is achieved by investing heavily in UML development tools. Presently, UML tools are used by developers as an afterthought for documentation purposes, for example, generation of a class diagram. The idea is for developers to use UML diagrams while developing.

- **Repository**: There will be investments in server products that will allow a core metadata repository for SOA services. This database technology will provide a centralized storage of composite application components and workflows along with web service contracts. It will also store configuration and discovery models that are required by system management tools. (We predict that this will probably be stored in the SSDS.)

This is Microsoft's approach to delivering SaaS for the next 10 years, so it shouldn't be underestimated. The aim of this approach is for companies to plug into Microsoft core cloud-based services and eventually even host them fully using Microsoft data centers. Most companies cannot afford the infrastructure investments that are required for SOA services, so if Microsoft can supply inexpensive cloud services, it could claim the market. Microsoft also recognizes that most companies will not just jump into the cloud without a reason, but making the development experience and software delivery compelling is likely to change perception. If you look at Visual Basic's adoption in the early '90s, you will understand this reasoning.

At the time of writing, we don't know exactly how ADO.NET Data Services will fit into this picture. However, we predict that ADO.NET Data Services will probably appear in the repository project as another service that can be used as part of the model. Microsoft also may bake the ADO.NET Data Services framework into its new WCF 4.0 approach, which will extend its current .NET 3.5 out-of-the-box REST support. WCF 4.0 will ship with a REST Starter Kit that provides the following Visual Studio project and item templates for common RESTful scenarios: REST Singleton Service, REST Collection Service, Atom Feed Service, Atom Publishing Protocol Service, and HTTP Plain XML Service.

Entity Framework V2.0

Entity Framework V1.0 is an extensive object relational mapping (ORM) for developers. Unfortunately, it currently has a number of shortfalls, which some people **really** don't like:

- Inordinate focus on the data aspects of entities leads to degraded entity architectures.

- Excess code is needed to deal with the lack of lazy loading.

- The shared canonical model contradicts software best practices.

- Lack of "persistence ignorance" causes business logic to be harder to read, write, and modify, causing development and maintenance costs.

- Excessive merge conflicts occur with source control in team environments.

The Entity Framework team created the framework using a traditional Microsoft design process, which prevented them from getting early feedback in the design process. The Entity Framework, although very usable, still has some way to go for a lot of mainstream developers. The Entity Framework team has recognized this and is now following the transparent design approach that was used as part of the ADO.NET Data Services project.

Following are some of the new features that will be in Entity Framework 2.0:

- Generating the database schema from the Entity Framework model instead of the other way around

- Using structural annotation of entity schemas instead of XML attributes

- Addressing persistence ignorance by supporting Plain Old CLR Types (POCO) classes and allowing bare .NET types to be used in the Entity Framework so that Entity Framework–specific attributes do not need to be added

- Support for implicit lazy loading of entities

- Transparent caching support

- Support of computed properties on Entity Data Models

What does the Entity Framework V2.0 mean for ADO.NET Data Services? Well, presently ADO.NET Data Services is not coupled to the Entity Framework; it only provides first-class support for the Entity Framework. Due to this integration, if we were using the Entity Framework to surface a data source, we wouldn't need to add anything extra onto the model because it just transparently provides support for querying and updating our data source. If the Entity Framework model were to change dramatically with no backward support, the ADO.NET Data Services team would have to align it to the new version.

Astoria vNext

The Astoria (ADO.NET Data Services) team is currently working on the next version of the framework, code-named Astoria vNext. Members of the initial ADO.NET Data Services project team took the approach of sharing their experiences with the public through a transparent design process. This helped the team to deliver a framework that customers really wanted. In the next version, the same approach will be taken, and the team will post day-to-day design challenges on its blog site (http://blogs.msdn.com/astoriateam). The team will also answer questions on bugs, queries, and so on, on its Microsoft forum page (http://forums.microsoft.com/MSDN/ShowForum.aspx?ForumID=1430). Also, to help illustrate some of these challenges, Channel 9, which you'll find on the blog site, will be used to post some short videos from the team.

The current version of the framework was created during the same time as Microsoft proposed a number of large initiatives such as SSDS, Entity Framework, and so forth. The goal of the next release is to align these technologies and to add functionality that wasn't included in the first release.

In particular, the following major points will be addressed in the next release of ADO.NET Data Services:

- Enriched data source plug-in interfaces to support high scalability such as Microsoft-hosted services and the needs of such infrastructures via dynamic metafeeds

- Enriched client programming support and deeper integration with current and future app framework investments across Microsoft

- Continued drive toward support for standards such as AtomPub

- Creation of a friendly feeds feature to enable rich mashup scenarios

- Offline ADO.NET data services

- Alignment with SQL Server Data Services

- Alignment with Entity Framework V2.0

- Plain Old XML Support

- ASP.NET DataServiceDataSource server control

The rest of this section expands upon some of the preceding points.

Enriched Data Source Plug-in to Support High Scale Needs

This is still early in the design process and will be used to address high-scalability requirements to help serve thousands of clients. The current concerns are that when too many .NET types are used to represent the model, a hit occurs on how the service represents these types. To address this concern, the new design will attempt to reduce the number of .NET types loaded by dynamically determining the metadata when the service is called.

Friendly Feeds

When a data source is surfaced to a data service, it can then be exposed to multiple clients using one of the two supported serialization formats, Atom and JSON. The choice of this format would depend on the type of client that it is intended for. For example, if the client is an AJAX application, you would opt for the JSON format; for other types of clients, you would use the Atom format because this is what is hard-coded into the client library. The rules of both these formats are fixed so that the client assembly knows exactly how to serialize the data into the appropriate entity types. The team received feedback on whether it would add the ability to control how this format is output from the service, which could be when the data needs to be ordered differently or if another type of client needs to access the data in a different format. This situation could occur in cases when the data is used in a mapping mashup. In such a mashup, you might want to combine geoencoded external data with a Virtual Earth display. In the current version of the Virtual Earth V5.0 API, there is now support to load a GeoRSS microformat feed that automatically displays RSS data in Virtual Earth. This cuts down on development time because all you need to do is to point Virtual Earth at the GeoRSS feed URL, and the API will take care of displaying the push-pin points in the map. Presently, if you wanted to create this mashup, you would need to read the Atom feed first and then add each of the push-pin points to the Virtual Earth map, which involves unnecessary code.

WHAT IS A GEORSS FEED?

GeoRSS, or Geographically Encoded Objects for RSS, is an initiative to help RSS readers digest geographically tagged feeds. It supports basic geometries in the format such as point, line, box, and polygon. The main usage of the format has been in mashups, where this data is used to display a number of points or polygons in a mapping interface such as Google Maps and Virtual Earth. For a neat example of what you can use this format for, see the Joey tracking application at `http://blog.ublip.com/archives/integrating-ublip-gps-tracking-with-tufts-university-bus-tracking-application`.

The team has recognized this need and is thinking of adding a feature that will allow developers to control ADO.NET Data Services serialization formats. The name of this enhancement is dubbed by the team as "friendly feeds." Obviously, this will break existing client code, so the team is working on adding protocol version numbers to the feeds that are produced by these customizations. The friendly feeds feature is intended to be used in Atom feed customizations and will not apply to any other nonfeed formats such as JSON; that is, its intention is not to enable building other serializations.

Offline ADO.NET Data Services

If you want to interact with a data service, you need to be online to connect to it and query against it; once you go offline you can't access the service. If you were developing a Silverlight application that accessed a service and you wanted to work on it on a plane while traveling to Australia, you would copy the database locally and resurface a copy of the data service. Once you landed, you would then need to point the Silverlight application to the real database. If you updated any important data in your local copy, you would need to write a script to extract this to the data service's live database. This is one of the situations that the offline ADO.NET Data Services feature aims to address.

This feature will be implemented by combining MSF to create offline-capable applications that have a local replica of the data. Once a network connection becomes available, the synchronization process using the MSF takes place. The user experience for this feature will be transparent:

1. In Visual Studio, the user will select to take data service offline.

2. The ADO.NET Data Services framework copies the metadata from the service and creates a SQL schema for it in a local SQL Server Compact 3.5 database.

3. An MSF replication profile is also created.

4. When the user chooses to make the data service online, a synchronization process is performed in the background between it and the hosted data service.

Alignment with SQL Server Data Services

There currently isn't any support in SQL Server Data Services for ADO.NET Data Services, even though REST can be used to access data in the cloud. The primary reason for this mismatch is that the teams initially had different objectives: one to provide on-premises cloud services, and the other to provide hosted infrastructure services. Ideally the same framework should be used in both situations. This alignment was originally thought to be straightforward, as it should just be the case of mapping the query language differences. However, there are a number of deep-rooted challenges in the fundamental way these two technologies work:

- ADO.NET data services work on a single consistency domain that maps to a single data source. This domain is similar to a Container in SSDS. However, in SSDS Containers can span multiple consistency domains, and queries can be made that span more than one. The alignment would need ADO.NET Data Services to be able to support more than one domain.

- Entities in SSDS do not require a schema, but in data services they require types that map to the EDM schema.

- Multi-tenancy is a fundamental concept in SSDS, but not in ADO.NET Data Services. This could have security implications for data services.

> ### WHAT IS MULTI-TENANCY?
>
> In multi-tenancy software architecture, an instance of a particular piece of software is used to serve multiple clients (the tenants). This is achieved by virtually partitioning the data and the service to each tenant. This ensures that there is further protection against unwanted visitors.

Many argue that the alignment is not necessary because they want SSDS to remain lightweight and flexible, and they feel that if they need to conform to the Entity Data Model, these aspects of SSDS will be killed. However, the SSDS team aims to please both parties by supplying support for both the Entity Framework EDM model and the flexible model of SSDS. This will be achieved by giving a choice as to whether the Containers are schema based or flex entities.

Time will tell how these technologies will be aligned.

ASP.NET DataServiceDataSource Server Control

In demonstrations, the ADO.NET Data Services team used an ASP.NET data server control to bind ASP.NET server controls to a data service. To do this, they used an ASP.NET `DataServiceDataSource` server control that has built-in binding features. The control operates in a fashion similar to the LINQ to SQL ASP.NET data source and can be used to cut down development time. The team has promised to release this control in the near future.

Summary

The future of computing will involve many changes over the coming years, with an increasing set of systems being placed in the cloud. ADO.NET Data Services will play an important role as the technology that will link the cloud to RIAs that will be written in technologies such as Silverlight and AJAX. This programming model is completely different from what a lot of developers are used to. We would suggest that you keep checking on the progress of the next version of the Entity Framework, Olso, and SQL Server Data Services.

We hope that this book has provided you with a grounding in many new and different technologies and how these operate with ADO.NET Data Services. Happy coding!

Index

You Need the Companion eBook

Your purchase of this book entitles you to buy the companion PDF-version eBook for only $10. Take the weightless companion with you anywhere.

We believe this Apress title will prove so indispensable that you'll want to carry it with you everywhere, which is why we are offering the companion eBook (in PDF format) for $10 to customers who purchase this book now. Convenient and fully searchable, the PDF version of any content-rich, page-heavy Apress book makes a valuable addition to your programming library. You can easily find and copy code—or perform examples by quickly toggling between instructions and the application. Even simultaneously tackling a donut, diet soda, and complex code becomes simplified with hands-free eBooks!

Once you purchase your book, getting the $10 companion eBook is simple:

❶ Visit **www.apress.com/promo/tendollars/**.

❷ Complete a basic registration form to receive a randomly generated question about this title.

❸ Answer the question correctly in 60 seconds, and you will receive a promotional code to redeem for the $10.00 eBook.

THE EXPERT'S VOICE™

2855 TELEGRAPH AVENUE | SUITE 600 | BERKELEY, CA 94705

Offer valid through 06/09.